CAPTAIN AMERICA

Loose Nuke

WRITER: RICK REMENDER

PENCILER: CARLOS PACHECO AND NIC KLEIN

INKERS: KLAUS JANSON, NIC KLEIN AND MARIANO TAIBO

COLOURS: DEAN WHITE, RACHELLE ROSENBERG, RAINIER BEREDO AND VAL STAPLES

LETTERS: VC's JOE CARAMAGNA

ASSISTANT EDITOR: JACOB THOMAS

EDITORS: TOM BREVOORT AND LAUREN SANKOVITCH

EDITOR IN CHIEF: AXEL ALONSO

CHIEF CREATIVE OFFICER: JOE QUESADA

PUBLISHER: DAN BUCKLEY

EXECUTIVE PRODUCER: ALAN FINE

COVER ART: CARLOS PACHECO

Do you have any comments or queries about this graphic novel? Email us at graphicnovels@panini.co.uk

TM & © 2013 and 2014 Marvel & Subs. Licensed by Marvel Characters B.V. through Panini S.p.A. Italy. All Rights Reserved. First printing 2014. Published by Panini Pu... ...Managing Editor. Mark Irvine, Production Ma... ...Gray, Designer. Office of publication: Brockb... ...not be sold, except by authorised deale... ...part of its cover or markings removed, nor i... ...he Minifigure figurine are trademarks or ... ...ed in particular decorations are not comme...

MARVEL GRAPHIC NOVEL

CAPTAIN AMERICA #11

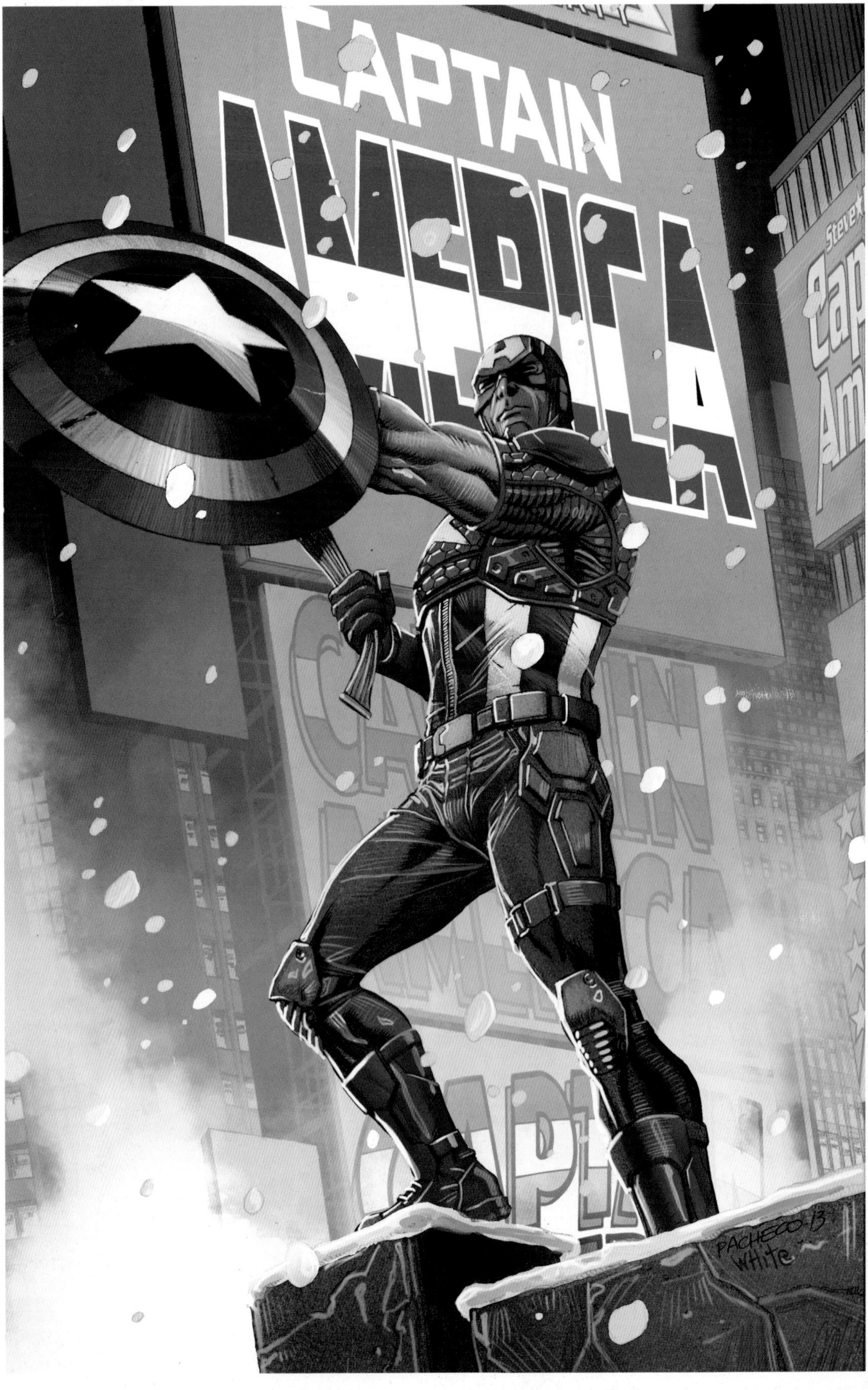
CAPTAIN AMERICA
PACHECO-13
White

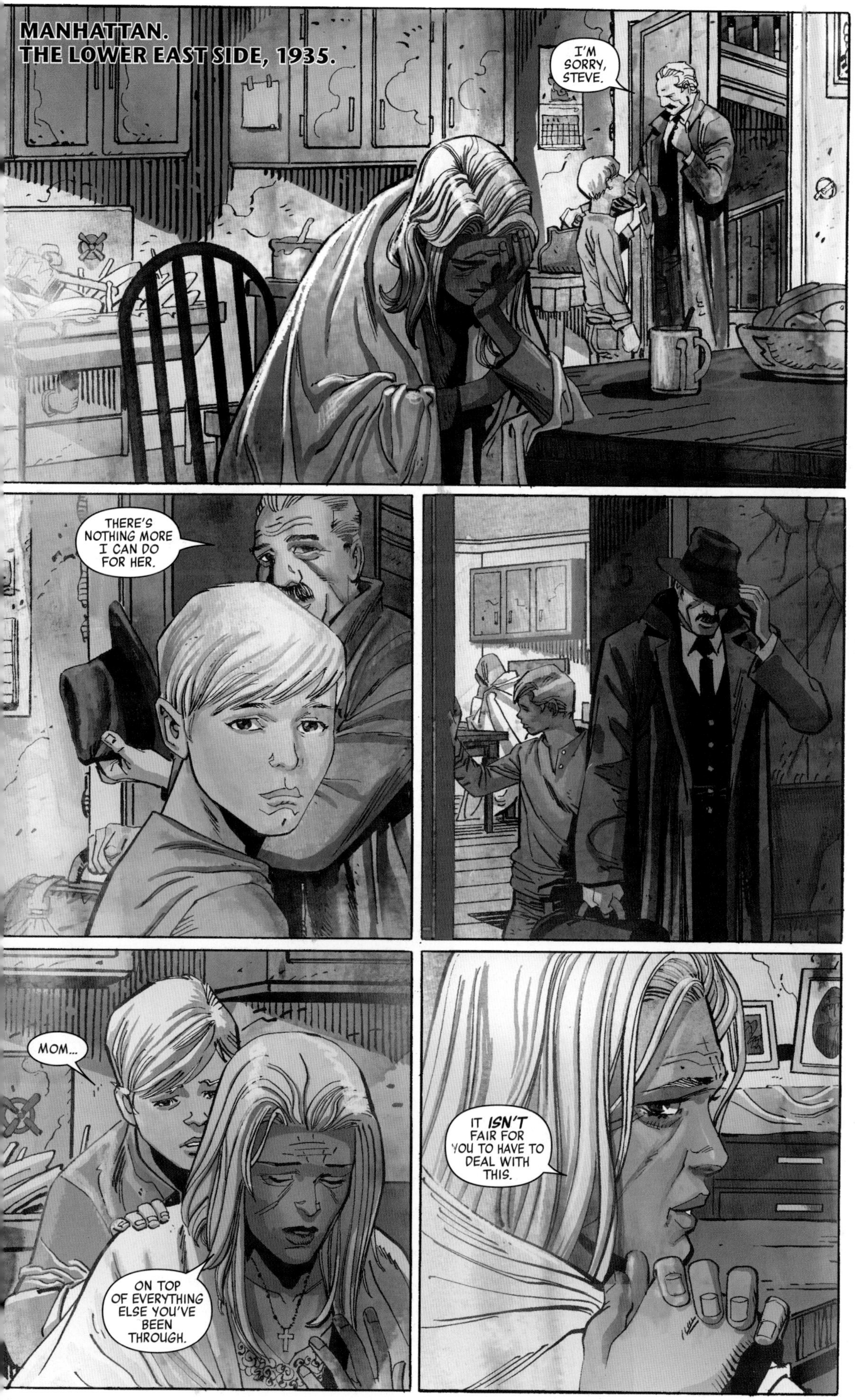
MANHATTAN.
THE LOWER EAST SIDE, 1935.
I'M SORRY, STEVE.
THERE'S NOTHING MORE I CAN DO FOR HER.
MOM...
ON TOP OF EVERYTHING ELSE YOU'VE BEEN THROUGH.
IT ISN'T FAIR FOR YOU TO HAVE TO DEAL WITH THIS.

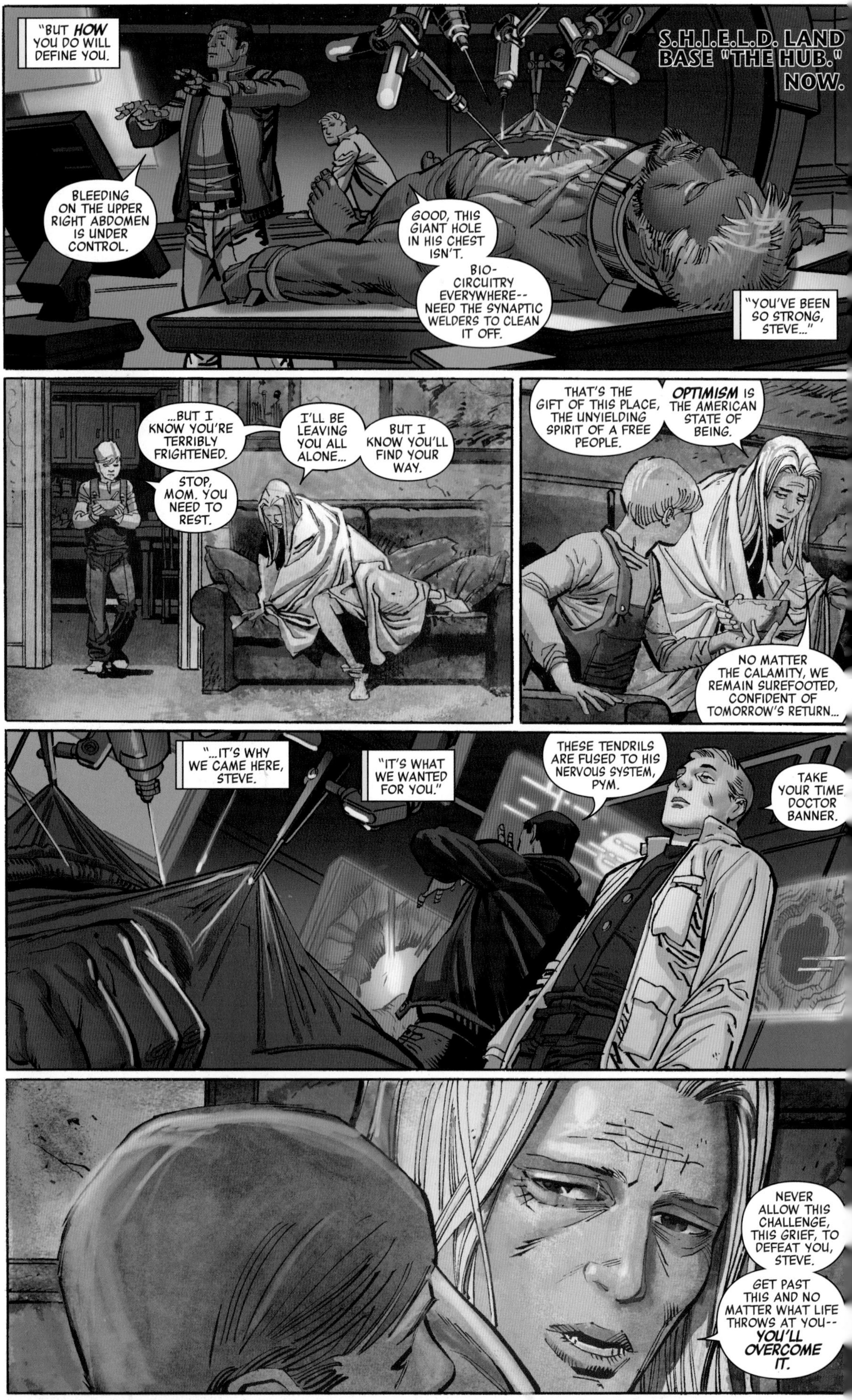
"BUT HOW YOU DO WILL DEFINE YOU.
S.H.I.E.L.D. LAND BASE "THE HUB." NOW.
BLEEDING ON THE UPPER RIGHT ABDOMEN IS UNDER CONTROL.
GOOD, THIS GIANT HOLE IN HIS CHEST ISN'T.
BIO-CIRCUITRY EVERYWHERE-- NEED THE SYNAPTIC WELDERS TO CLEAN IT OFF.
"YOU'VE BEEN SO STRONG, STEVE..."
...BUT I KNOW YOU'RE TERRIBLY FRIGHTENED.
STOP, MOM. YOU NEED TO REST.
I'LL BE LEAVING YOU ALL ALONE...
BUT I KNOW YOU'LL FIND YOUR WAY.
THAT'S THE GIFT OF THIS PLACE, THE UNYIELDING SPIRIT OF A FREE PEOPLE.
OPTIMISM IS THE AMERICAN STATE OF BEING.
NO MATTER THE CALAMITY, WE REMAIN SUREFOOTED, CONFIDENT OF TOMORROW'S RETURN...
"...IT'S WHY WE CAME HERE, STEVE.
"IT'S WHAT WE WANTED FOR YOU."
THESE TENDRILS ARE FUSED TO HIS NERVOUS SYSTEM, PYM.
TAKE YOUR TIME DOCTOR BANNER.
NEVER ALLOW THIS CHALLENGE, THIS GRIEF, TO DEFEAT YOU, STEVE.
GET PAST THIS AND NO MATTER WHAT LIFE THROWS AT YOU-- YOU'LL OVERCOME IT.

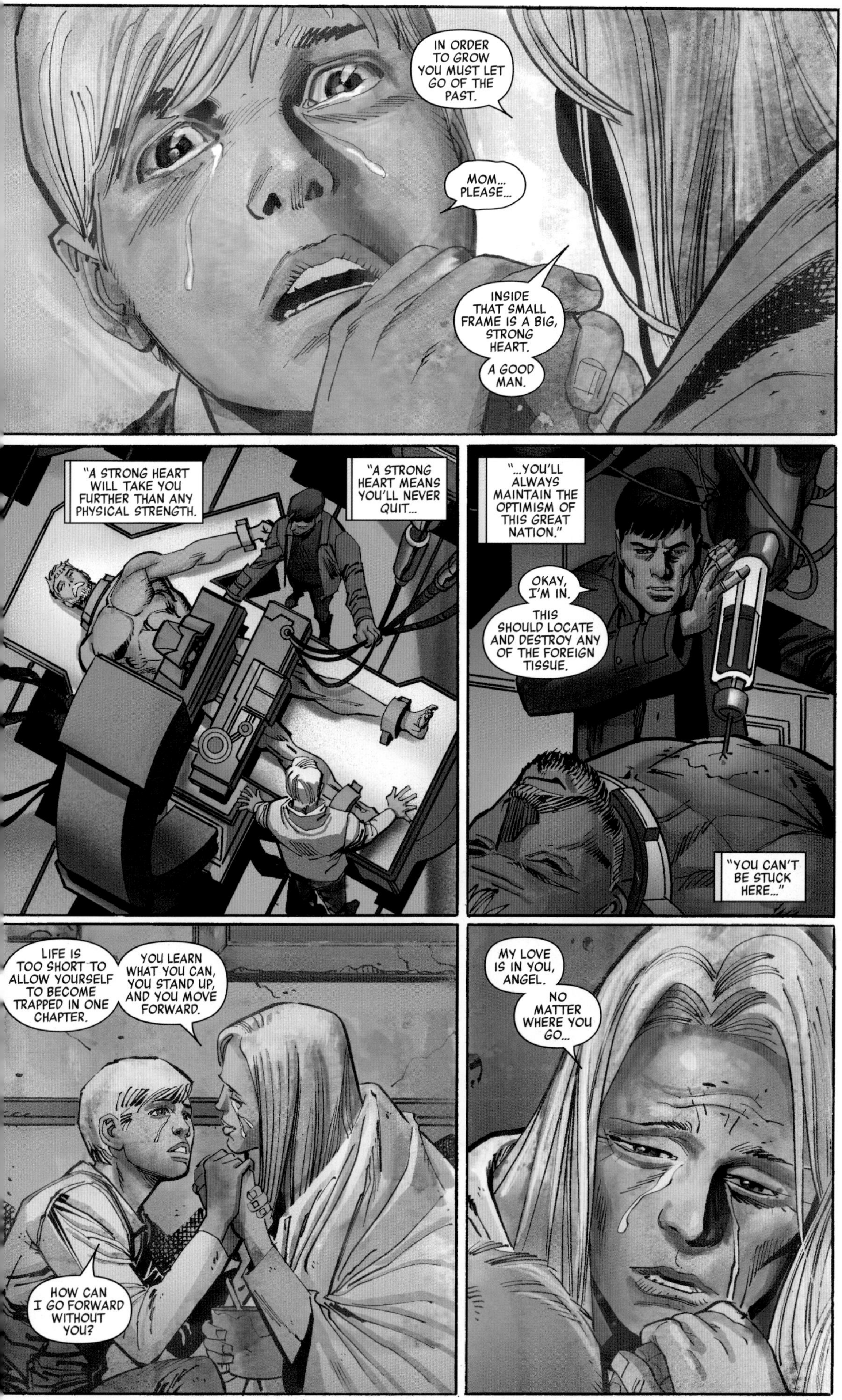
IN ORDER TO GROW YOU MUST LET GO OF THE PAST.
MOM... PLEASE...
INSIDE THAT SMALL FRAME IS A BIG, STRONG HEART.
A GOOD MAN.
"A STRONG HEART WILL TAKE YOU FURTHER THAN ANY PHYSICAL STRENGTH.
"A STRONG HEART MEANS YOU'LL NEVER QUIT...
"...YOU'LL ALWAYS MAINTAIN THE OPTIMISM OF THIS GREAT NATION."
OKAY, I'M IN.
THIS SHOULD LOCATE AND DESTROY ANY OF THE FOREIGN TISSUE.
"YOU CAN'T BE STUCK HERE..."
LIFE IS TOO SHORT TO ALLOW YOURSELF TO BECOME TRAPPED IN ONE CHAPTER.
YOU LEARN WHAT YOU CAN, YOU STAND UP, AND YOU MOVE FORWARD.
HOW CAN I GO FORWARD WITHOUT YOU?
MY LOVE IS IN YOU, ANGEL.
NO MATTER WHERE YOU GO...

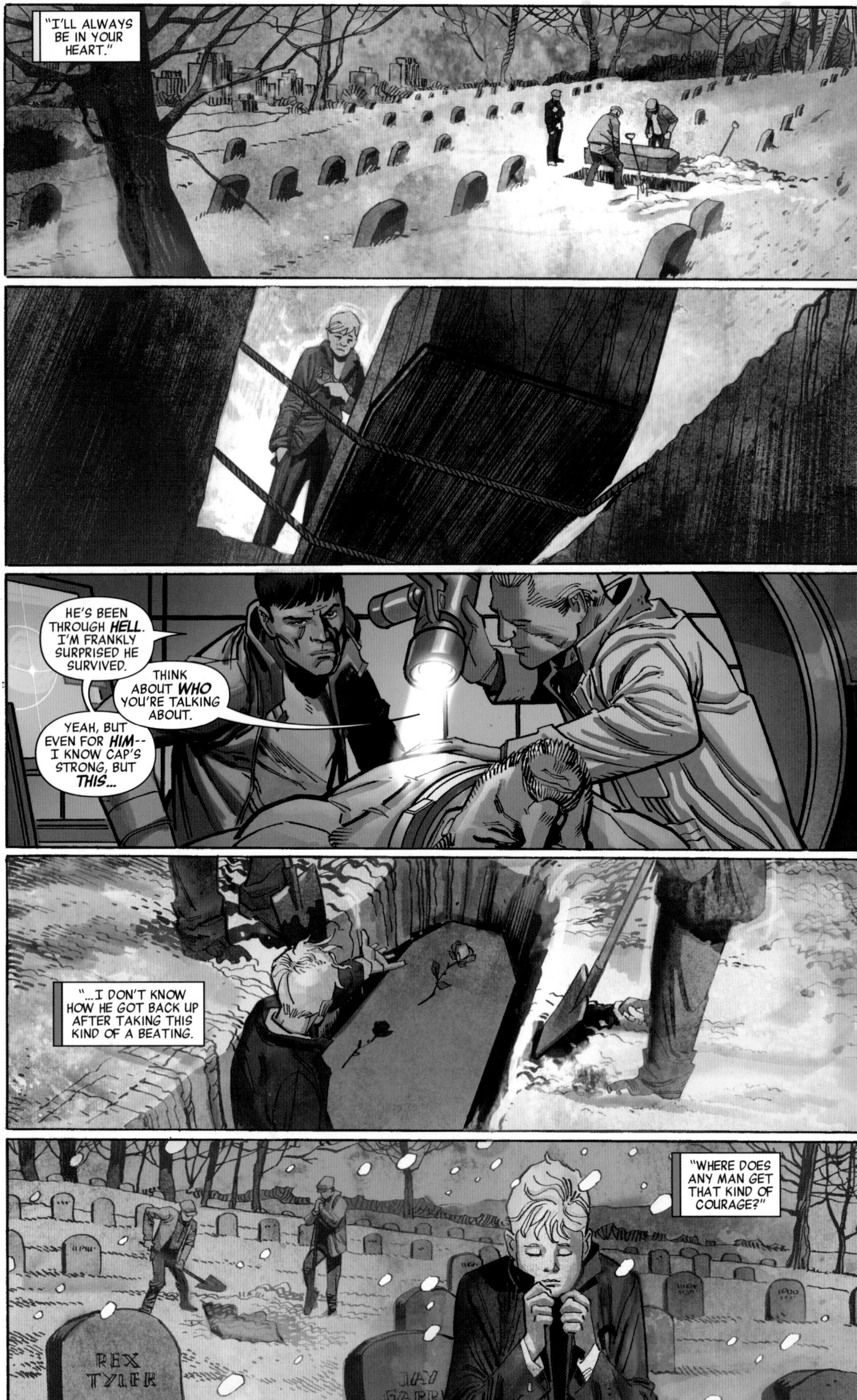
"I'LL ALWAYS BE IN YOUR HEART."
HE'S BEEN THROUGH HELL. I'M FRANKLY SURPRISED HE SURVIVED.
THINK ABOUT WHO YOU'RE TALKING ABOUT.
YEAH, BUT EVEN FOR HIM-- I KNOW CAP'S STRONG, BUT THIS...
"...I DON'T KNOW HOW HE GOT BACK UP AFTER TAKING THIS KIND OF A BEATING.
"WHERE DOES ANY MAN GET THAT KIND OF COURAGE?"
REX TYLER

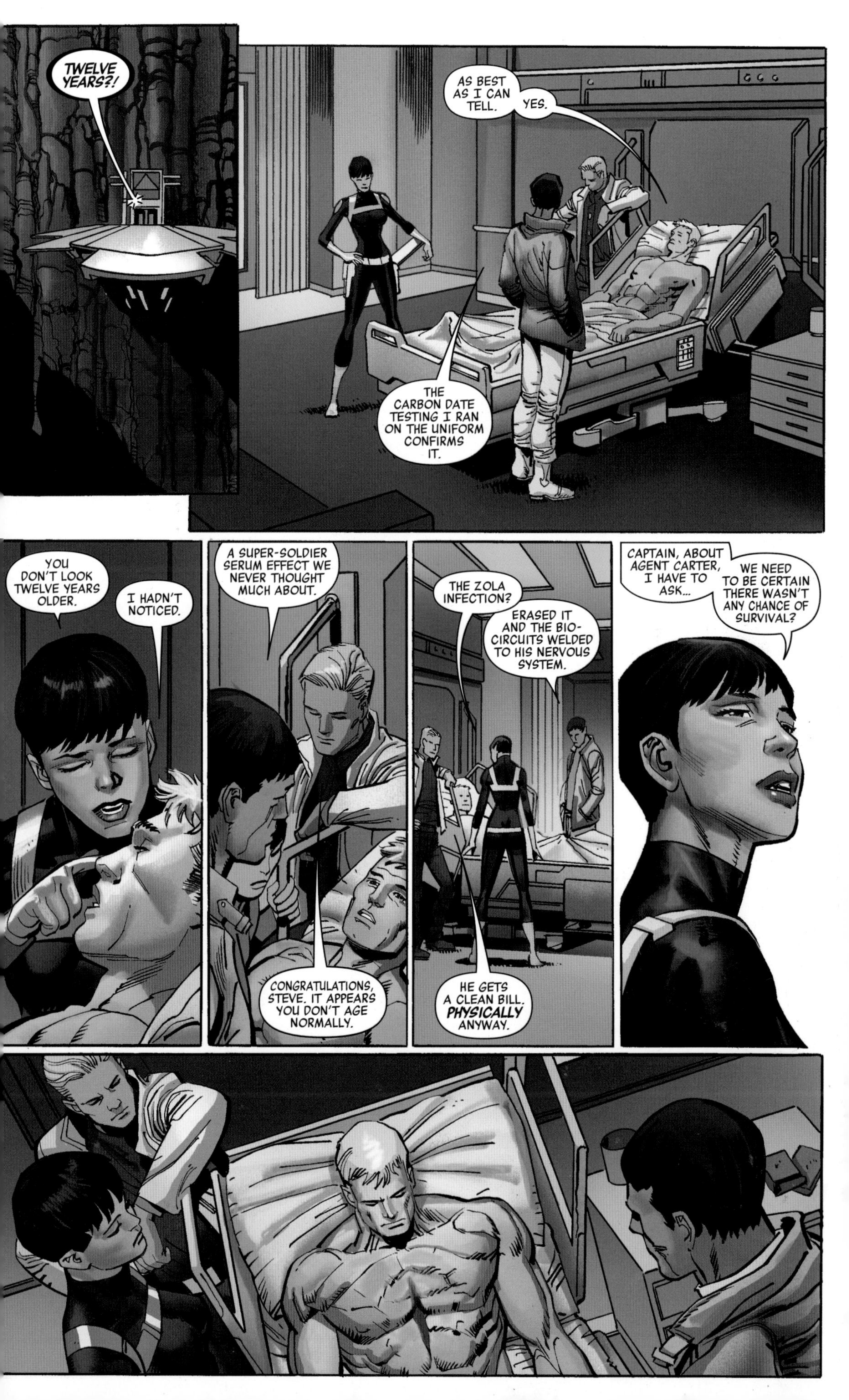
TWELVE YEARS?!
AS BEST AS I CAN TELL.
YES.
THE CARBON DATE TESTING I RAN ON THE UNIFORM CONFIRMS IT.
YOU DON'T LOOK TWELVE YEARS OLDER.
I HADN'T NOTICED.
A SUPER-SOLDIER SERUM EFFECT WE NEVER THOUGHT MUCH ABOUT.
CONGRATULATIONS, STEVE. IT APPEARS YOU DON'T AGE NORMALLY.
THE ZOLA INFECTION?
ERASED IT AND THE BIO-CIRCUITS WELDED TO HIS NERVOUS SYSTEM.
HE GETS A CLEAN BILL. PHYSICALLY ANYWAY.
CAPTAIN, ABOUT AGENT CARTER, I HAVE TO ASK...
WE NEED TO BE CERTAIN THERE WASN'T ANY CHANCE OF SURVIVAL?

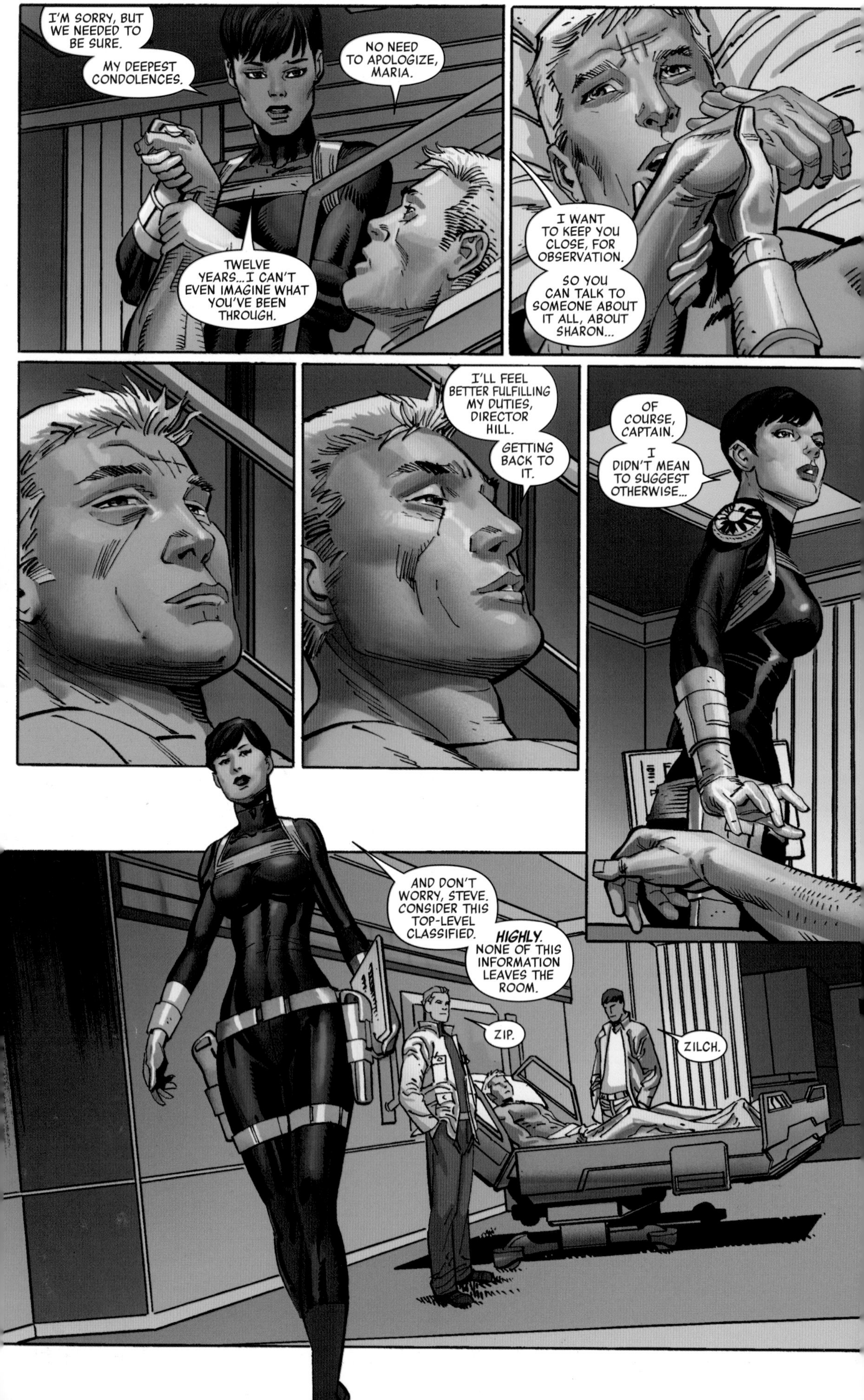
I'M SORRY, BUT WE NEEDED TO BE SURE.
MY DEEPEST CONDOLENCES.
NO NEED TO APOLOGIZE, MARIA.
TWELVE YEARS...I CAN'T EVEN IMAGINE WHAT YOU'VE BEEN THROUGH.
I WANT TO KEEP YOU CLOSE, FOR OBSERVATION.
SO YOU CAN TALK TO SOMEONE ABOUT IT ALL, ABOUT SHARON...
I'LL FEEL BETTER FULFILLING MY DUTIES, DIRECTOR HILL.
GETTING BACK TO IT.
OF COURSE, CAPTAIN.
I DIDN'T MEAN TO SUGGEST OTHERWISE...
AND DON'T WORRY, STEVE. CONSIDER THIS TOP-LEVEL CLASSIFIED.
HIGHLY. NONE OF THIS INFORMATION LEAVES THE ROOM.
ZIP.
ZILCH.

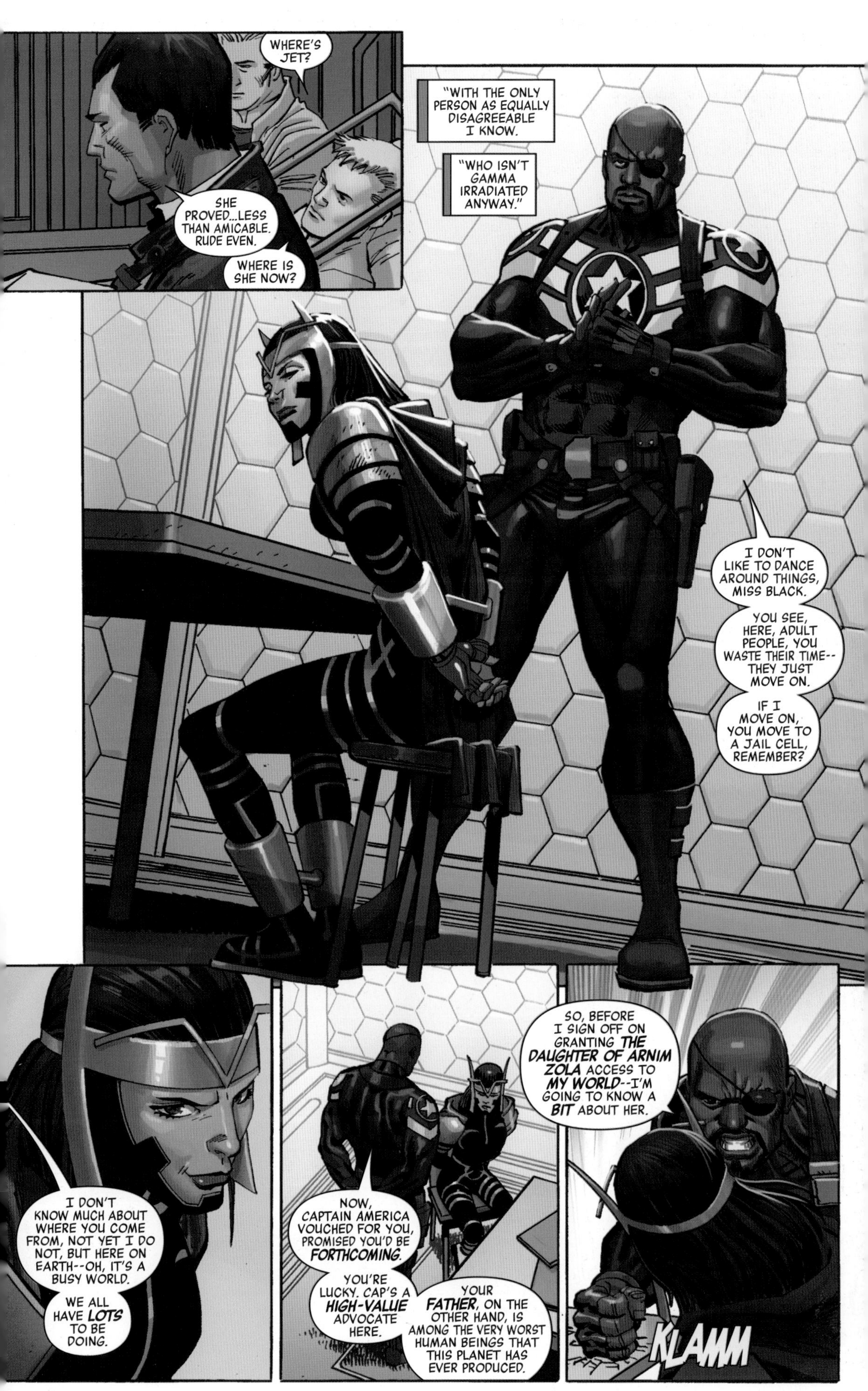
WHERE'S JET?
SHE PROVED...LESS THAN AMICABLE. RUDE EVEN.
WHERE IS SHE NOW?
"WITH THE ONLY PERSON AS EQUALLY DISAGREEABLE I KNOW.
"WHO ISN'T GAMMA IRRADIATED ANYWAY."
I DON'T LIKE TO DANCE AROUND THINGS, MISS BLACK.
YOU SEE, HERE, ADULT PEOPLE, YOU WASTE THEIR TIME--THEY JUST MOVE ON.
IF I MOVE ON, YOU MOVE TO A JAIL CELL, REMEMBER?
I DON'T KNOW MUCH ABOUT WHERE YOU COME FROM, NOT YET I DO NOT, BUT HERE ON EARTH--OH, IT'S A BUSY WORLD.
WE ALL HAVE LOTS TO BE DOING.
NOW, CAPTAIN AMERICA VOUCHED FOR YOU, PROMISED YOU'D BE FORTHCOMING.
YOU'RE LUCKY. CAP'S A HIGH-VALUE ADVOCATE HERE.
YOUR FATHER, ON THE OTHER HAND, IS AMONG THE VERY WORST HUMAN BEINGS THAT THIS PLANET HAS EVER PRODUCED.
SO, BEFORE I SIGN OFF ON GRANTING THE DAUGHTER OF ARNIM ZOLA ACCESS TO MY WORLD--I'M GOING TO KNOW A BIT ABOUT HER.
KLAMM

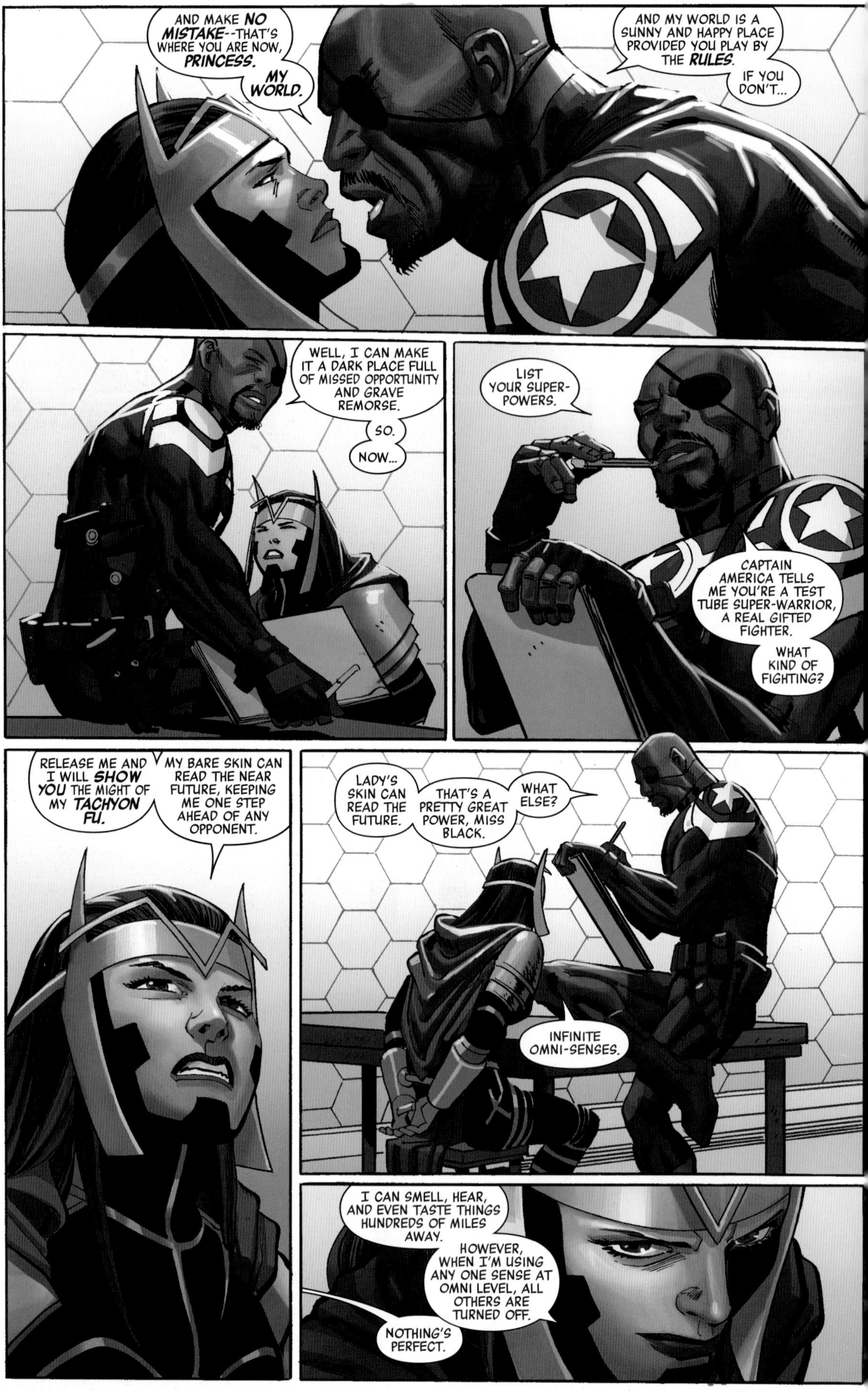
AND MAKE NO MISTAKE--THAT'S WHERE YOU ARE NOW, PRINCESS.
MY WORLD.
AND MY WORLD IS A SUNNY AND HAPPY PLACE PROVIDED YOU PLAY BY THE RULES.
IF YOU DON'T...
WELL, I CAN MAKE IT A DARK PLACE FULL OF MISSED OPPORTUNITY AND GRAVE REMORSE.
SO.
NOW...
LIST YOUR SUPER-POWERS.
CAPTAIN AMERICA TELLS ME YOU'RE A TEST TUBE SUPER-WARRIOR, A REAL GIFTED FIGHTER.
WHAT KIND OF FIGHTING?
RELEASE ME AND I WILL SHOW YOU THE MIGHT OF MY TACHYON FU.
MY BARE SKIN CAN READ THE NEAR FUTURE, KEEPING ME ONE STEP AHEAD OF ANY OPPONENT.
LADY'S SKIN CAN READ THE FUTURE.
THAT'S A PRETTY GREAT POWER, MISS BLACK.
WHAT ELSE?
INFINITE OMNI-SENSES.
I CAN SMELL, HEAR, AND EVEN TASTE THINGS HUNDREDS OF MILES AWAY.
HOWEVER, WHEN I'M USING ANY ONE SENSE AT OMNI LEVEL, ALL OTHERS ARE TURNED OFF.
NOTHING'S PERFECT.

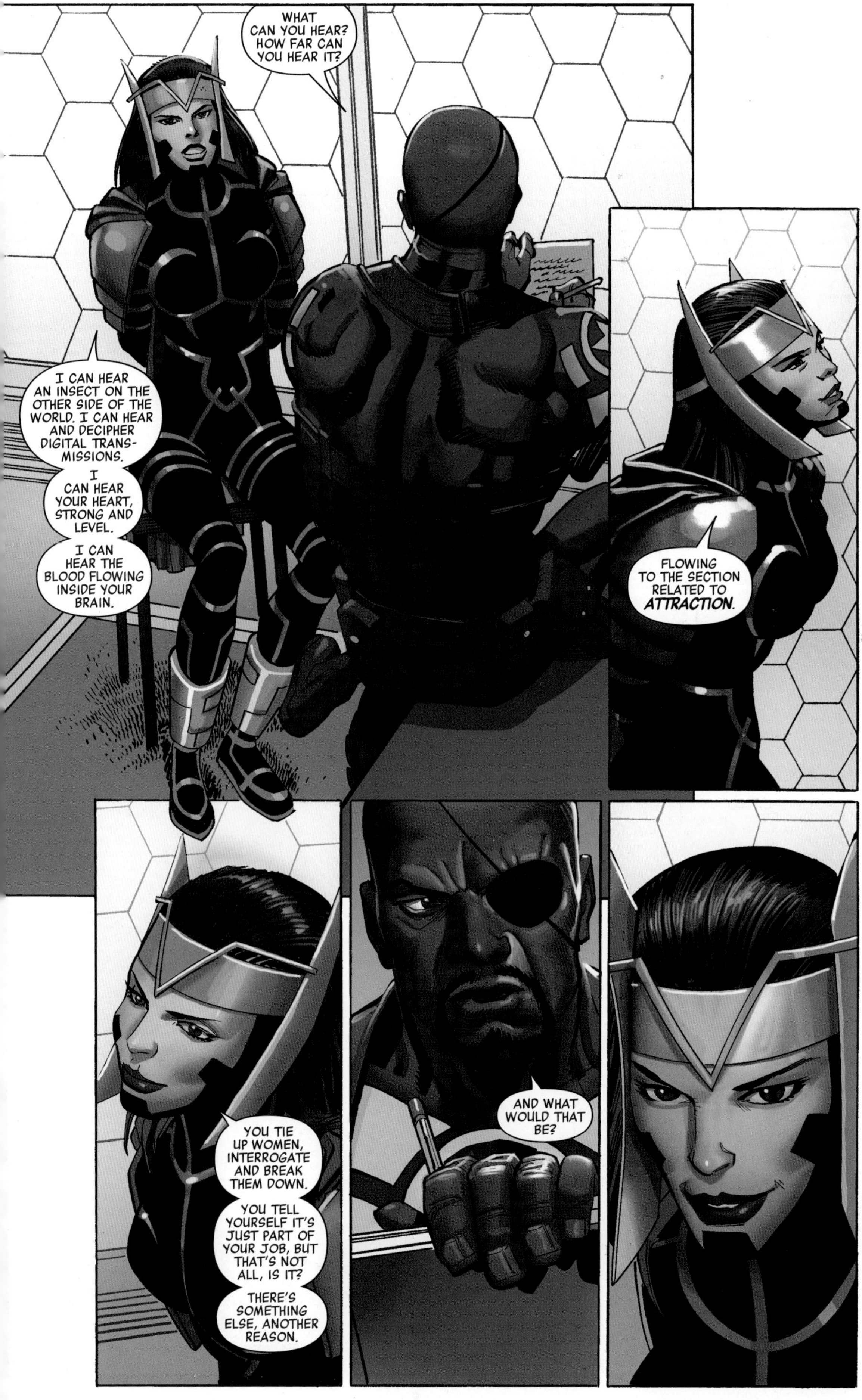
WHAT CAN YOU HEAR? HOW FAR CAN YOU HEAR IT?
I CAN HEAR AN INSECT ON THE OTHER SIDE OF THE WORLD. I CAN HEAR AND DECIPHER DIGITAL TRANS-MISSIONS.
I CAN HEAR YOUR HEART, STRONG AND LEVEL.
I CAN HEAR THE BLOOD FLOWING INSIDE YOUR BRAIN.
FLOWING TO THE SECTION RELATED TO *ATTRACTION*.
YOU TIE UP WOMEN, INTERROGATE AND BREAK THEM DOWN.
YOU TELL YOURSELF IT'S JUST PART OF YOUR JOB, BUT THAT'S NOT ALL, IS IT?
THERE'S SOMETHING ELSE, ANOTHER REASON.
AND WHAT WOULD THAT BE?

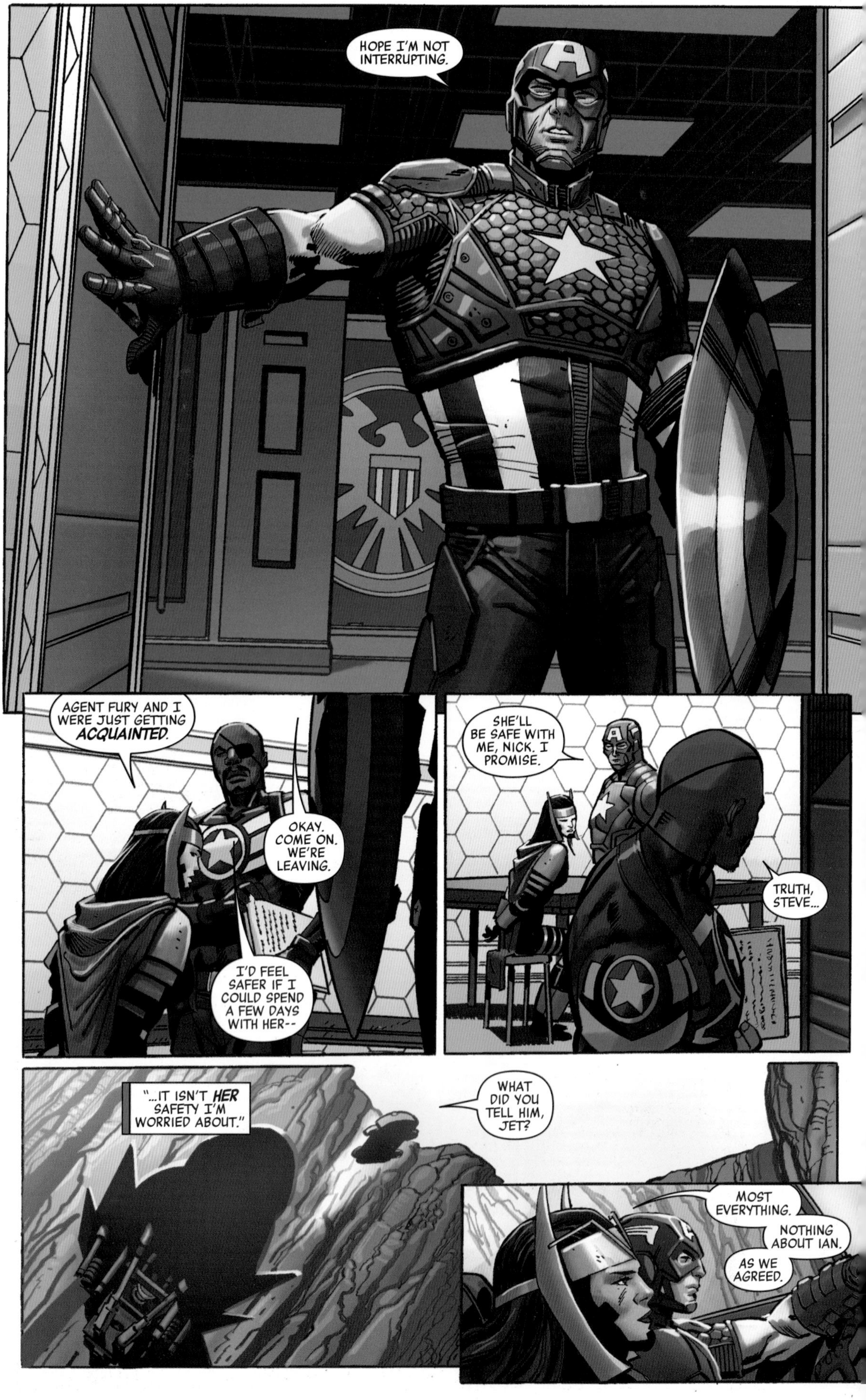
HOPE I'M NOT INTERRUPTING.
AGENT FURY AND I WERE JUST GETTING ACQUAINTED.
OKAY. COME ON. WE'RE LEAVING.
I'D FEEL SAFER IF I COULD SPEND A FEW DAYS WITH HER--
SHE'LL BE SAFE WITH ME, NICK. I PROMISE.
TRUTH, STEVE...
"...IT ISN'T HER SAFETY I'M WORRIED ABOUT."
WHAT DID YOU TELL HIM, JET?
MOST EVERYTHING.
NOTHING ABOUT IAN.
AS WE AGREED.

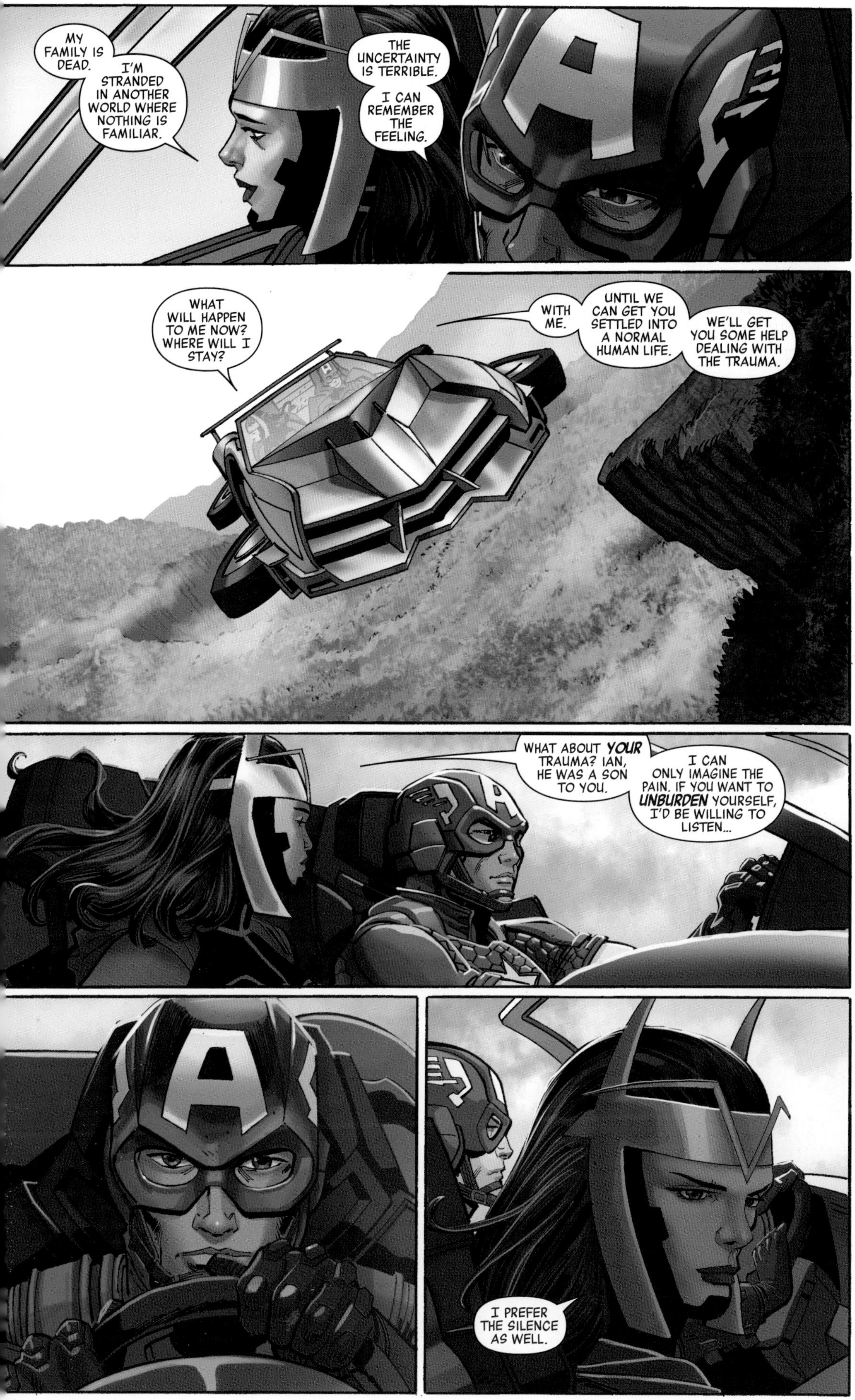
MY FAMILY IS DEAD.
I'M STRANDED IN ANOTHER WORLD WHERE NOTHING IS FAMILIAR.
THE UNCERTAINTY IS TERRIBLE.
I CAN REMEMBER THE FEELING.
WHAT WILL HAPPEN TO ME NOW? WHERE WILL I STAY?
WITH ME.
UNTIL WE CAN GET YOU SETTLED INTO A NORMAL HUMAN LIFE.
WE'LL GET YOU SOME HELP DEALING WITH THE TRAUMA.
WHAT ABOUT *YOUR* TRAUMA? IAN, HE WAS A SON TO YOU.
I CAN ONLY IMAGINE THE PAIN. IF YOU WANT TO *UNBURDEN* YOURSELF, I'D BE WILLING TO LISTEN...
I PREFER THE SILENCE AS WELL.

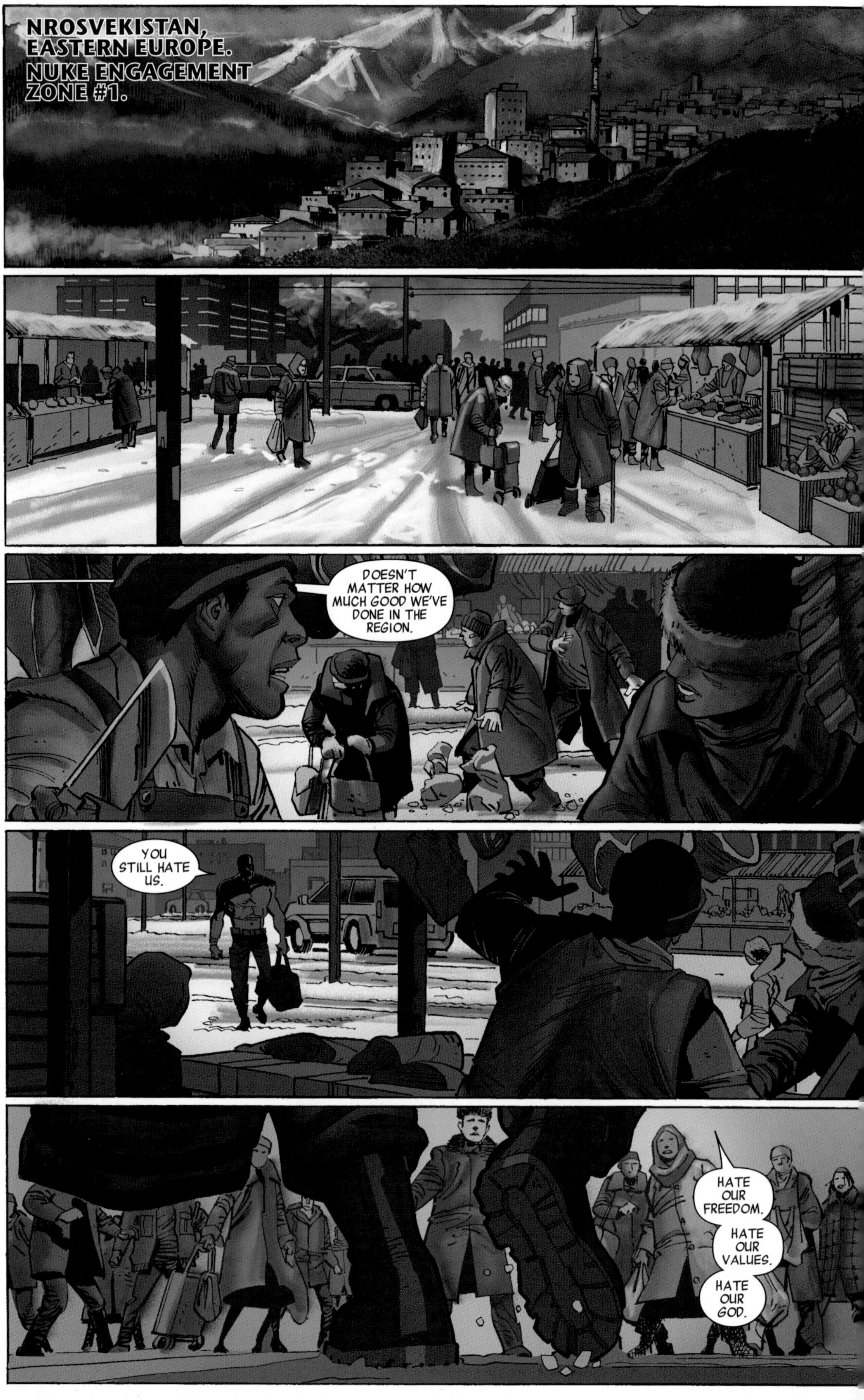
NROSVEKISTAN, EASTERN EUROPE.
NUKE ENGAGEMENT ZONE #1.
DOESN'T MATTER HOW MUCH GOOD WE'VE DONE IN THE REGION.
YOU STILL HATE US.
HATE OUR FREEDOM.
HATE OUR VALUES.
HATE OUR GOD.

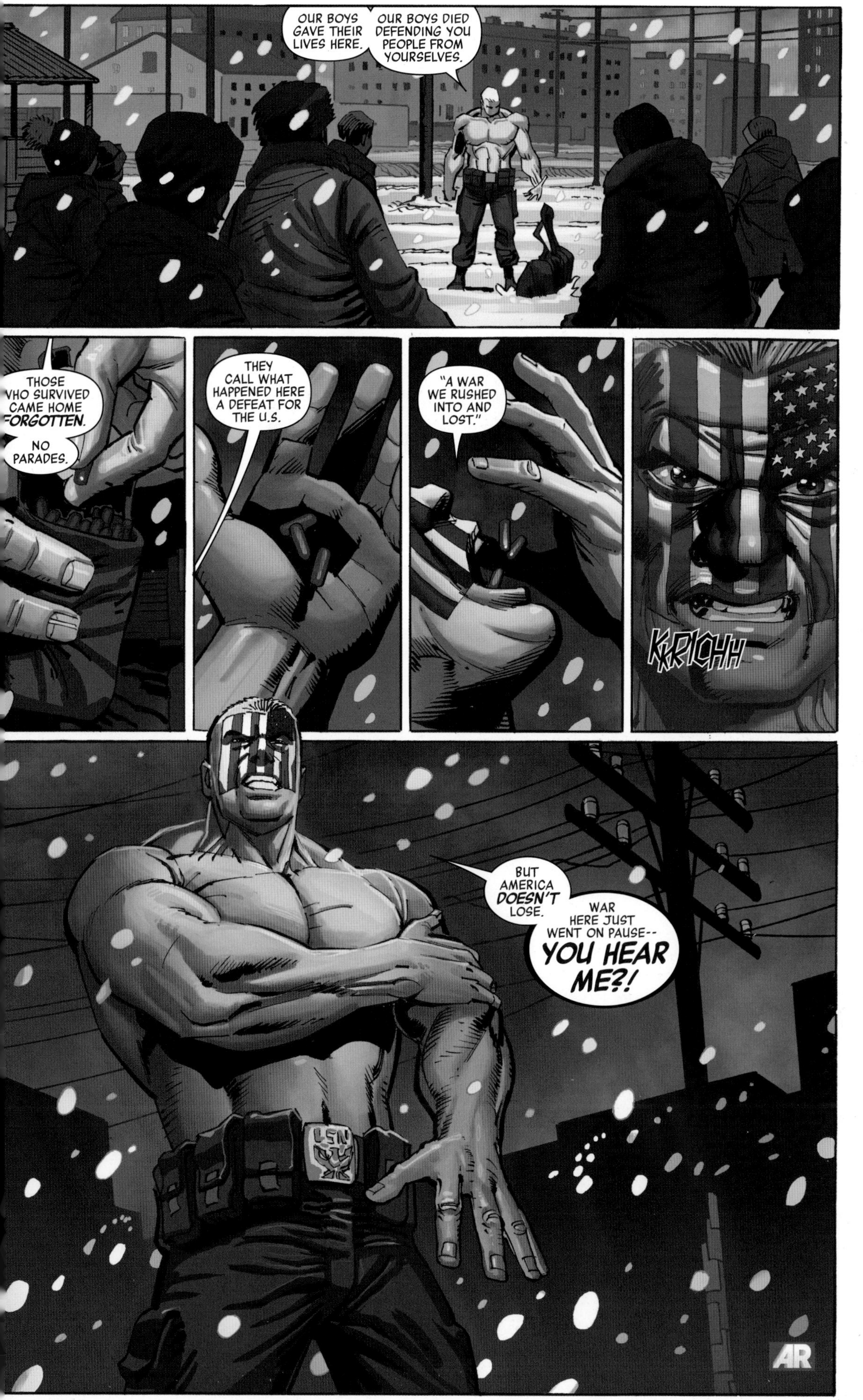
OUR BOYS GAVE THEIR LIVES HERE.
OUR BOYS DIED DEFENDING YOU PEOPLE FROM YOURSELVES.
THOSE WHO SURVIVED CAME HOME FORGOTTEN.
NO PARADES.
THEY CALL WHAT HAPPENED HERE A DEFEAT FOR THE U.S.
"A WAR WE RUSHED INTO AND LOST."
KKKRICHH
BUT AMERICA DOESN'T LOSE.
WAR HERE JUST WENT ON PAUSE--
YOU HEAR ME?!

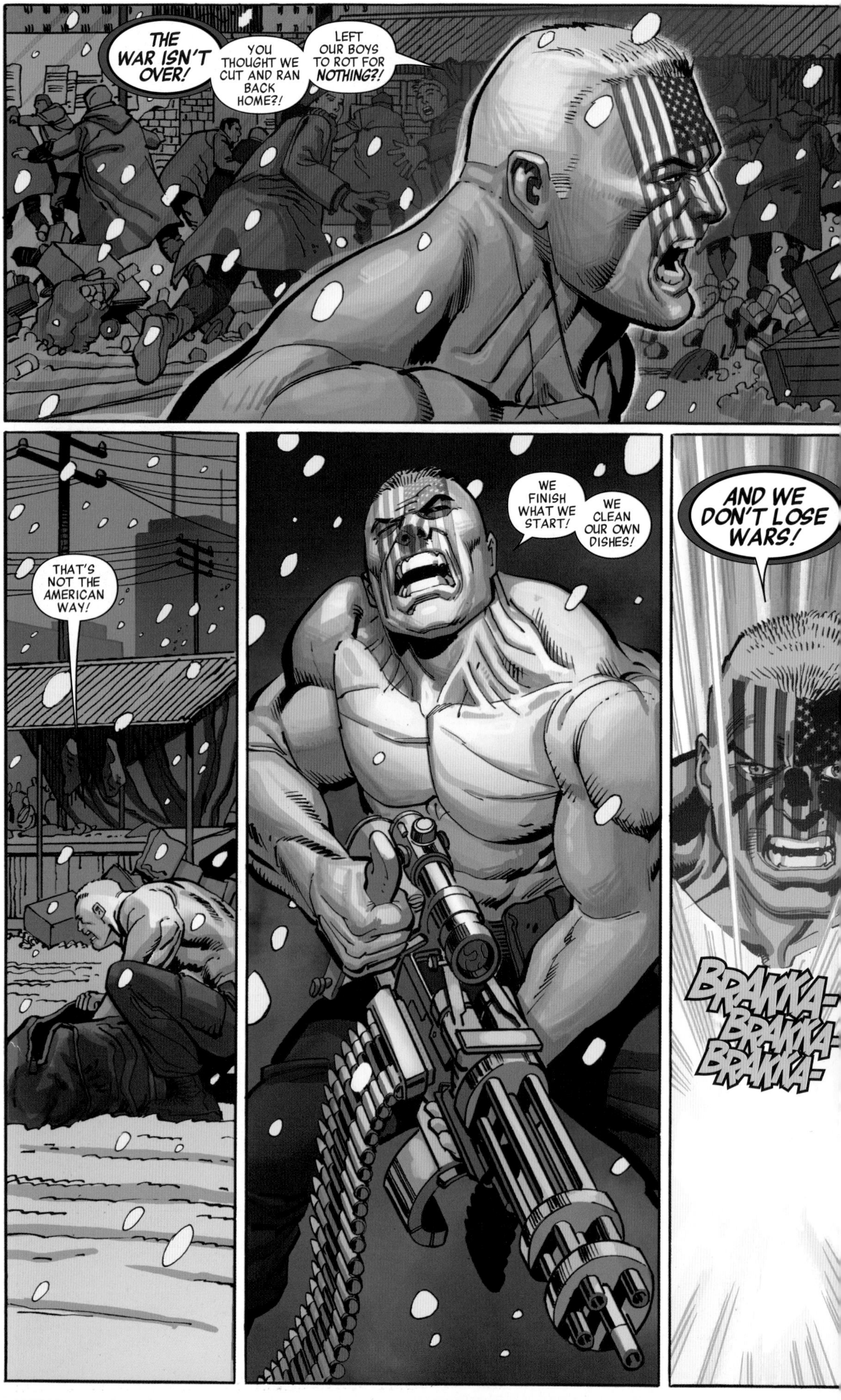
THE WAR ISN'T OVER!
YOU THOUGHT WE CUT AND RAN BACK HOME?!
LEFT OUR BOYS TO ROT FOR NOTHING?!
THAT'S NOT THE AMERICAN WAY!
WE FINISH WHAT WE START!
WE CLEAN OUR OWN DISHES!
AND WE DON'T LOSE WARS!
BRAKKA-BRAKKA-BRAKKA-

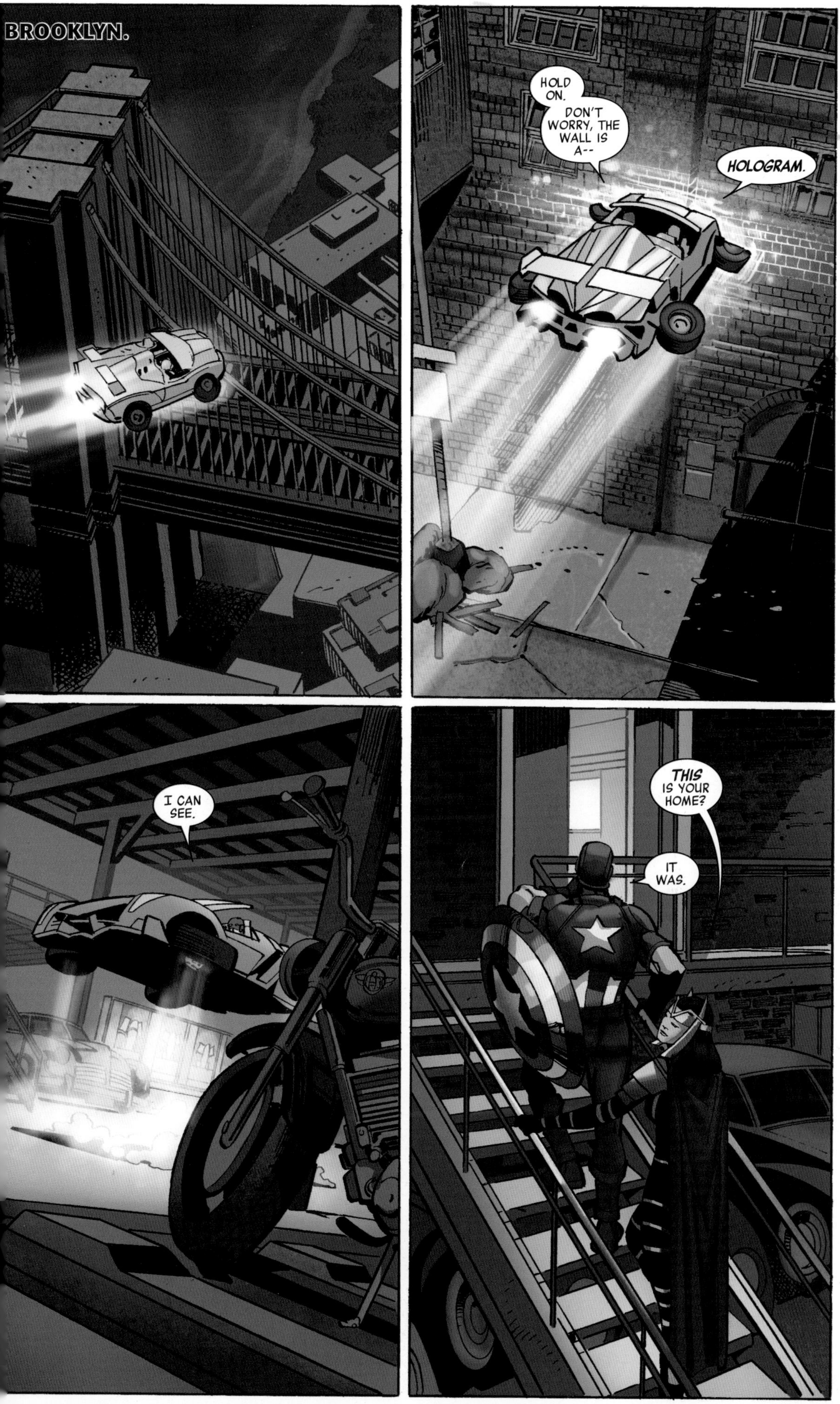
BROOKLYN.
HOLD ON.
DON'T WORRY, THE WALL IS A--
HOLOGRAM.
I CAN SEE.
THIS IS YOUR HOME?
IT WAS.

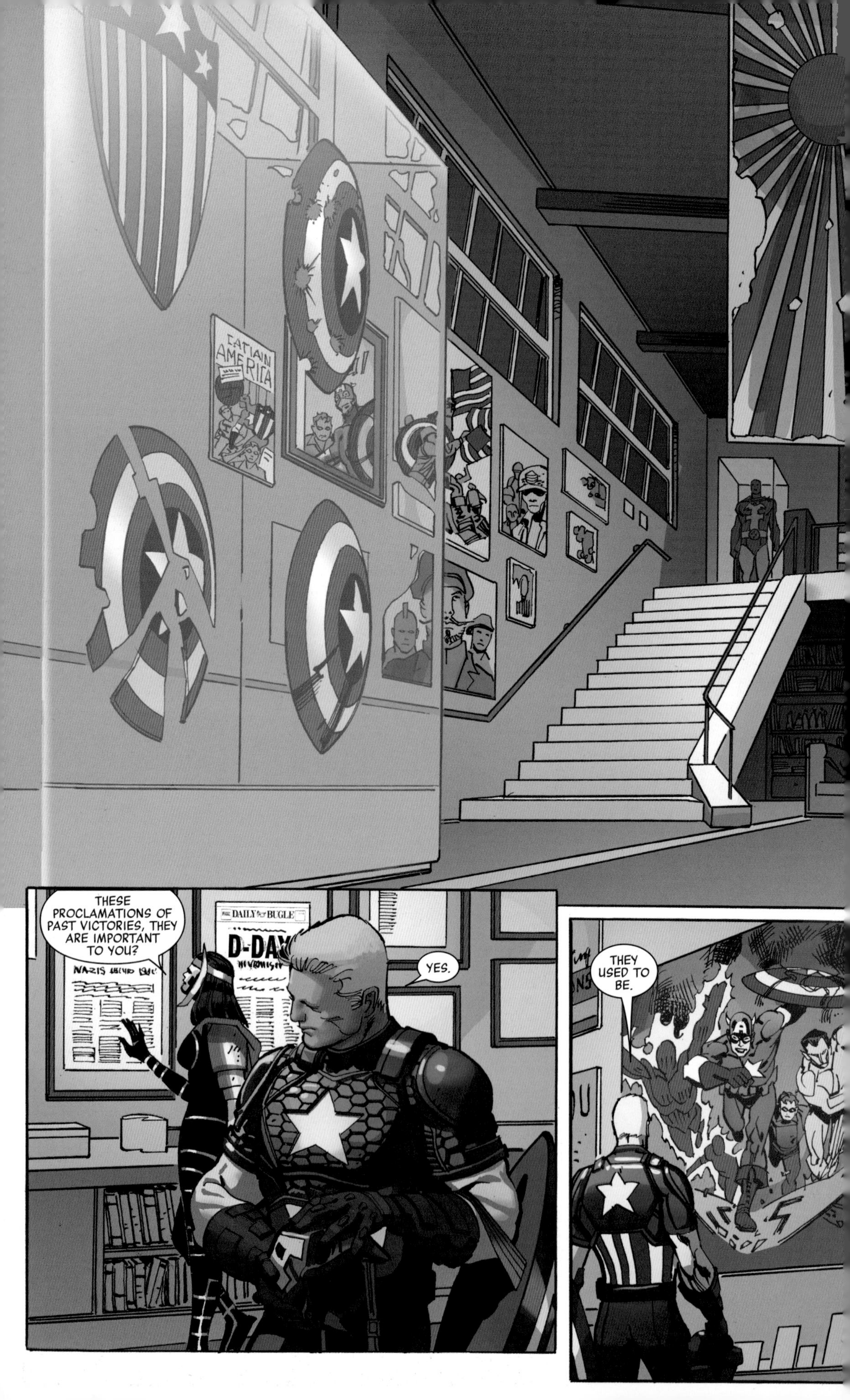
CAPTAIN AMERICA
DAILY BUGLE
D-DAY
NAZIS
THESE PROCLAMATIONS OF PAST VICTORIES, THEY ARE IMPORTANT TO YOU?
YES.
THEY USED TO BE.

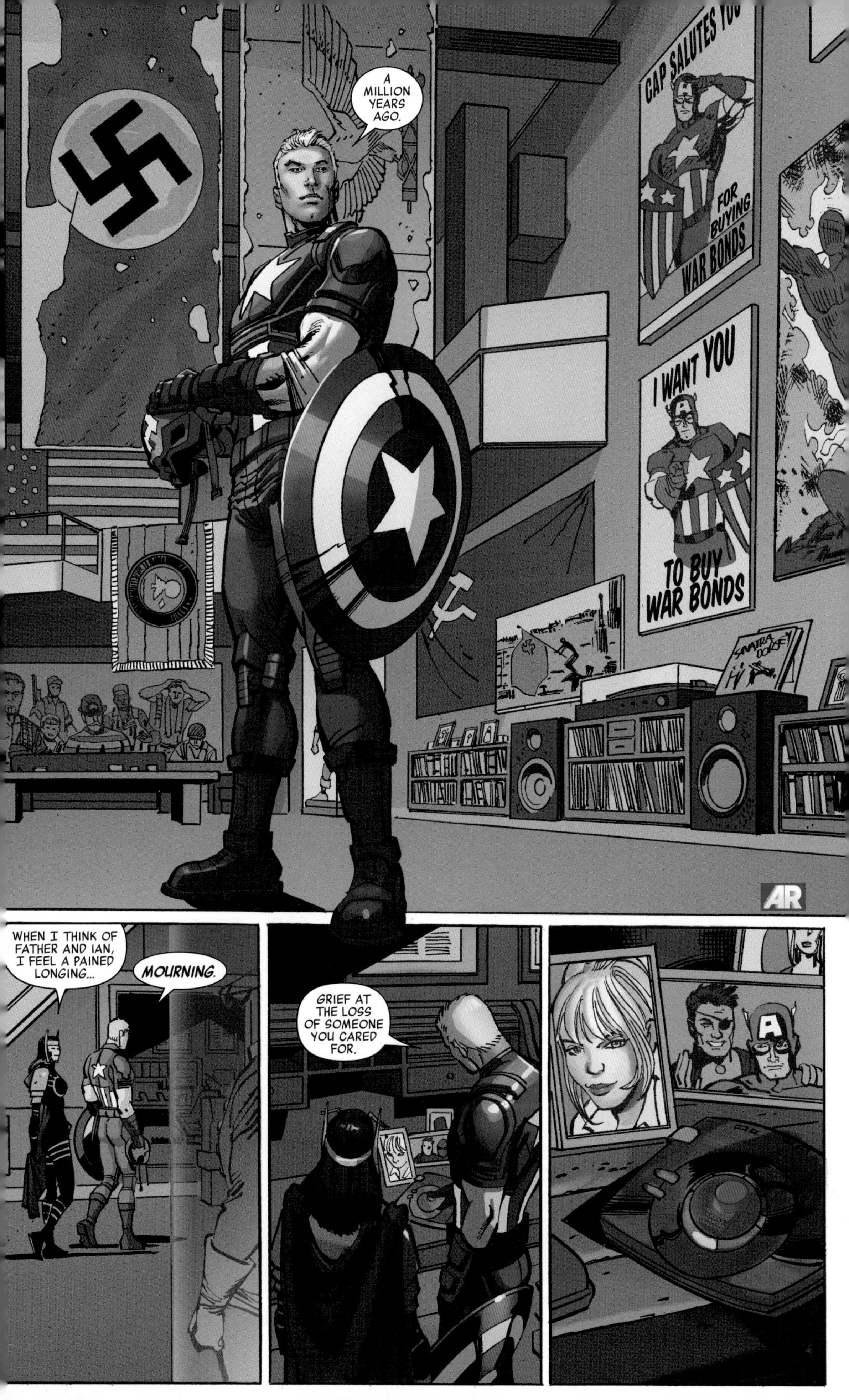
A MILLION YEARS AGO.
CAP SALUTES YOU
FOR BUYING WAR BONDS
I WANT YOU
TO BUY WAR BONDS
WHEN I THINK OF FATHER AND IAN, I FEEL A PAINED LONGING...
MOURNING.
GRIEF AT THE LOSS OF SOMEONE YOU CARED FOR.

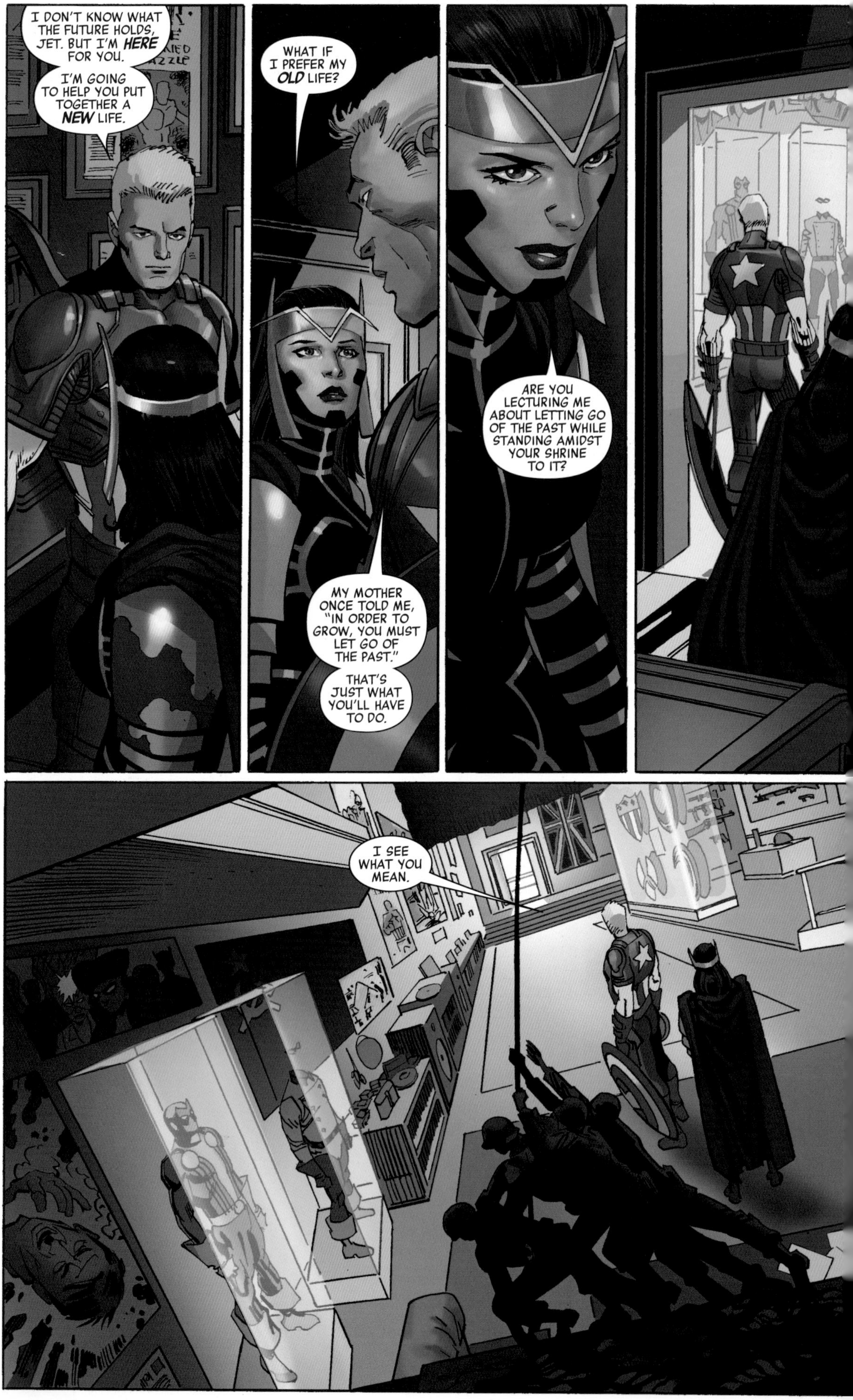
I DON'T KNOW WHAT THE FUTURE HOLDS, JET. BUT I'M HERE FOR YOU.
I'M GOING TO HELP YOU PUT TOGETHER A NEW LIFE.
WHAT IF I PREFER MY OLD LIFE?
MY MOTHER ONCE TOLD ME, "IN ORDER TO GROW, YOU MUST LET GO OF THE PAST."
THAT'S JUST WHAT YOU'LL HAVE TO DO.
ARE YOU LECTURING ME ABOUT LETTING GO OF THE PAST WHILE STANDING AMIDST YOUR SHRINE TO IT?
I SEE WHAT YOU MEAN.

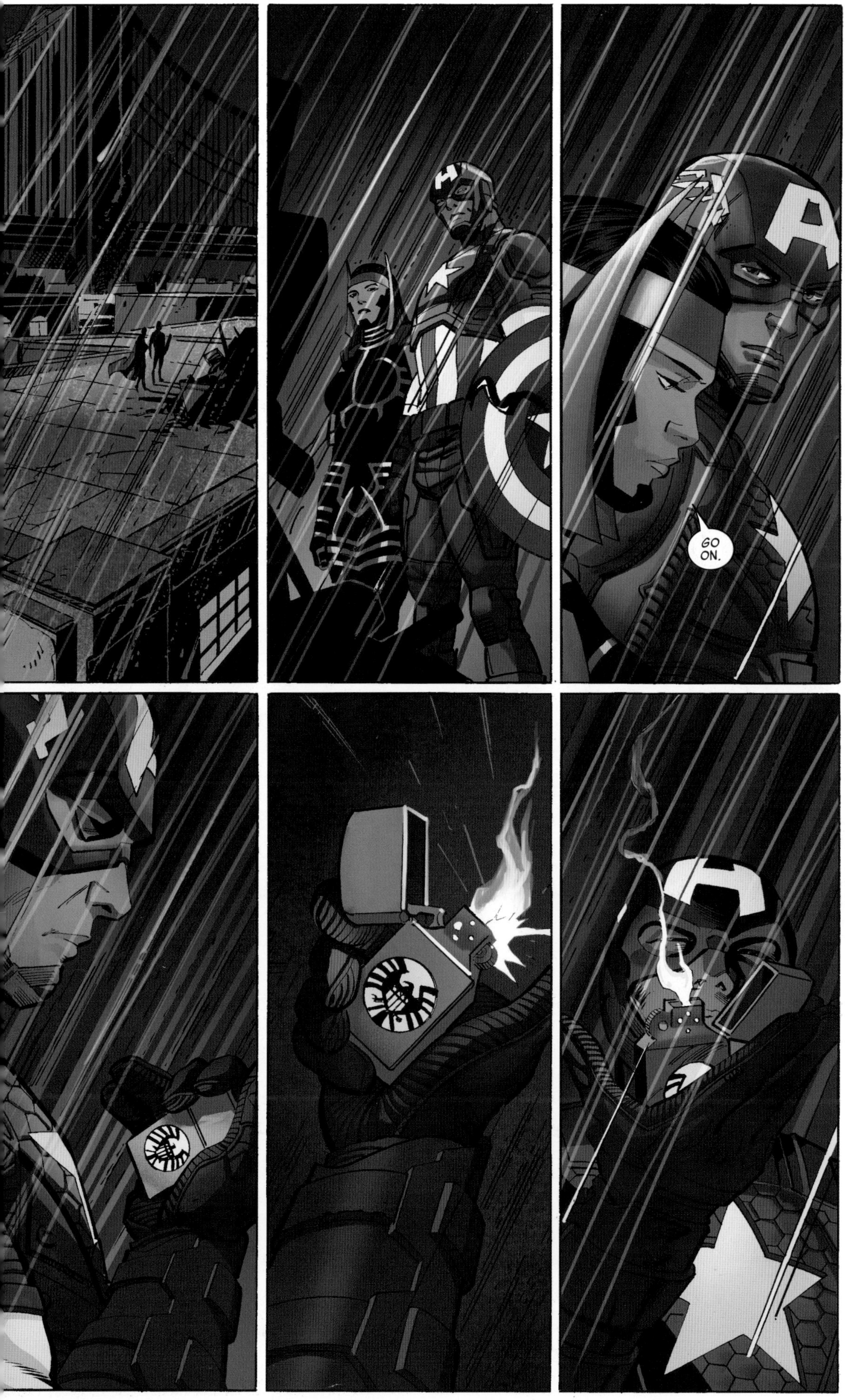
GO ON.

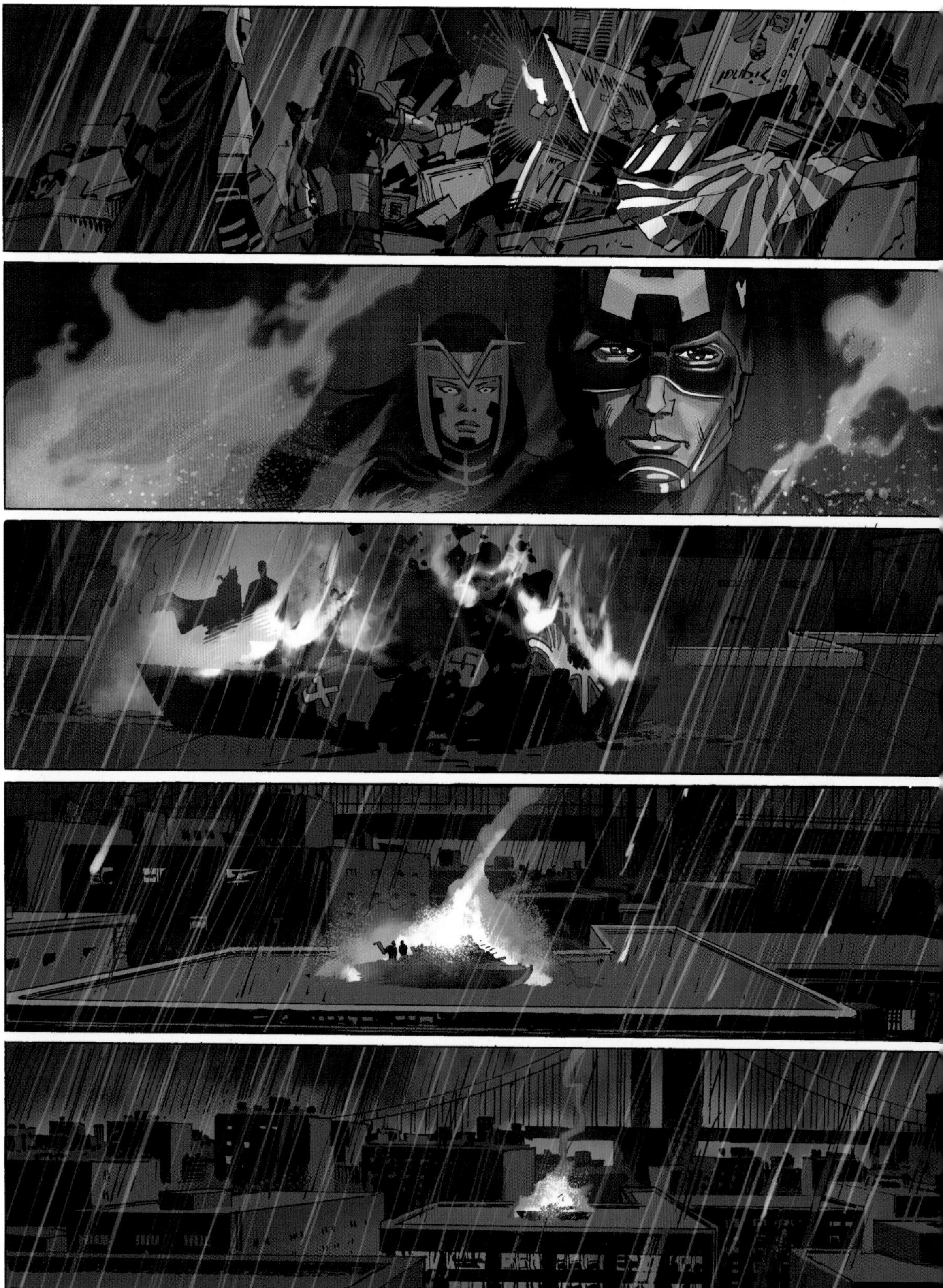

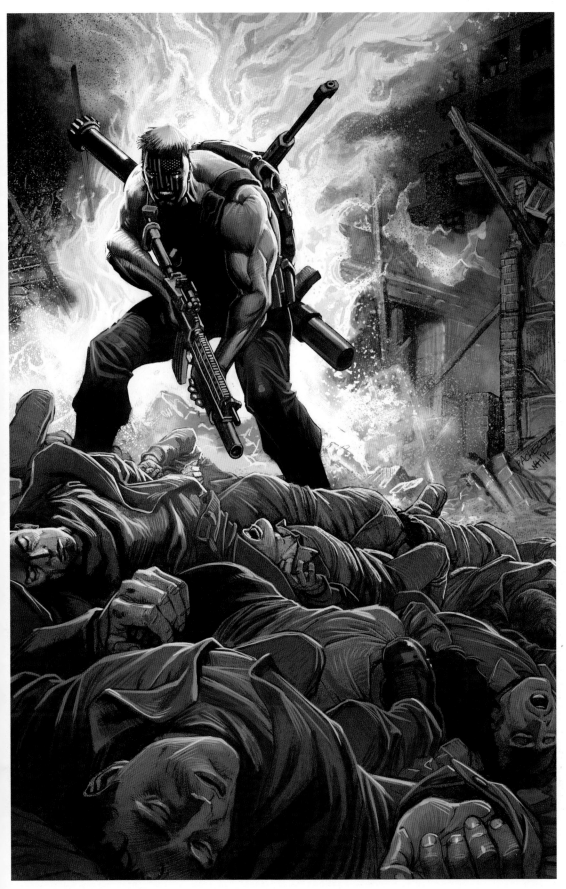

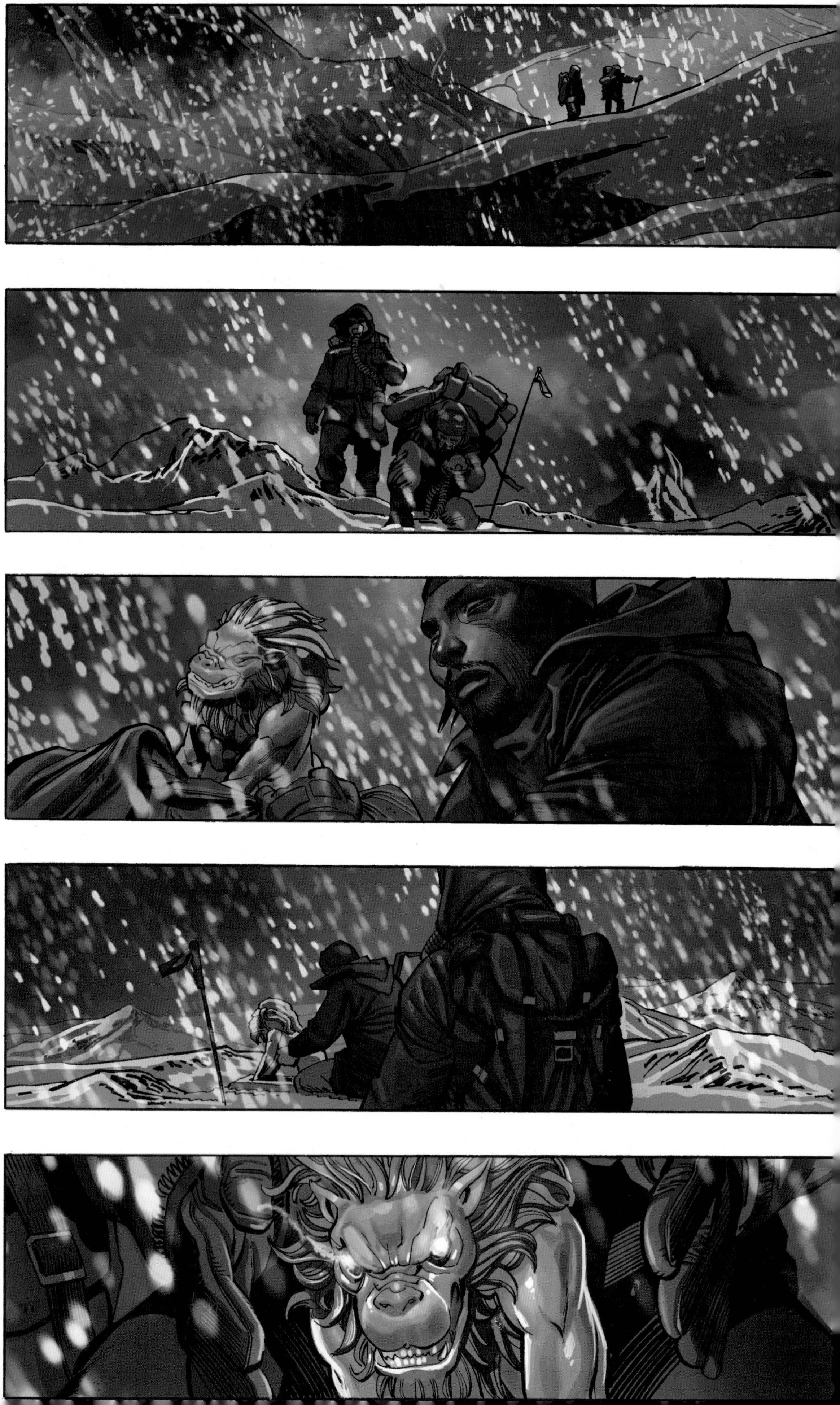

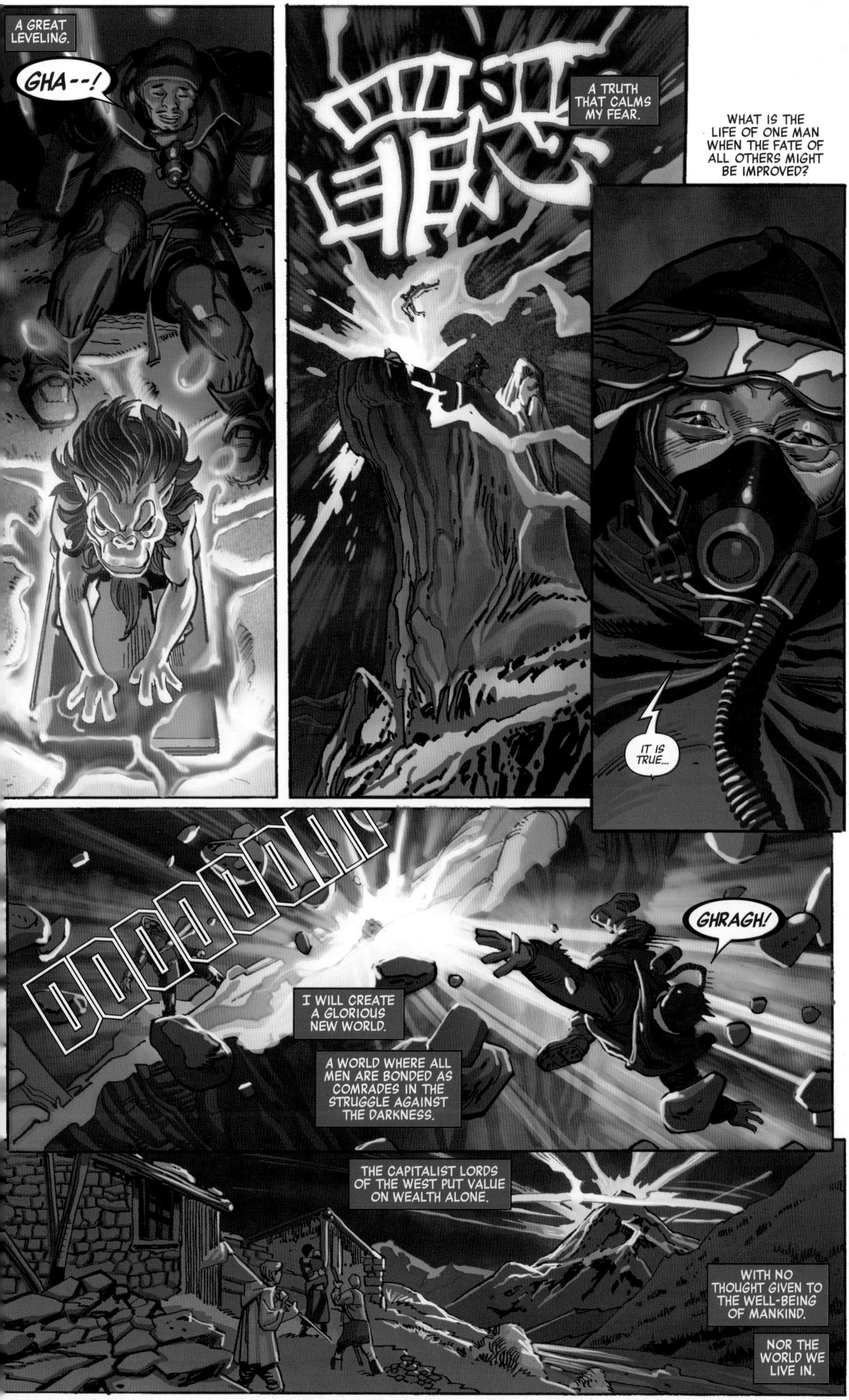
A GREAT LEVELING.
GHA--!
A TRUTH THAT CALMS MY FEAR.
WHAT IS THE LIFE OF ONE MAN WHEN THE FATE OF ALL OTHERS MIGHT BE IMPROVED?
IT IS TRUE...
GHRAGH!
I WILL CREATE A GLORIOUS NEW WORLD.
A WORLD WHERE ALL MEN ARE BONDED AS COMRADES IN THE STRUGGLE AGAINST THE DARKNESS.
THE CAPITALIST LORDS OF THE WEST PUT VALUE ON WEALTH ALONE.
WITH NO THOUGHT GIVEN TO THE WELL-BEING OF MANKIND.
NOR THE WORLD WE LIVE IN.

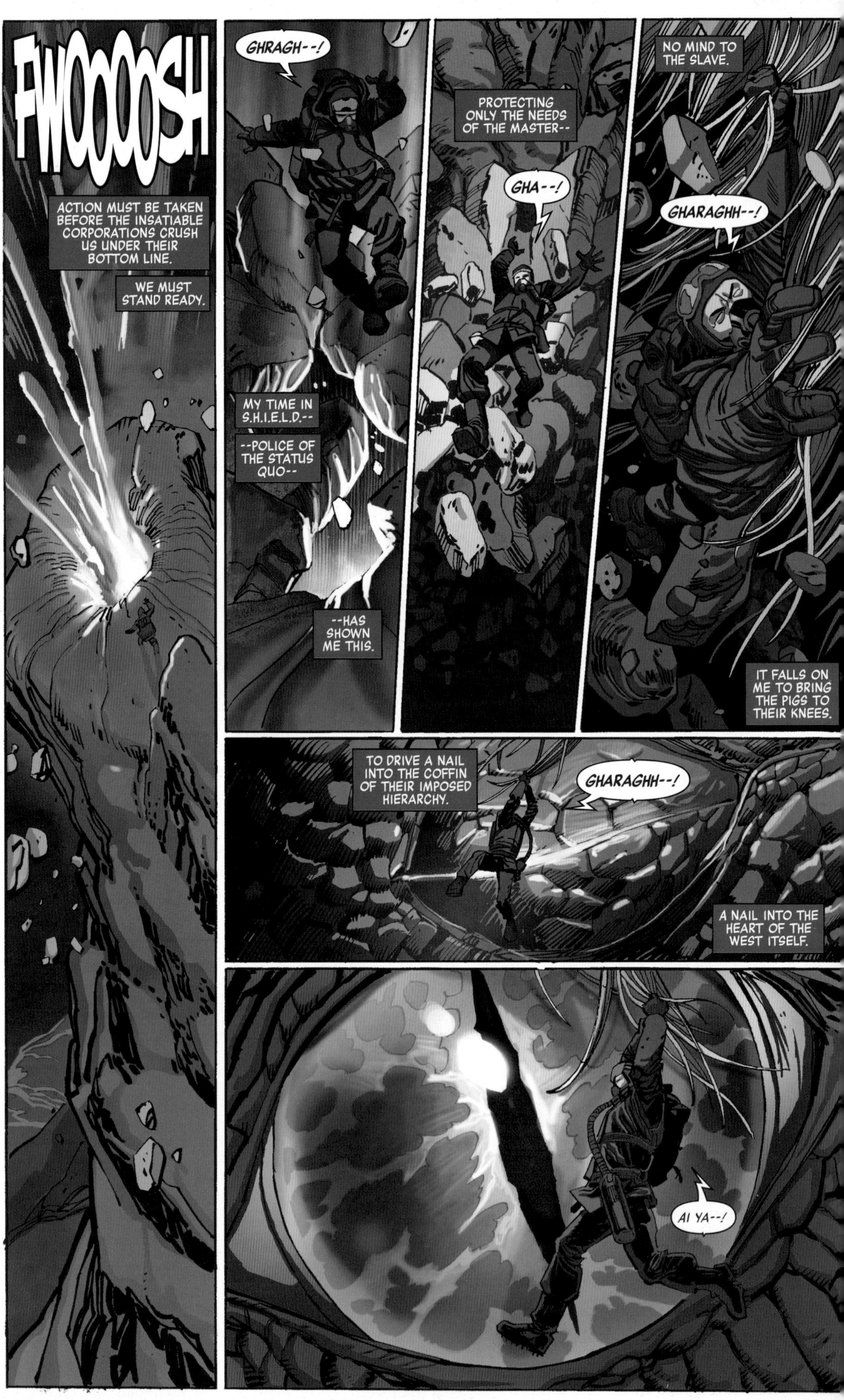
FWOOOOSH
ACTION MUST BE TAKEN BEFORE THE INSATIABLE CORPORATIONS CRUSH US UNDER THEIR BOTTOM LINE.
WE MUST STAND READY.
GHRAGH--!
MY TIME IN S.H.I.E.L.D.--
--POLICE OF THE STATUS QUO--
--HAS SHOWN ME THIS.
PROTECTING ONLY THE NEEDS OF THE MASTER--
GHA--!
NO MIND TO THE SLAVE.
GHARAGHH--!
IT FALLS ON ME TO BRING THE PIGS TO THEIR KNEES.
TO DRIVE A NAIL INTO THE COFFIN OF THEIR IMPOSED HIERARCHY.
GHARAGHH--!
A NAIL INTO THE HEART OF THE WEST ITSELF.
AI YA--!

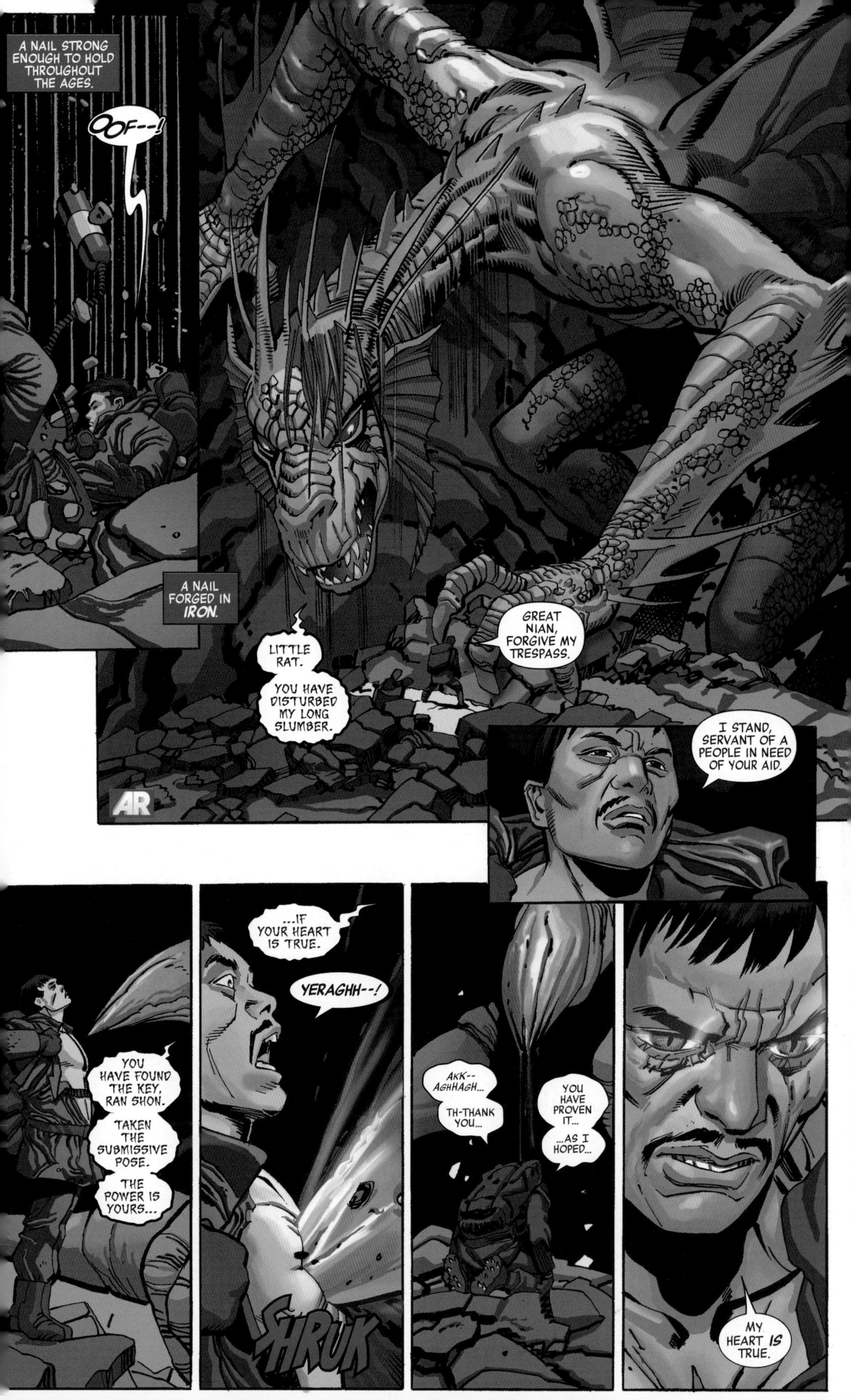
A NAIL STRONG ENOUGH TO HOLD THROUGHOUT THE AGES.
OOF--!
A NAIL FORGED IN IRON.
LITTLE RAT.
YOU HAVE DISTURBED MY LONG SLUMBER.
GREAT NIAN, FORGIVE MY TRESPASS.
I STAND, SERVANT OF A PEOPLE IN NEED OF YOUR AID.
YOU HAVE FOUND THE KEY, RAN SHON.
TAKEN THE SUBMISSIVE POSE.
THE POWER IS YOURS...
...IF YOUR HEART IS TRUE.
YERAGHH--!
SHRUK
AKK--AGHHAGH...
TH-THANK YOU...
YOU HAVE PROVEN IT...
...AS I HOPED...
MY HEART IS TRUE.

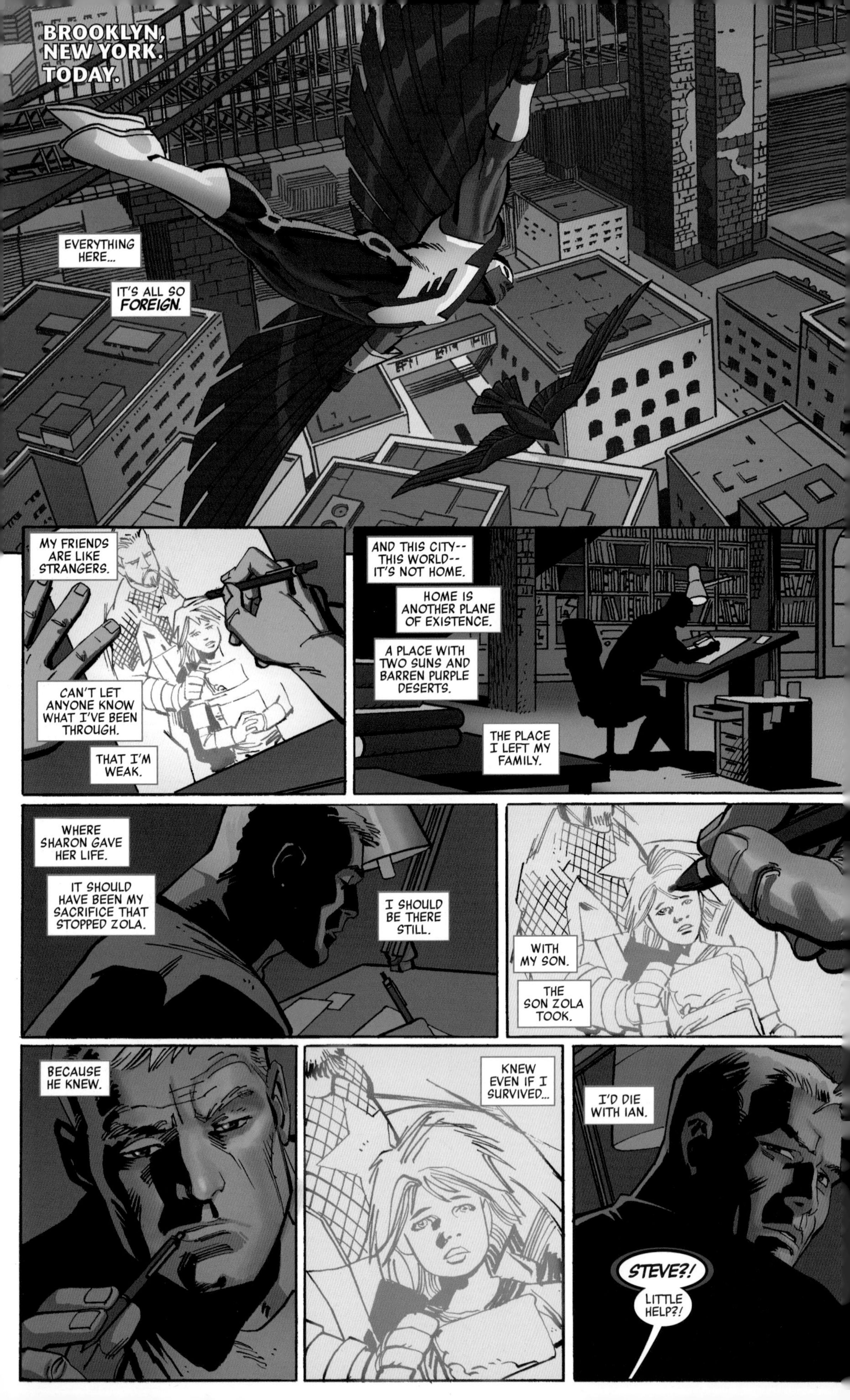
BROOKLYN, NEW YORK. TODAY.
EVERYTHING HERE...
IT'S ALL SO *FOREIGN*.
MY FRIENDS ARE LIKE STRANGERS.
CAN'T LET ANYONE KNOW WHAT I'VE BEEN THROUGH.
THAT I'M WEAK.
AND THIS CITY-- THIS WORLD-- IT'S NOT HOME.
HOME IS ANOTHER PLANE OF EXISTENCE.
A PLACE WITH TWO SUNS AND BARREN PURPLE DESERTS.
THE PLACE I LEFT MY FAMILY.
WHERE SHARON GAVE HER LIFE.
IT SHOULD HAVE BEEN MY SACRIFICE THAT STOPPED ZOLA.
I SHOULD BE THERE STILL.
WITH MY SON.
THE SON ZOLA TOOK.
BECAUSE HE KNEW.
KNEW EVEN IF I SURVIVED...
I'D DIE WITH IAN.
STEVE?!
LITTLE HELP?!

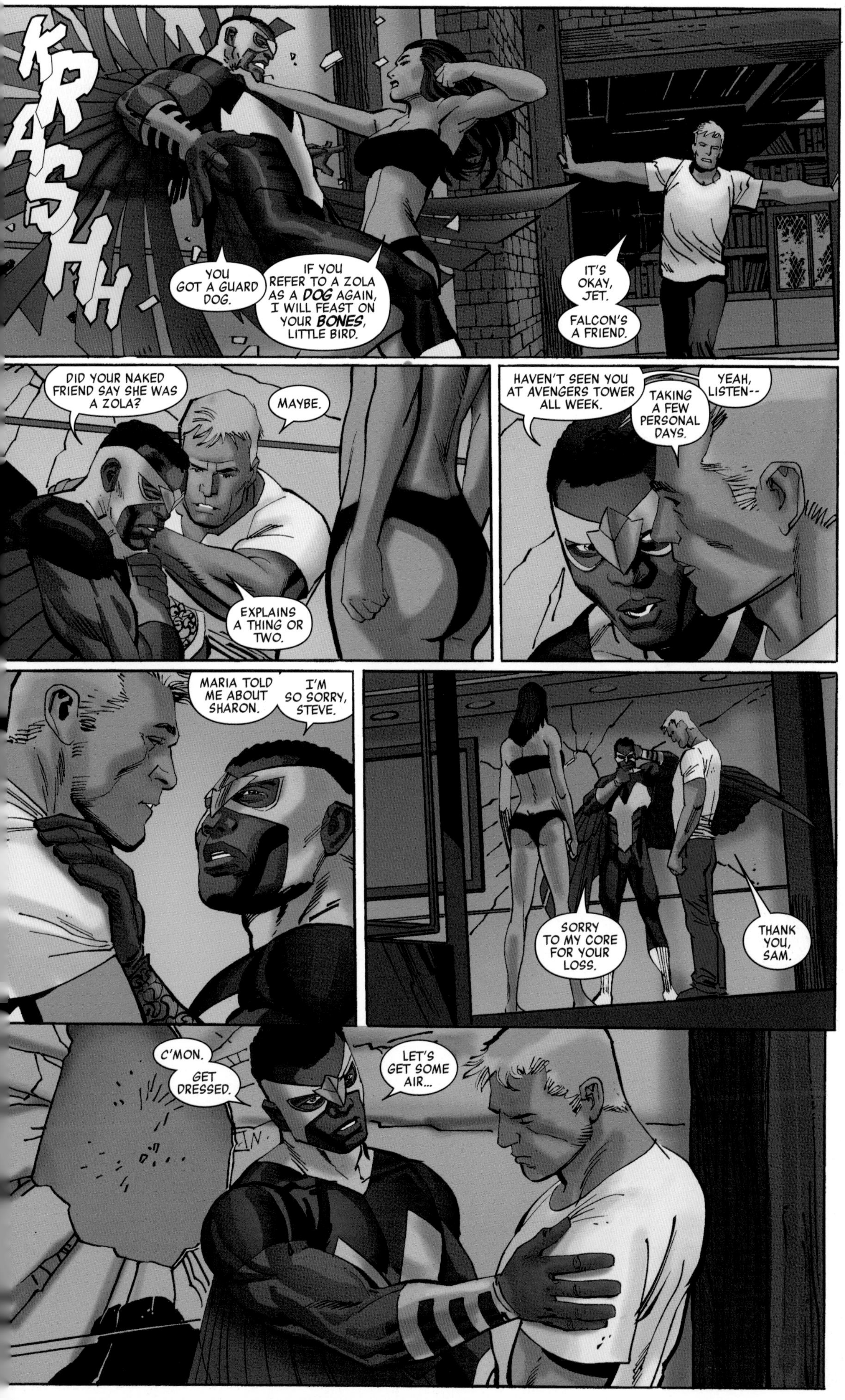
KRASHH
YOU GOT A GUARD DOG.
IF YOU REFER TO A ZOLA AS A DOG AGAIN, I WILL FEAST ON YOUR BONES, LITTLE BIRD.
IT'S OKAY, JET.
FALCON'S A FRIEND.
DID YOUR NAKED FRIEND SAY SHE WAS A ZOLA?
MAYBE.
EXPLAINS A THING OR TWO.
HAVEN'T SEEN YOU AT AVENGERS TOWER ALL WEEK.
YEAH, LISTEN--
TAKING A FEW PERSONAL DAYS.
MARIA TOLD ME ABOUT SHARON.
I'M SO SORRY, STEVE.
SORRY TO MY CORE FOR YOUR LOSS.
THANK YOU, SAM.
C'MON.
GET DRESSED.
LET'S GET SOME AIR...

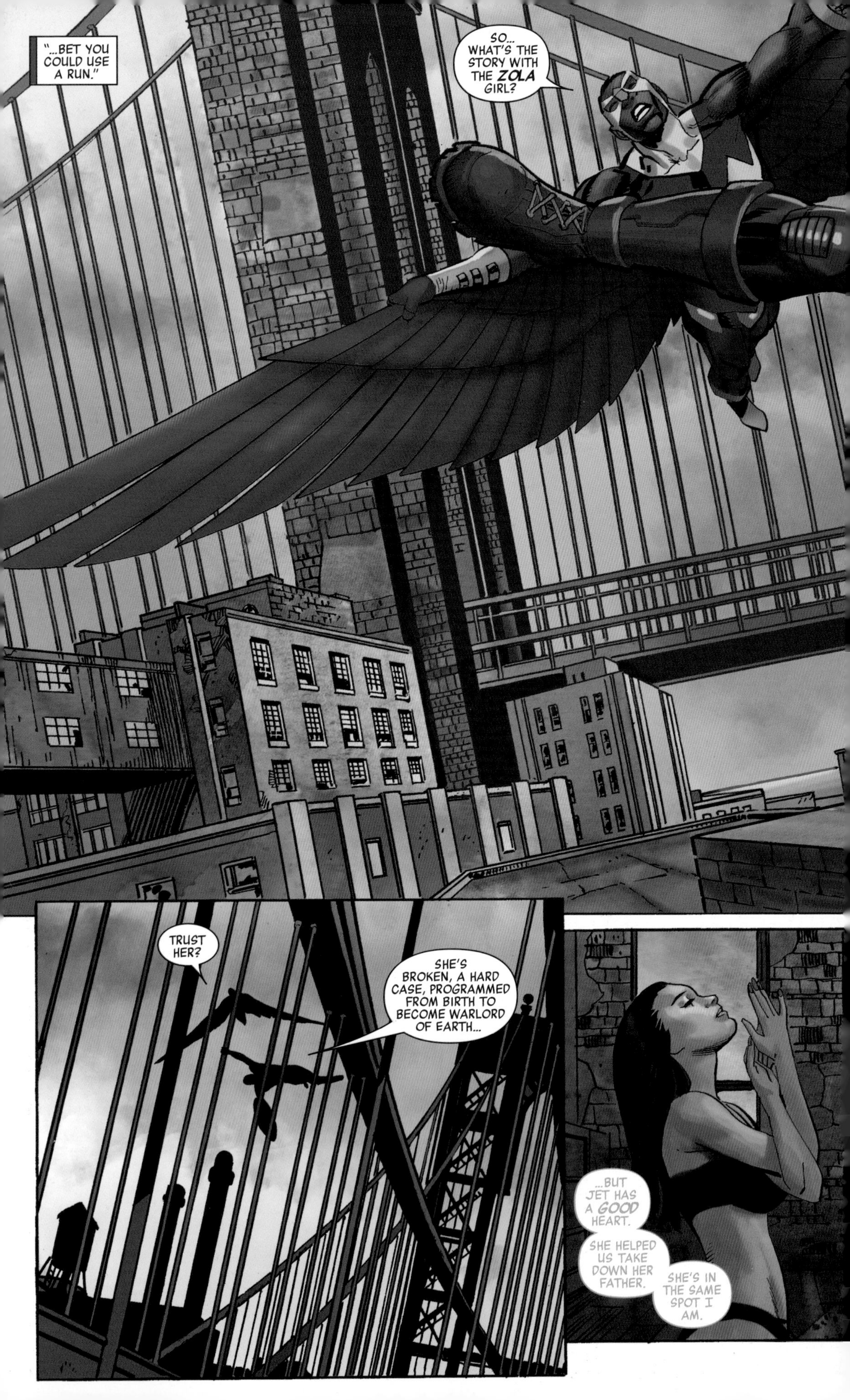
"...BET YOU COULD USE A RUN."
SO... WHAT'S THE STORY WITH THE ZOLA GIRL?
TRUST HER?
SHE'S BROKEN, A HARD CASE, PROGRAMMED FROM BIRTH TO BECOME WARLORD OF EARTH...
...BUT JET HAS A GOOD HEART.
SHE HELPED US TAKE DOWN HER FATHER.
SHE'S IN THE SAME SPOT I AM.

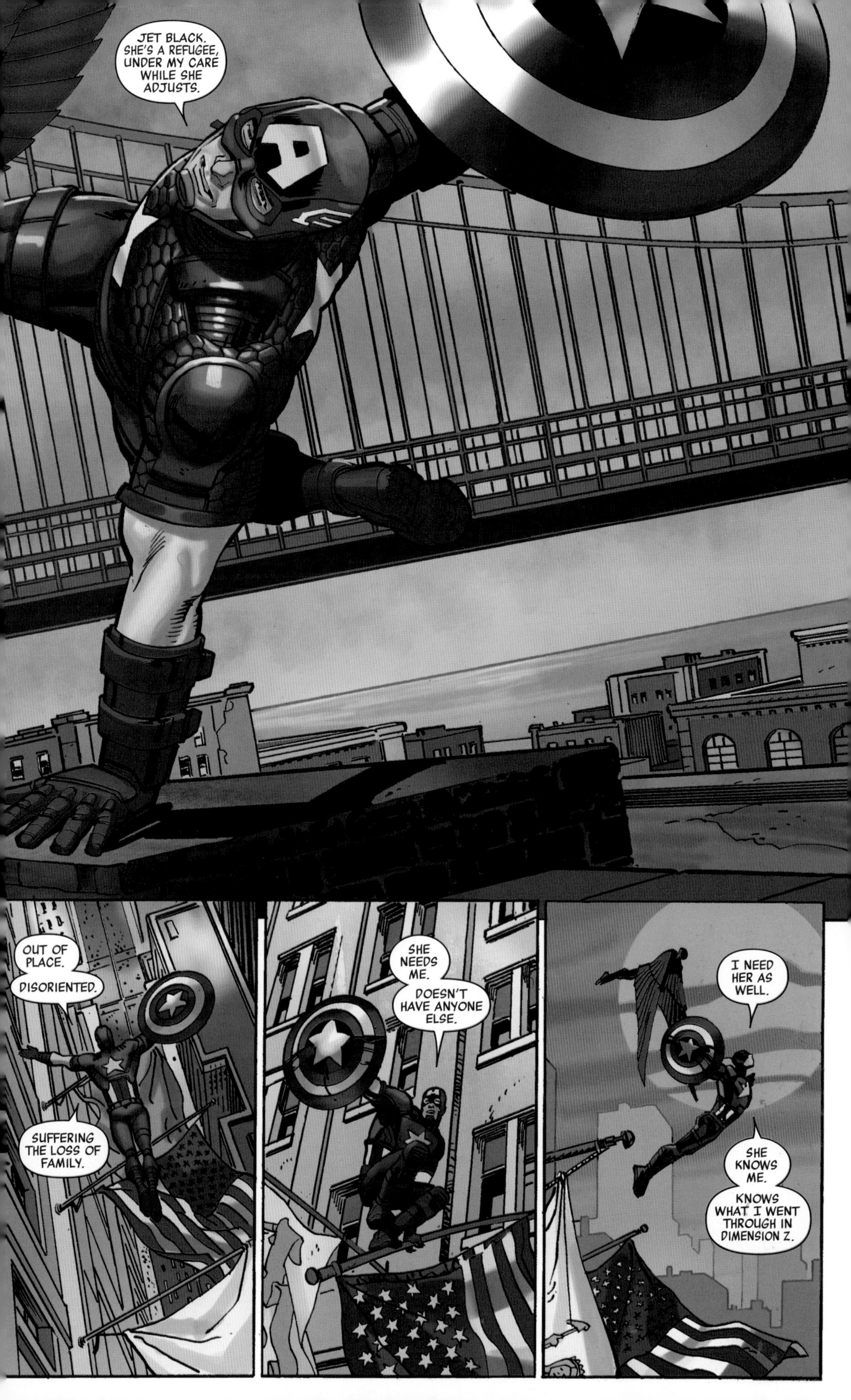
JET BLACK. SHE'S A REFUGEE, UNDER MY CARE WHILE SHE ADJUSTS.
OUT OF PLACE.
DISORIENTED.
SUFFERING THE LOSS OF FAMILY.
SHE NEEDS ME.
DOESN'T HAVE ANYONE ELSE.
I NEED HER AS WELL.
SHE KNOWS ME.
KNOWS WHAT I WENT THROUGH IN DIMENSION Z.

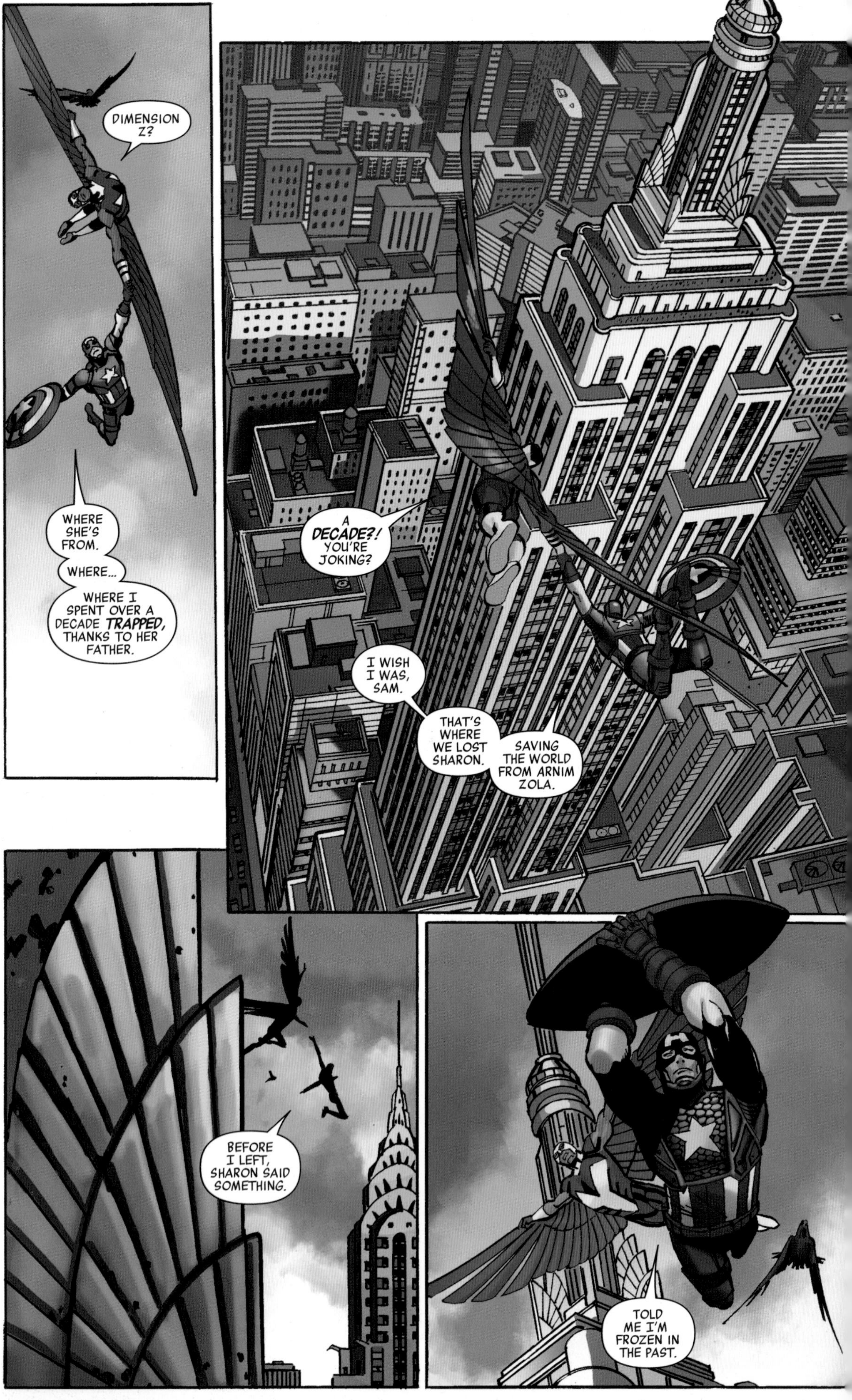
DIMENSION Z?
WHERE SHE'S FROM.
WHERE...
WHERE I SPENT OVER A DECADE TRAPPED, THANKS TO HER FATHER.
A DECADE?! YOU'RE JOKING?
I WISH I WAS, SAM.
THAT'S WHERE WE LOST SHARON.
SAVING THE WORLD FROM ARNIM ZOLA.
BEFORE I LEFT, SHARON SAID SOMETHING.
TOLD ME I'M FROZEN IN THE PAST.

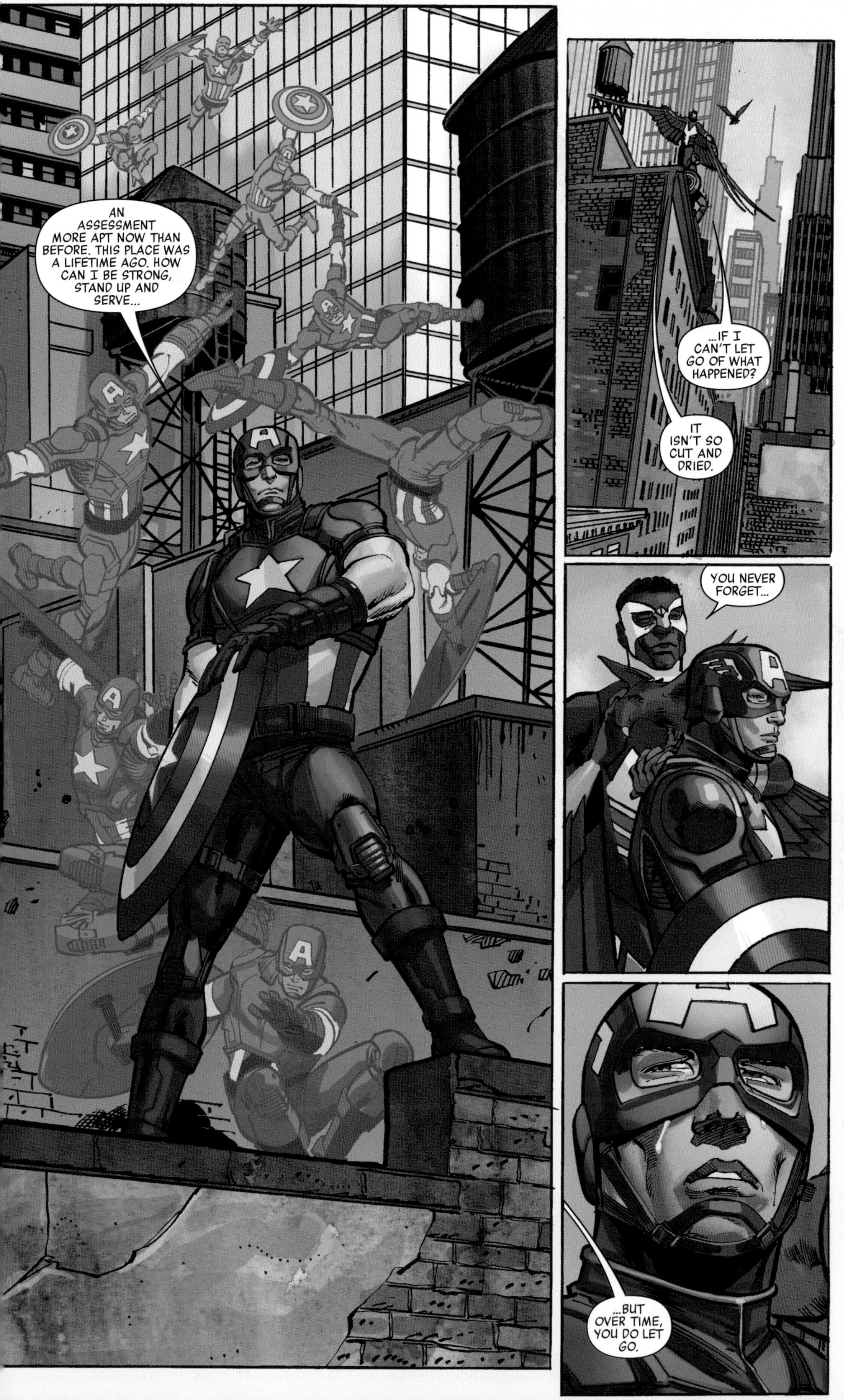
AN ASSESSMENT MORE APT NOW THAN BEFORE. THIS PLACE WAS A LIFETIME AGO. HOW CAN I BE STRONG, STAND UP AND SERVE...
...IF I CAN'T LET GO OF WHAT HAPPENED?
IT ISN'T SO CUT AND DRIED.
YOU NEVER FORGET...
...BUT OVER TIME, YOU DO LET GO.

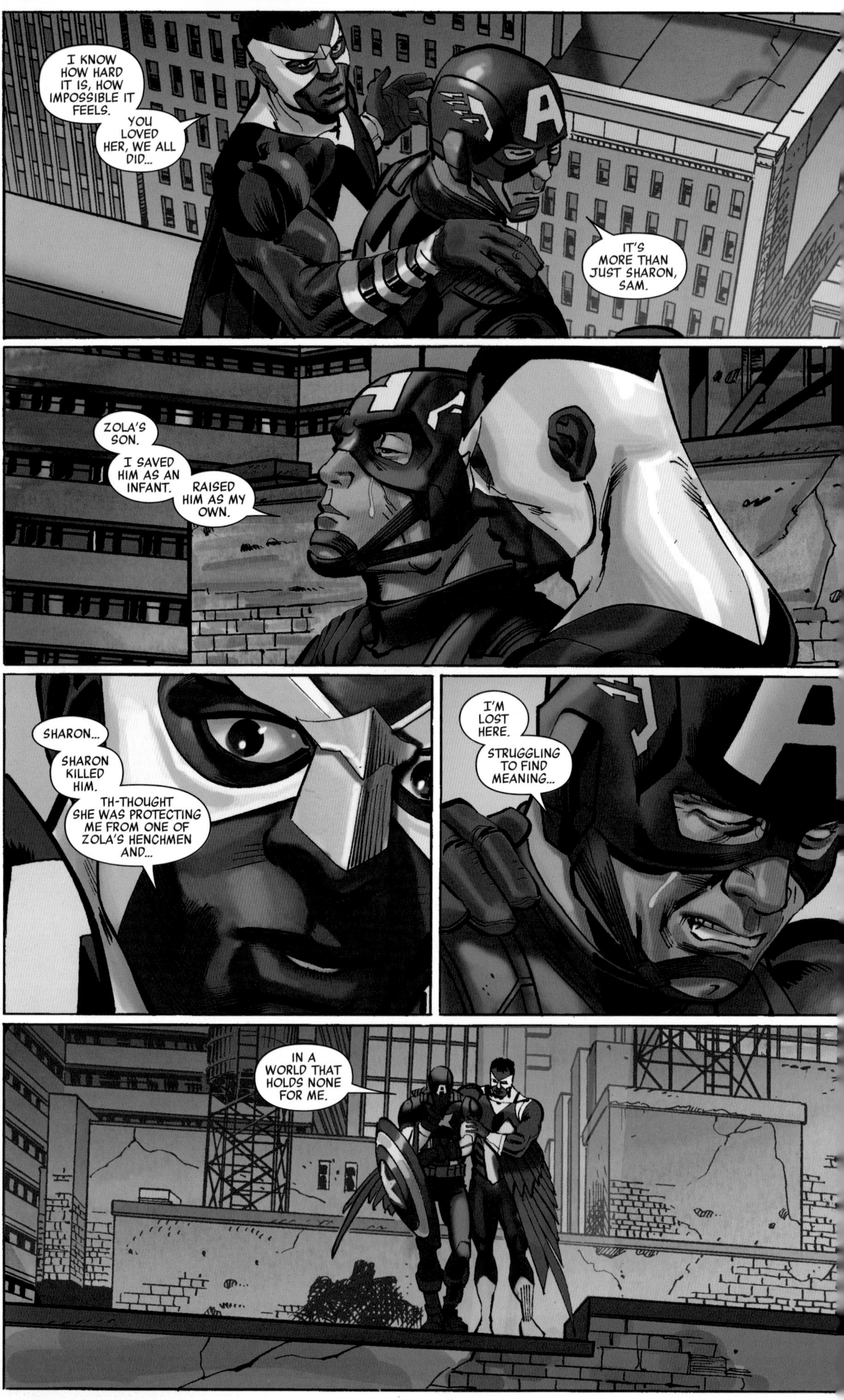

I KNOW HOW HARD IT IS, HOW IMPOSSIBLE IT FEELS.
YOU LOVED HER, WE ALL DID...
IT'S MORE THAN JUST SHARON, SAM.
ZOLA'S SON.
I SAVED HIM AS AN INFANT.
RAISED HIM AS MY OWN.
SHARON...
SHARON KILLED HIM.
TH-THOUGHT SHE WAS PROTECTING ME FROM ONE OF ZOLA'S HENCHMEN AND...
I'M LOST HERE.
STRUGGLING TO FIND MEANING...
IN A WORLD THAT HOLDS NONE FOR ME.

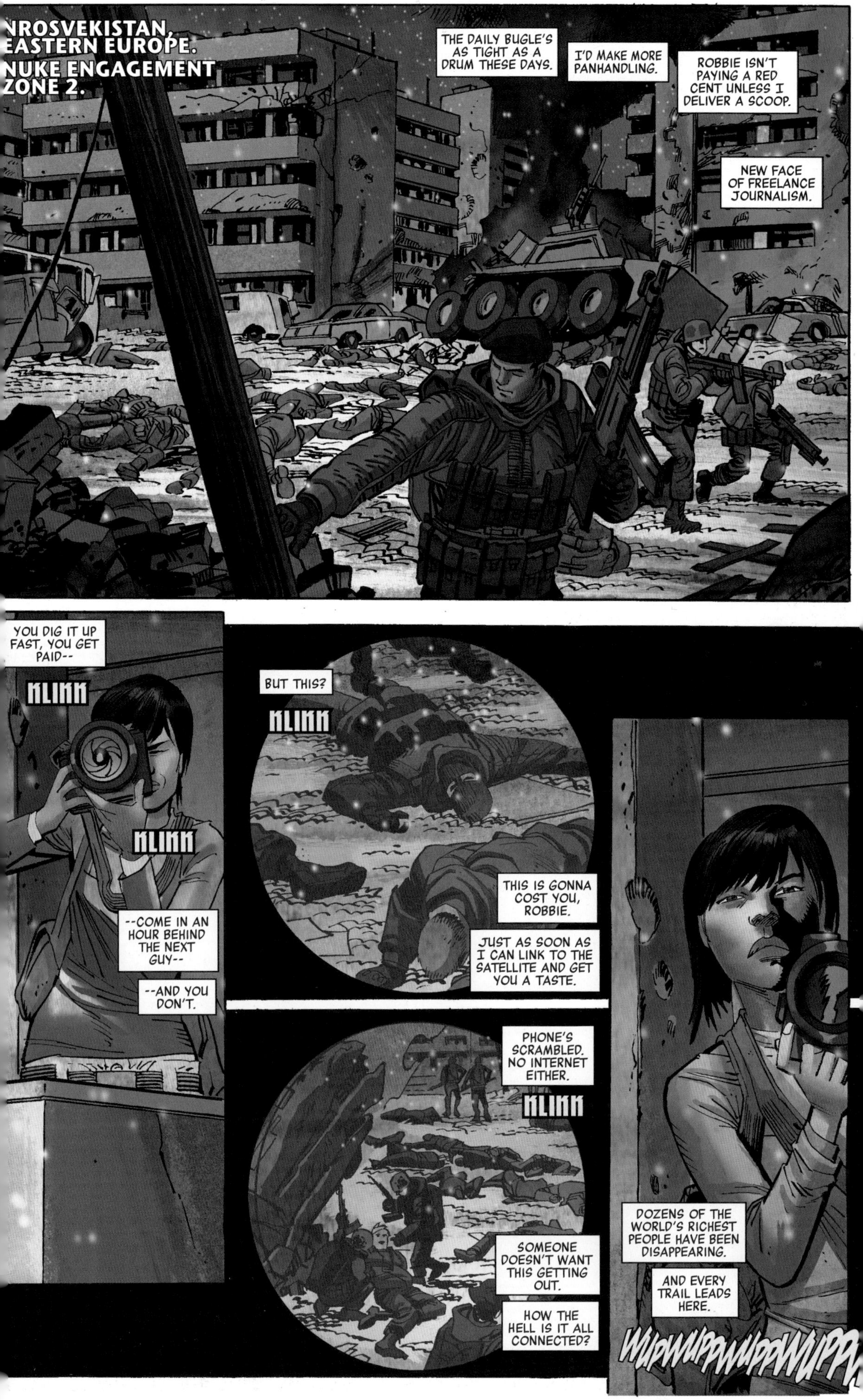

NROSVEKISTAN, EASTERN EUROPE.
NUKE ENGAGEMENT ZONE 2.
THE DAILY BUGLE'S AS TIGHT AS A DRUM THESE DAYS.
I'D MAKE MORE PANHANDLING.
ROBBIE ISN'T PAYING A RED CENT UNLESS I DELIVER A SCOOP.
NEW FACE OF FREELANCE JOURNALISM.
YOU DIG IT UP FAST, YOU GET PAID--
KLIKK
KLIKK
--COME IN AN HOUR BEHIND THE NEXT GUY--
--AND YOU DON'T.
BUT THIS?
KLIKK
THIS IS GONNA COST YOU, ROBBIE.
JUST AS SOON AS I CAN LINK TO THE SATELLITE AND GET YOU A TASTE.
PHONE'S SCRAMBLED. NO INTERNET EITHER.
KLIKK
SOMEONE DOESN'T WANT THIS GETTING OUT.
HOW THE HELL IS IT ALL CONNECTED?
DOZENS OF THE WORLD'S RICHEST PEOPLE HAVE BEEN DISAPPEARING.
AND EVERY TRAIL LEADS HERE.
WUPWUPPWUPPWUPP

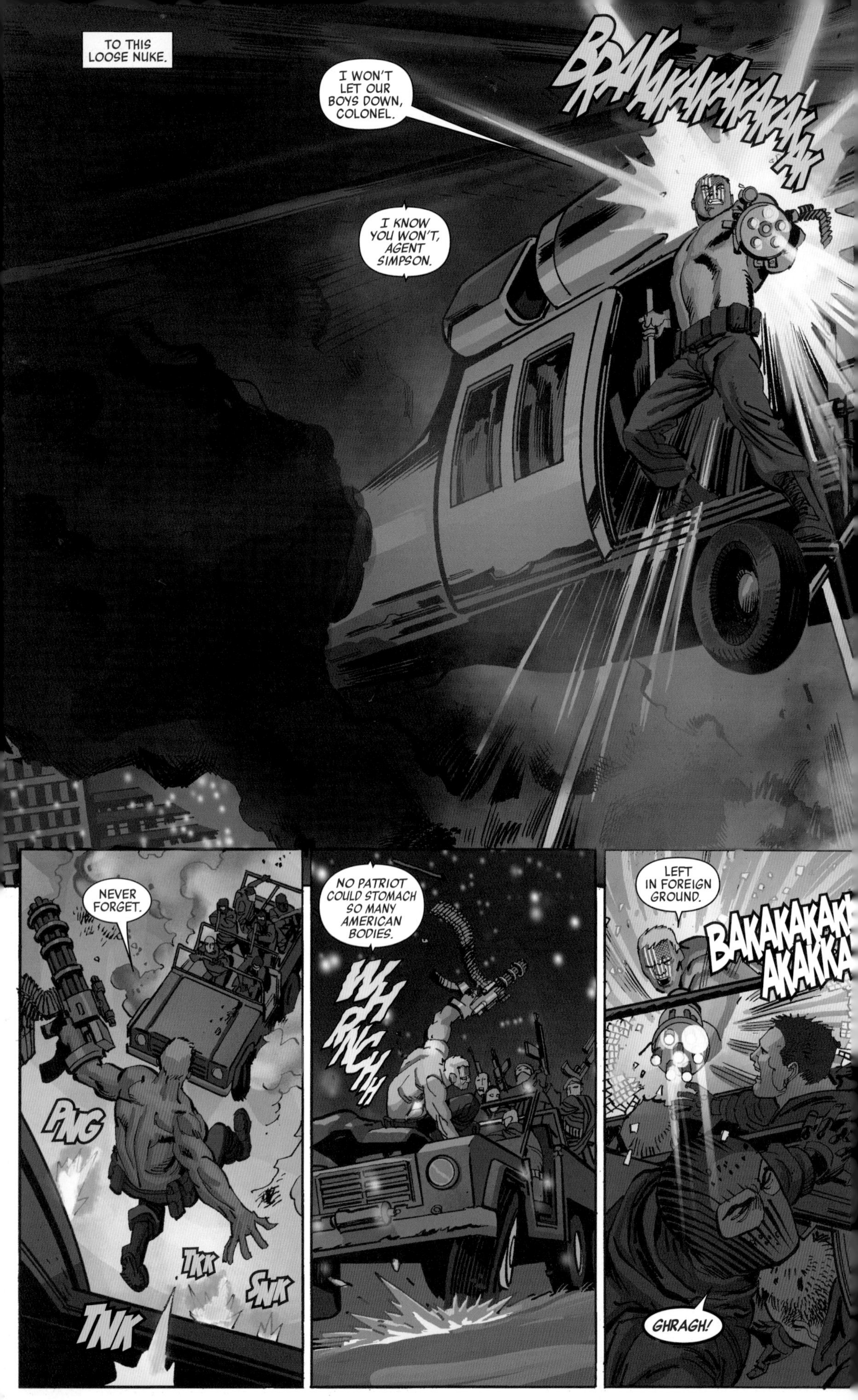
TO THIS LOOSE NUKE.
BRAKAKAKAKAKAKAKAKAK
I WON'T LET OUR BOYS DOWN, COLONEL.
I KNOW YOU WON'T, AGENT SIMPSON.
NEVER FORGET.
PNG
TKK
SNK
TNK
NO PATRIOT COULD STOMACH SO MANY AMERICAN BODIES.
WHRNCHH
LEFT IN FOREIGN GROUND.
BAKAKAKAKI AKAKKA
GHRAGH!

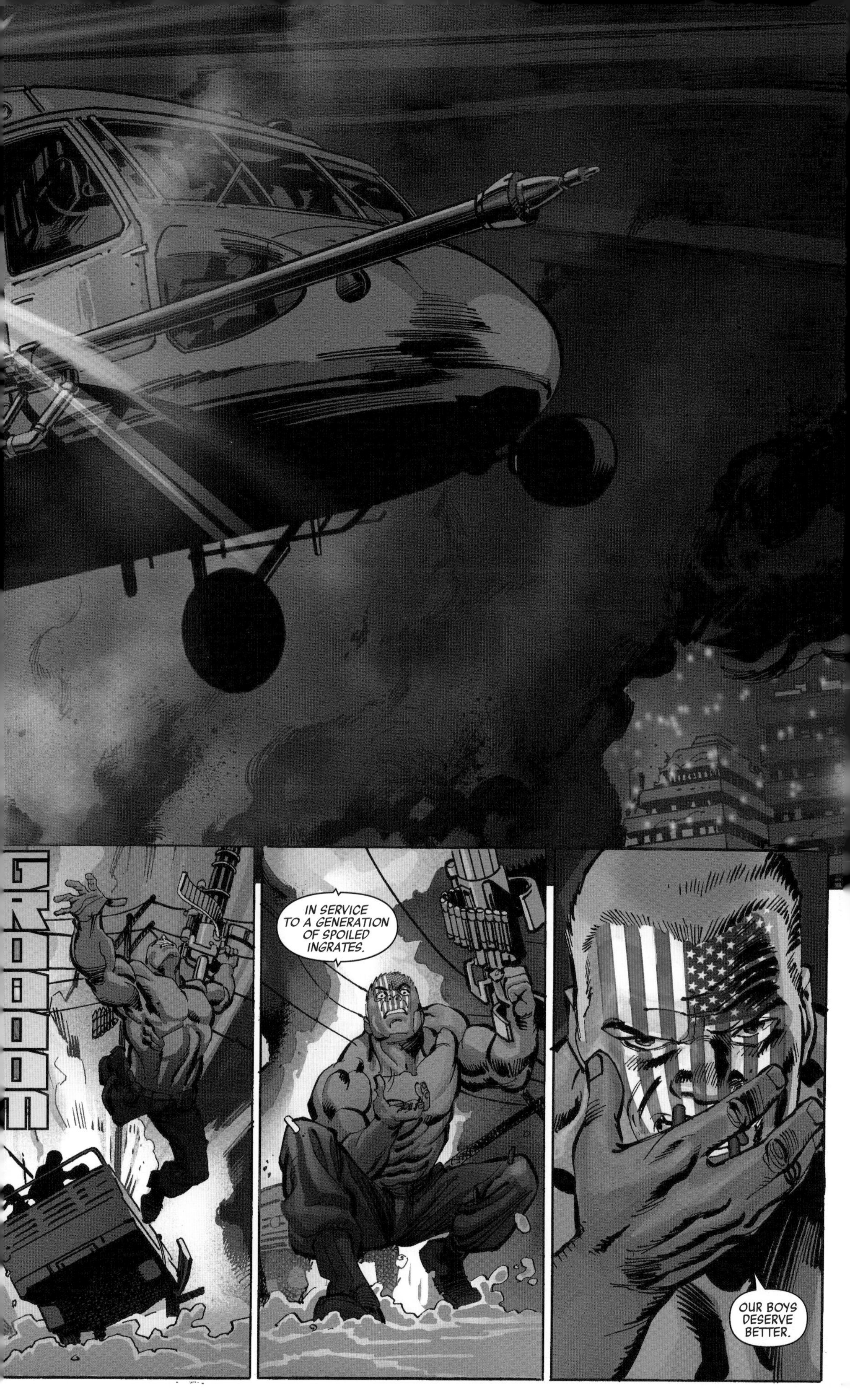
GROOOOM
IN SERVICE TO A GENERATION OF SPOILED INGRATES.
OUR BOYS DESERVE BETTER.

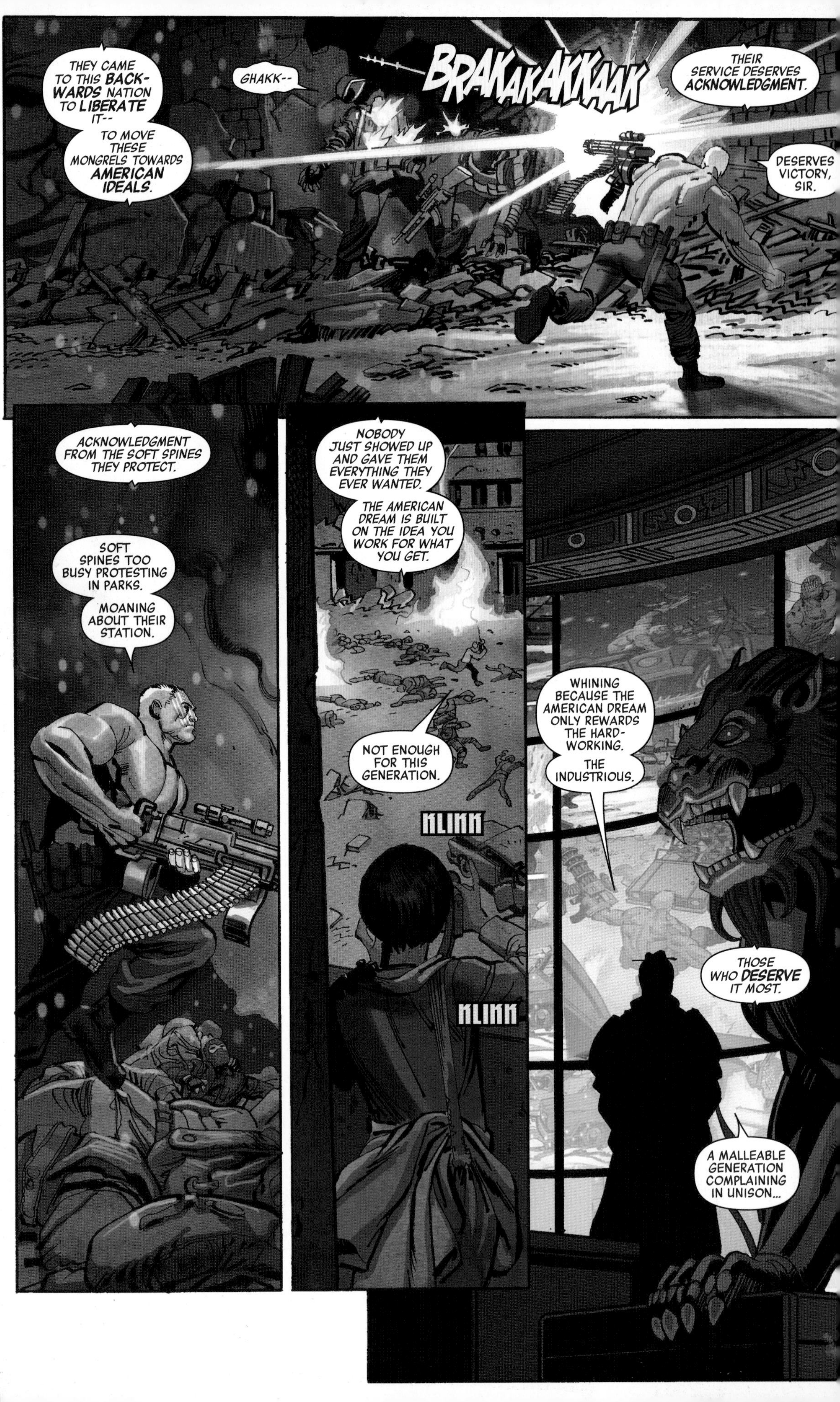

THEY CAME TO THIS BACKWARDS NATION TO LIBERATE IT--
TO MOVE THESE MONGRELS TOWARDS AMERICAN IDEALS.
GHAKK--
BRAKAKAKKAAK
THEIR SERVICE DESERVES ACKNOWLEDGMENT.
DESERVES VICTORY, SIR.
ACKNOWLEDGMENT FROM THE SOFT SPINES THEY PROTECT.
SOFT SPINES TOO BUSY PROTESTING IN PARKS.
MOANING ABOUT THEIR STATION.
NOBODY JUST SHOWED UP AND GAVE THEM EVERYTHING THEY EVER WANTED.
THE AMERICAN DREAM IS BUILT ON THE IDEA YOU WORK FOR WHAT YOU GET.
NOT ENOUGH FOR THIS GENERATION.
KLIKK
KLIKK
WHINING BECAUSE THE AMERICAN DREAM ONLY REWARDS THE HARD-WORKING.
THE INDUSTRIOUS.
THOSE WHO DESERVE IT MOST.
A MALLEABLE GENERATION COMPLAINING IN UNISON...

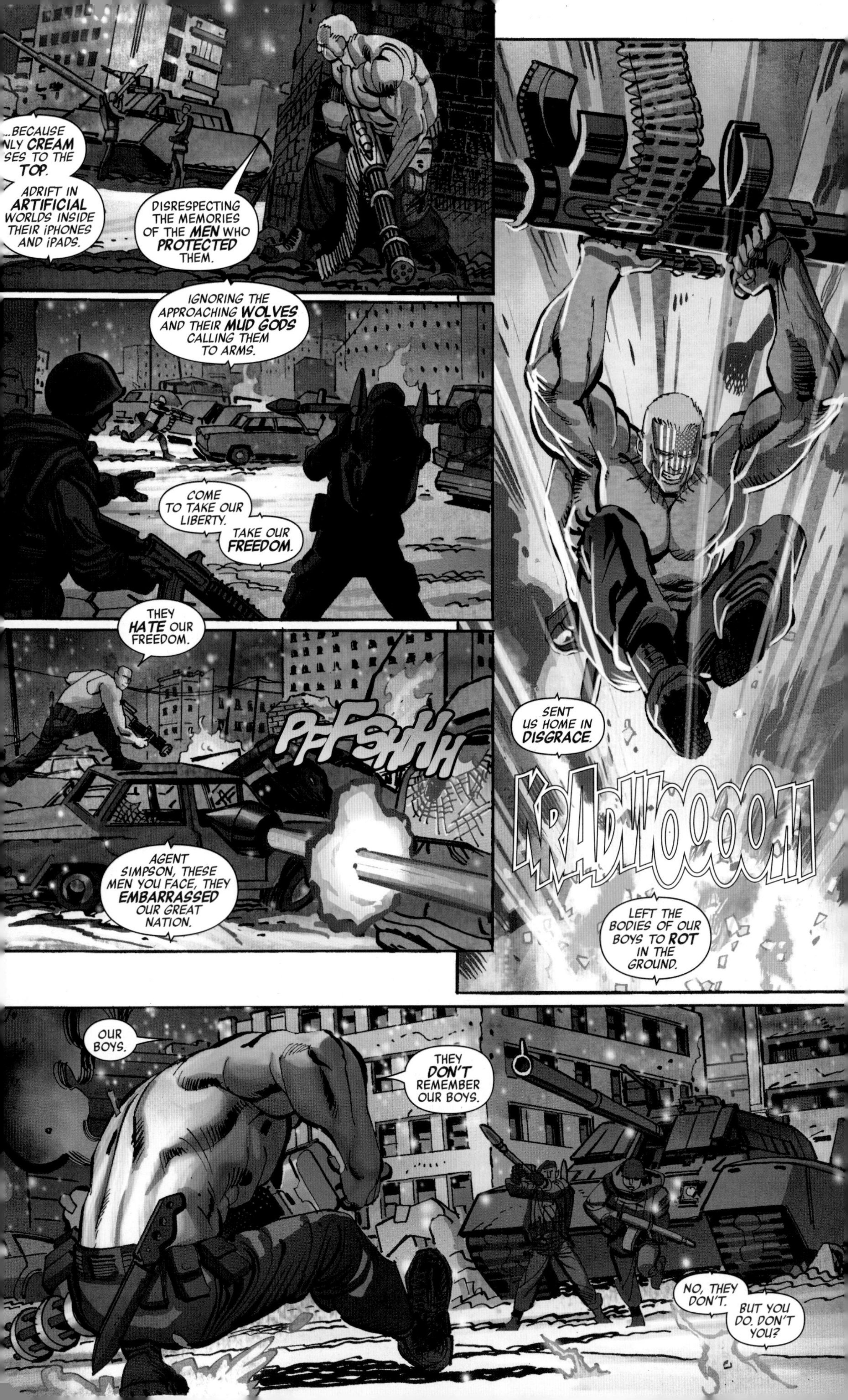

...BECAUSE
NLY CREAM
SES TO THE
TOP.
ADRIFT IN ARTIFICIAL WORLDS INSIDE THEIR iPHONES AND iPADS.
DISRESPECTING THE MEMORIES OF THE MEN WHO PROTECTED THEM.
IGNORING THE APPROACHING WOLVES AND THEIR MUD GODS CALLING THEM TO ARMS.
COME TO TAKE OUR LIBERTY.
TAKE OUR FREEDOM.
THEY HATE OUR FREEDOM.
PFFSHHH
AGENT SIMPSON, THESE MEN YOU FACE, THEY EMBARRASSED OUR GREAT NATION.
SENT US HOME IN DISGRACE.
KRADWOOOOM
LEFT THE BODIES OF OUR BOYS TO ROT IN THE GROUND.
OUR BOYS.
THEY DON'T REMEMBER OUR BOYS.
NO, THEY DON'T.
BUT YOU DO. DON'T YOU?

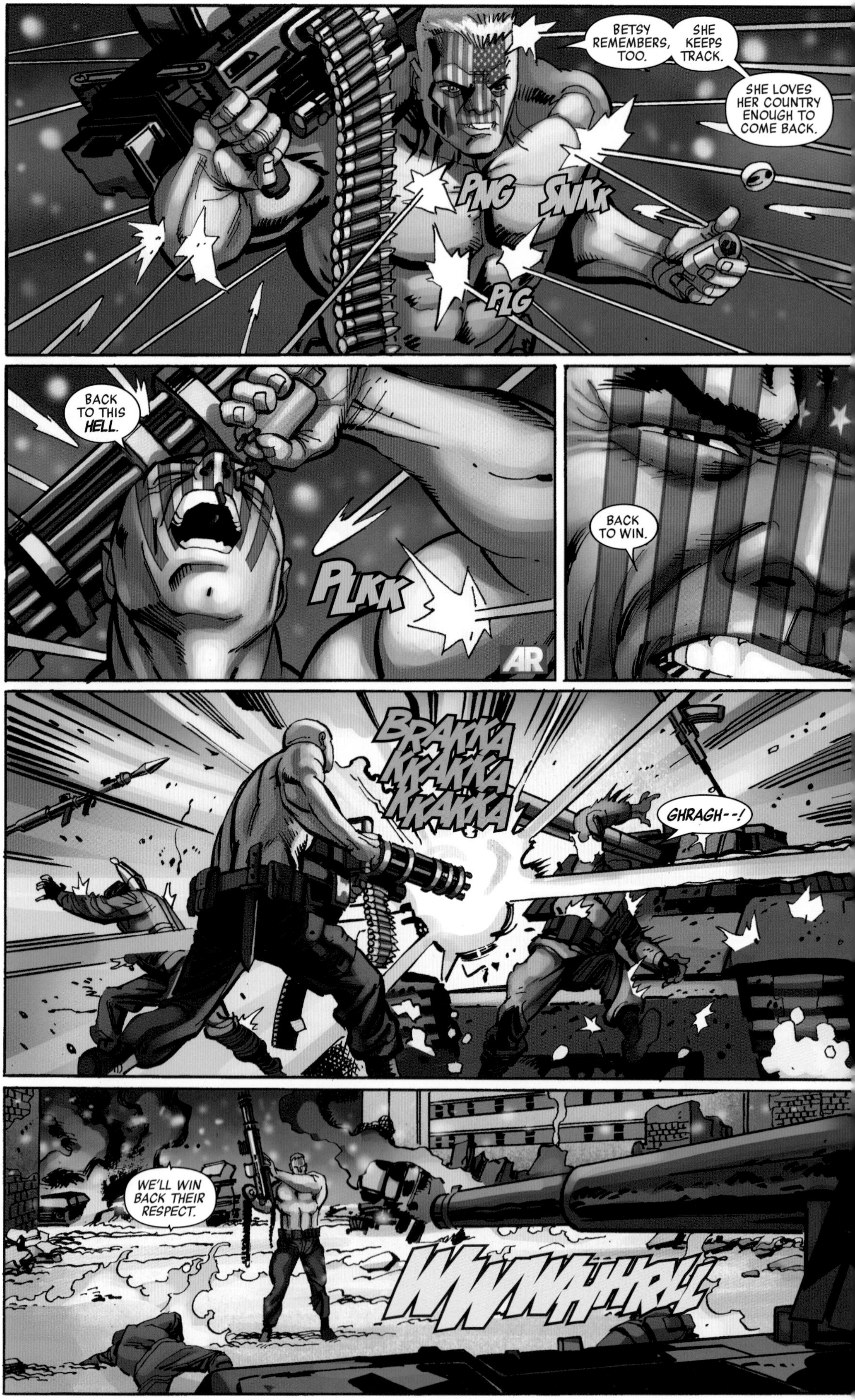
BETSY REMEMBERS, TOO.
SHE KEEPS TRACK.
SHE LOVES HER COUNTRY ENOUGH TO COME BACK.
PNG
SNKK
PLG
BACK TO THIS HELL.
PLKK
BACK TO WIN.
BRAKKA KKAKKA KKAKKA
GHRAGH--!
WE'LL WIN BACK THEIR RESPECT.

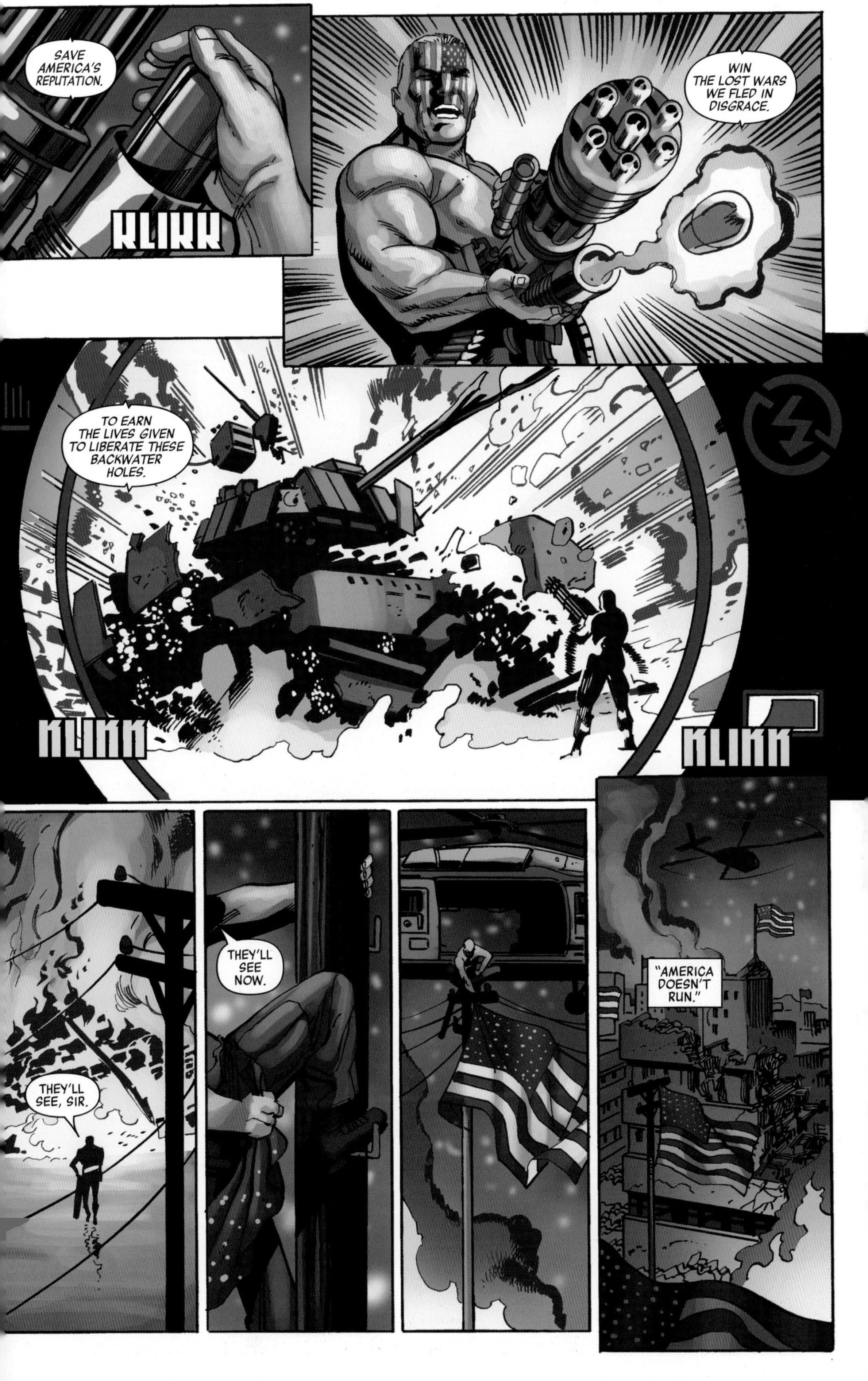
SAVE AMERICA'S REPUTATION.
KLIKK
WIN THE LOST WARS WE FLED IN DISGRACE.
TO EARN THE LIVES GIVEN TO LIBERATE THESE BACKWATER HOLES.
KLIKK
KLIKK
THEY'LL SEE, SIR.
THEY'LL SEE NOW.
"AMERICA DOESN'T RUN."

"AMERICA DOESN'T LOSE."

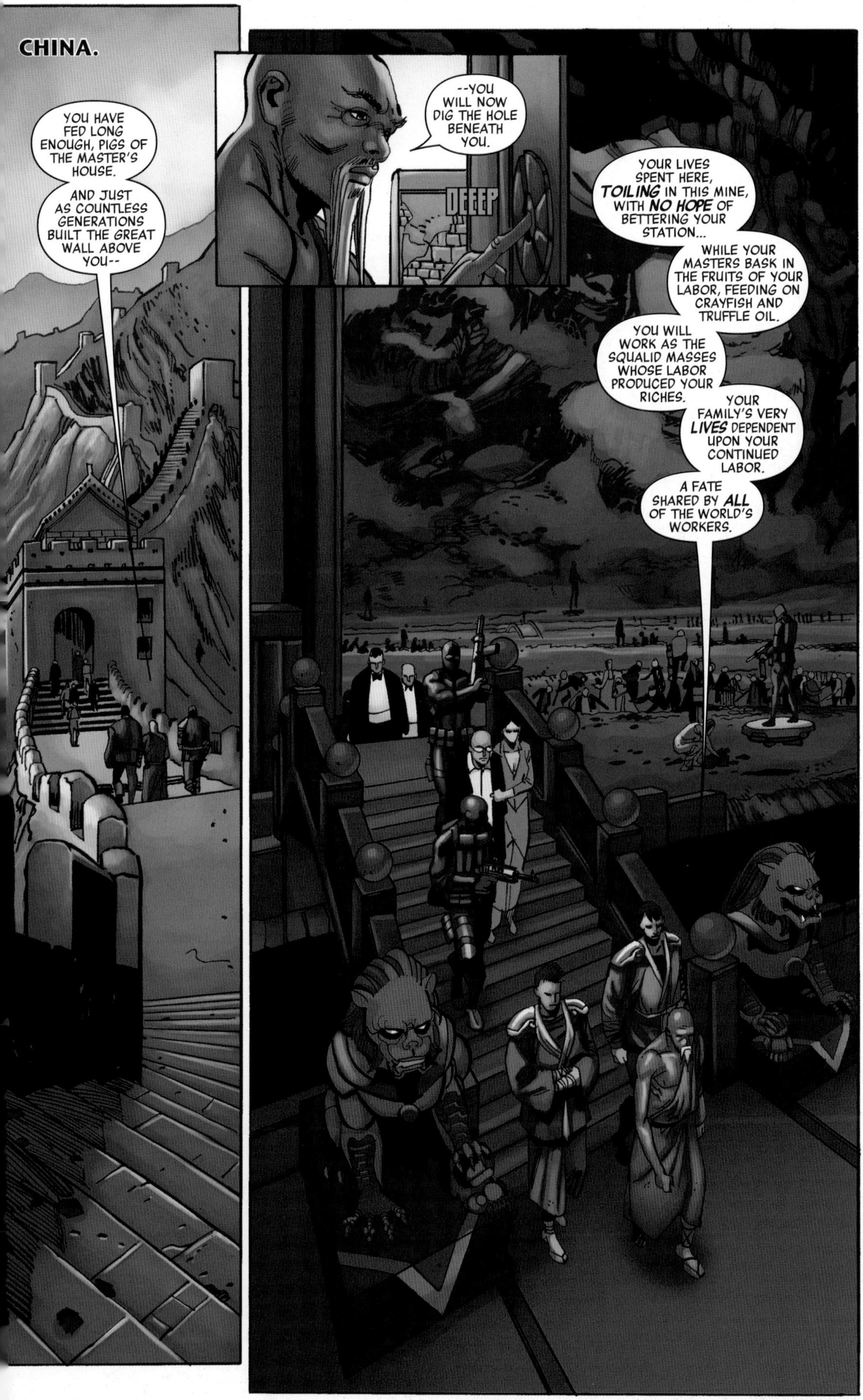
CHINA.
YOU HAVE FED LONG ENOUGH, PIGS OF THE MASTER'S HOUSE.
AND JUST AS COUNTLESS GENERATIONS BUILT THE GREAT WALL ABOVE YOU--
--YOU WILL NOW DIG THE HOLE BENEATH YOU.
DEEEP
YOUR LIVES SPENT HERE, TOILING IN THIS MINE, WITH NO HOPE OF BETTERING YOUR STATION...
WHILE YOUR MASTERS BASK IN THE FRUITS OF YOUR LABOR, FEEDING ON CRAYFISH AND TRUFFLE OIL.
YOU WILL WORK AS THE SQUALID MASSES WHOSE LABOR PRODUCED YOUR RICHES.
YOUR FAMILY'S VERY LIVES DEPENDENT UPON YOUR CONTINUED LABOR.
A FATE SHARED BY ALL OF THE WORLD'S WORKERS.

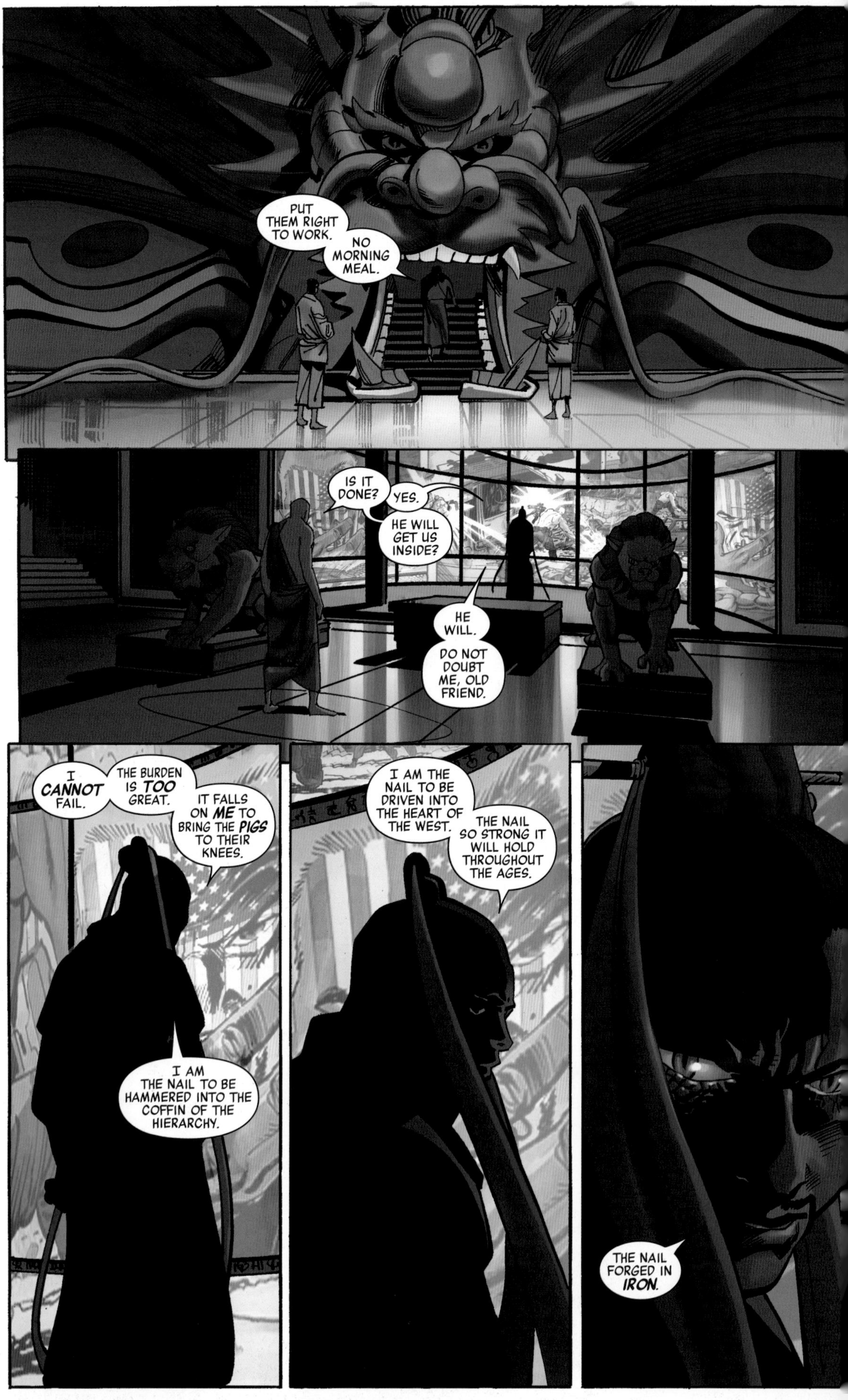
PUT THEM RIGHT TO WORK.
NO MORNING MEAL.
IS IT DONE?
YES.
HE WILL GET US INSIDE?
HE WILL.
DO NOT DOUBT ME, OLD FRIEND.
I CANNOT FAIL.
THE BURDEN IS TOO GREAT.
IT FALLS ON ME TO BRING THE PIGS TO THEIR KNEES.
I AM THE NAIL TO BE HAMMERED INTO THE COFFIN OF THE HIERARCHY.
I AM THE NAIL TO BE DRIVEN INTO THE HEART OF THE WEST.
THE NAIL SO STRONG IT WILL HOLD THROUGHOUT THE AGES.
THE NAIL FORGED IN IRON.

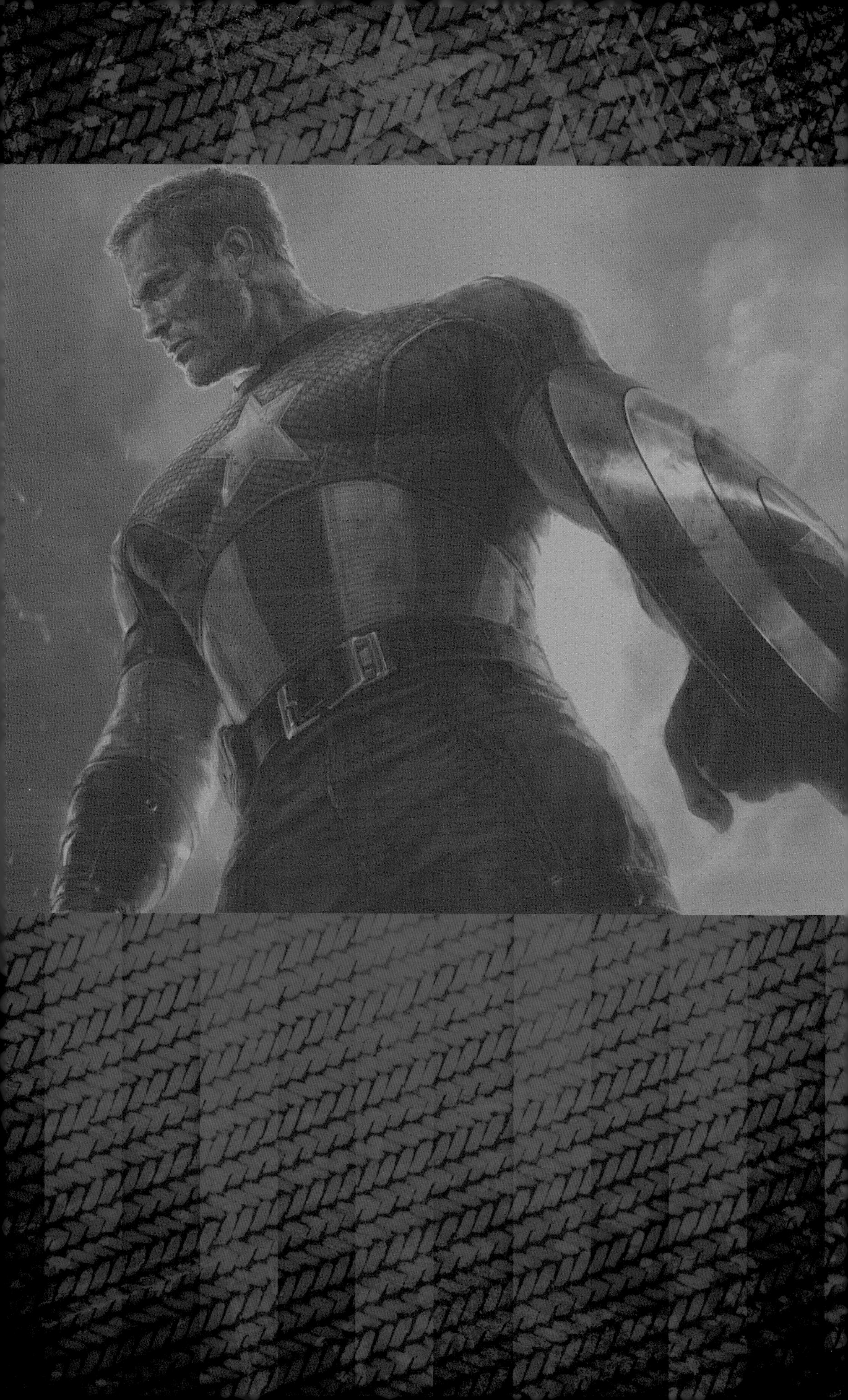

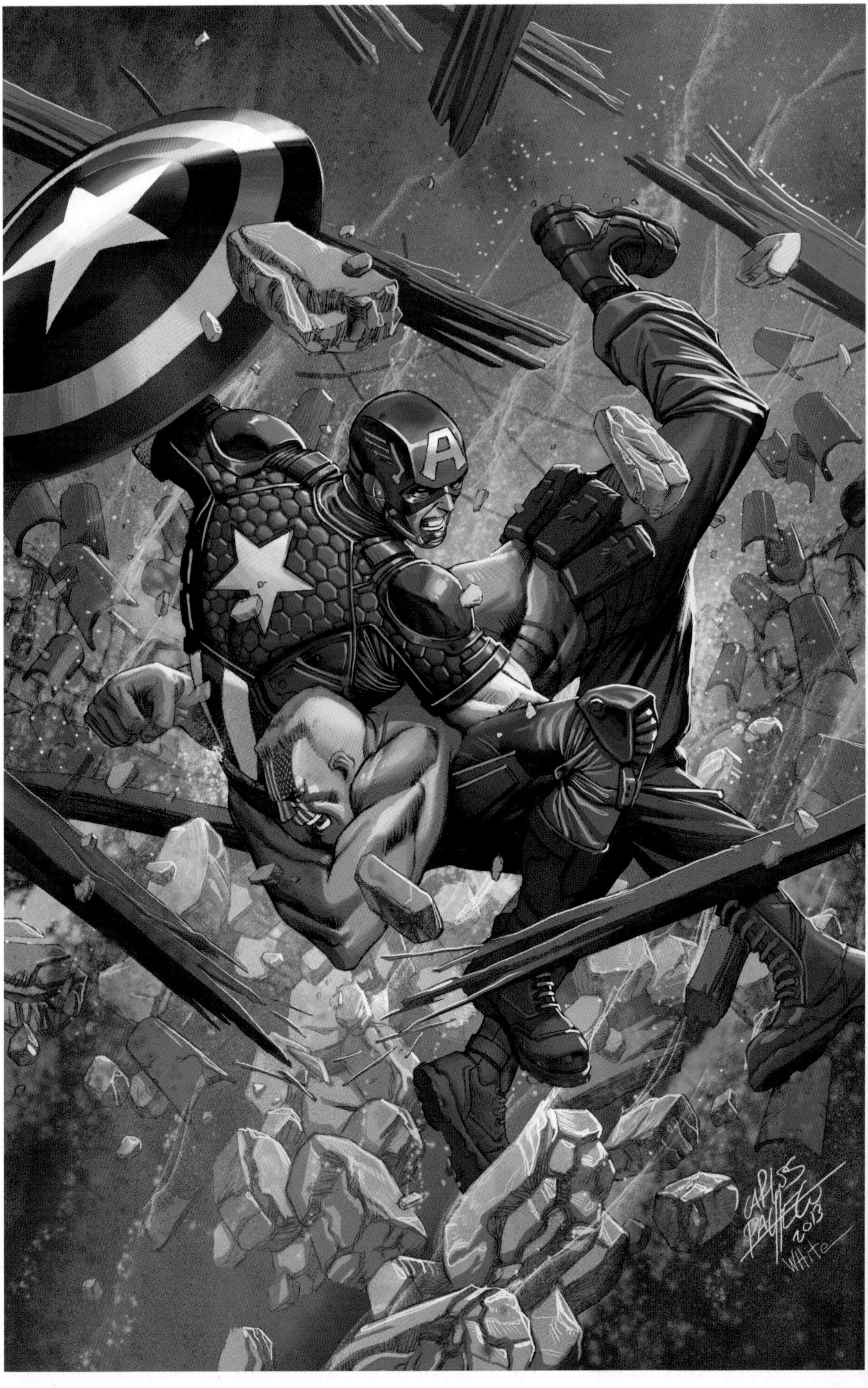
CARLOS PACHECO 2013
White

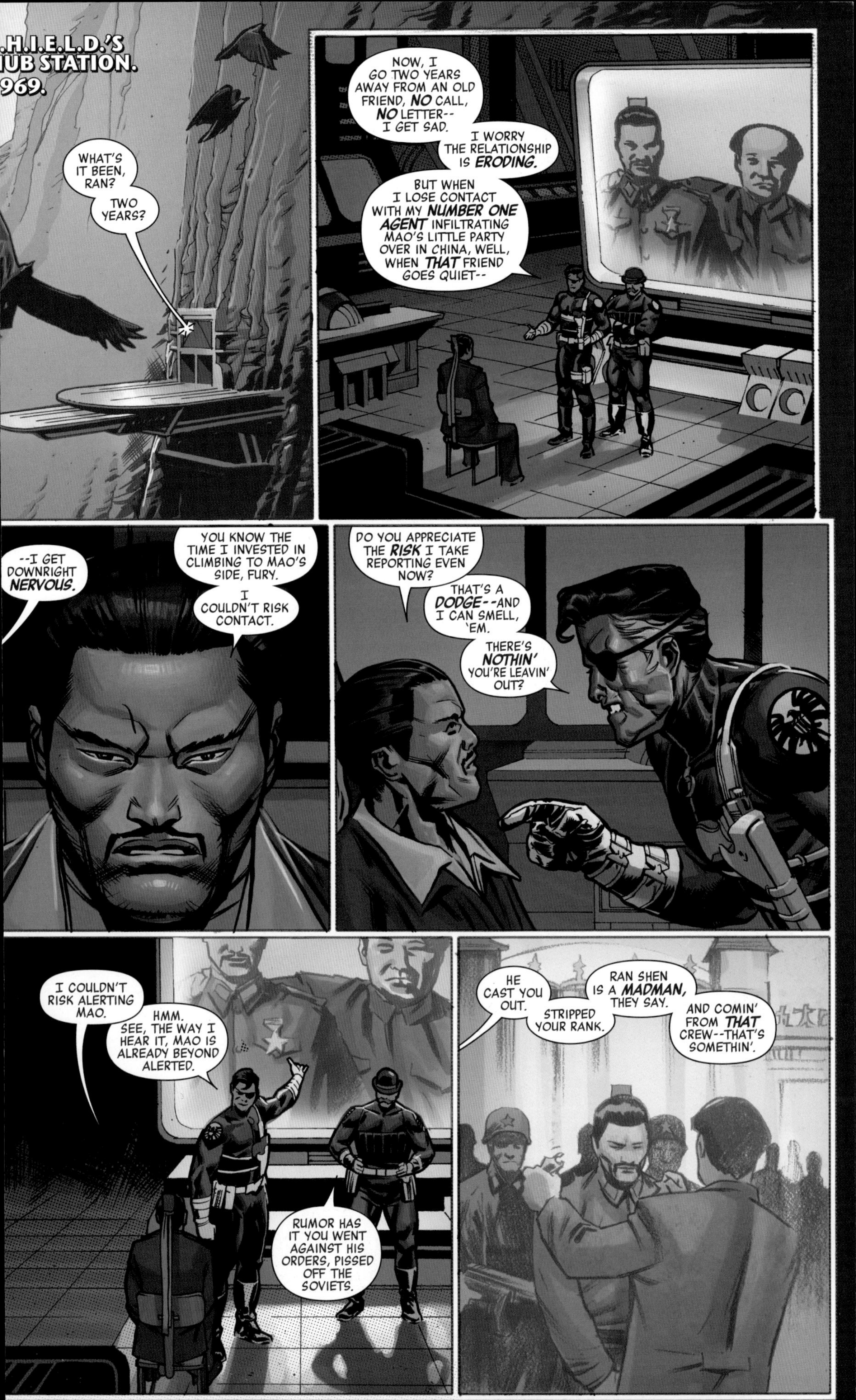
.H.I.E.L.D.'S
HUB STATION.
969.
WHAT'S IT BEEN, RAN?
TWO YEARS?
NOW, I GO TWO YEARS AWAY FROM AN OLD FRIEND, NO CALL, NO LETTER-- I GET SAD.
I WORRY THE RELATIONSHIP IS ERODING.
BUT WHEN I LOSE CONTACT WITH MY NUMBER ONE AGENT INFILTRATING MAO'S LITTLE PARTY OVER IN CHINA, WELL, WHEN THAT FRIEND GOES QUIET--
--I GET DOWNRIGHT NERVOUS.
YOU KNOW THE TIME I INVESTED IN CLIMBING TO MAO'S SIDE, FURY.
I COULDN'T RISK CONTACT.
DO YOU APPRECIATE THE RISK I TAKE REPORTING EVEN NOW?
THAT'S A DODGE--AND I CAN SMELL, 'EM.
THERE'S NOTHIN' YOU'RE LEAVIN' OUT?
I COULDN'T RISK ALERTING MAO.
HMM. SEE, THE WAY I HEAR IT, MAO IS ALREADY BEYOND ALERTED.
RUMOR HAS IT YOU WENT AGAINST HIS ORDERS, PISSED OFF THE SOVIETS.
HE CAST YOU OUT.
STRIPPED YOUR RANK.
RAN SHEN IS A MADMAN, THEY SAY.
AND COMIN' FROM THAT CREW--THAT'S SOMETHIN'.

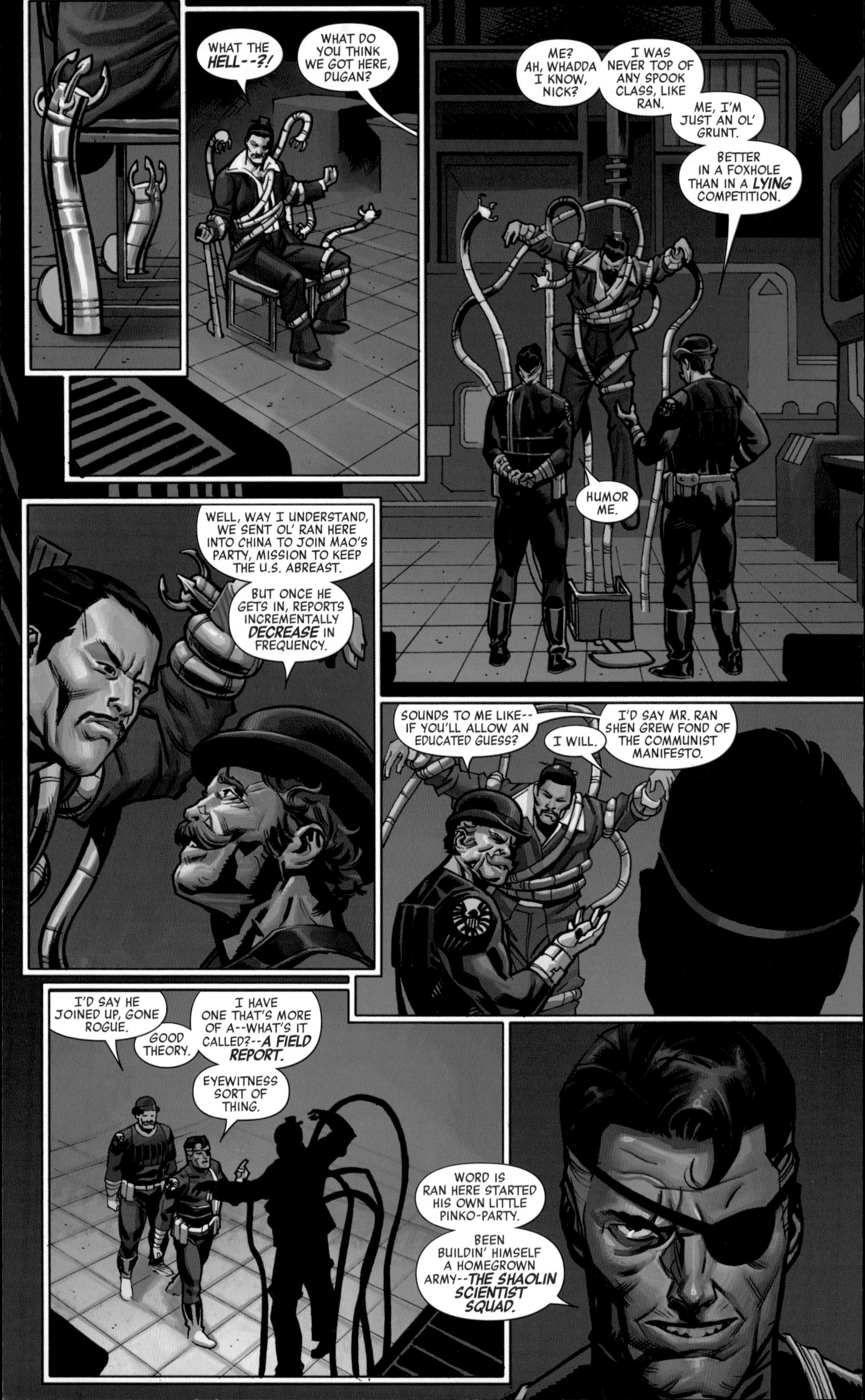
WHAT THE HELL--?!
WHAT DO YOU THINK WE GOT HERE, DUGAN?
ME? AH, WHADDA I KNOW, NICK?
I WAS NEVER TOP OF ANY SPOOK CLASS, LIKE RAN.
ME, I'M JUST AN OL' GRUNT.
BETTER IN A FOXHOLE THAN IN A LYING COMPETITION.
HUMOR ME.
WELL, WAY I UNDERSTAND, WE SENT OL' RAN HERE INTO CHINA TO JOIN MAO'S PARTY, MISSION TO KEEP THE U.S. ABREAST.
BUT ONCE HE GETS IN, REPORTS INCREMENTALLY DECREASE IN FREQUENCY.
SOUNDS TO ME LIKE-- IF YOU'LL ALLOW AN EDUCATED GUESS?
I WILL.
I'D SAY MR. RAN SHEN GREW FOND OF THE COMMUNIST MANIFESTO.
I'D SAY HE JOINED UP, GONE ROGUE.
GOOD THEORY.
I HAVE ONE THAT'S MORE OF A--WHAT'S IT CALLED?--A FIELD REPORT.
EYEWITNESS SORT OF THING.
WORD IS RAN HERE STARTED HIS OWN LITTLE PINKO-PARTY.
BEEN BUILDIN' HIMSELF A HOMEGROWN ARMY--THE SHAOLIN SCIENTIST SQUAD.

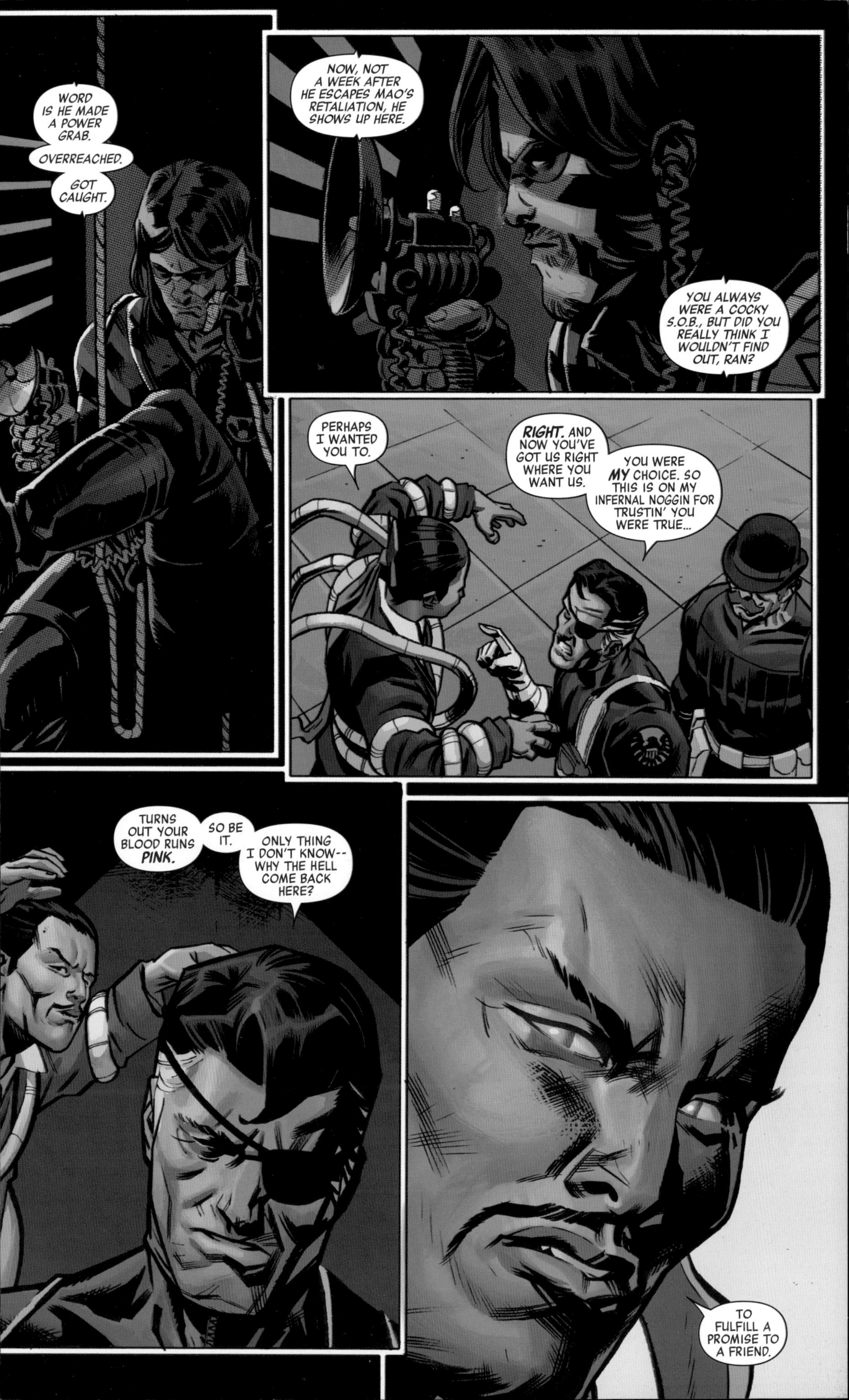
WORD IS HE MADE A POWER GRAB.
OVERREACHED.
GOT CAUGHT.
NOW, NOT A WEEK AFTER HE ESCAPES MAO'S RETALIATION, HE SHOWS UP HERE.
YOU ALWAYS WERE A COCKY S.O.B., BUT DID YOU REALLY THINK I WOULDN'T FIND OUT, RAN?
PERHAPS I WANTED YOU TO.
RIGHT. AND NOW YOU'VE GOT US RIGHT WHERE YOU WANT US.
YOU WERE MY CHOICE. SO THIS IS ON MY INFERNAL NOGGIN FOR TRUSTIN' YOU WERE TRUE...
TURNS OUT YOUR BLOOD RUNS PINK.
SO BE IT.
ONLY THING I DON'T KNOW-- WHY THE HELL COME BACK HERE?
TO FULFILL A PROMISE TO A FRIEND.

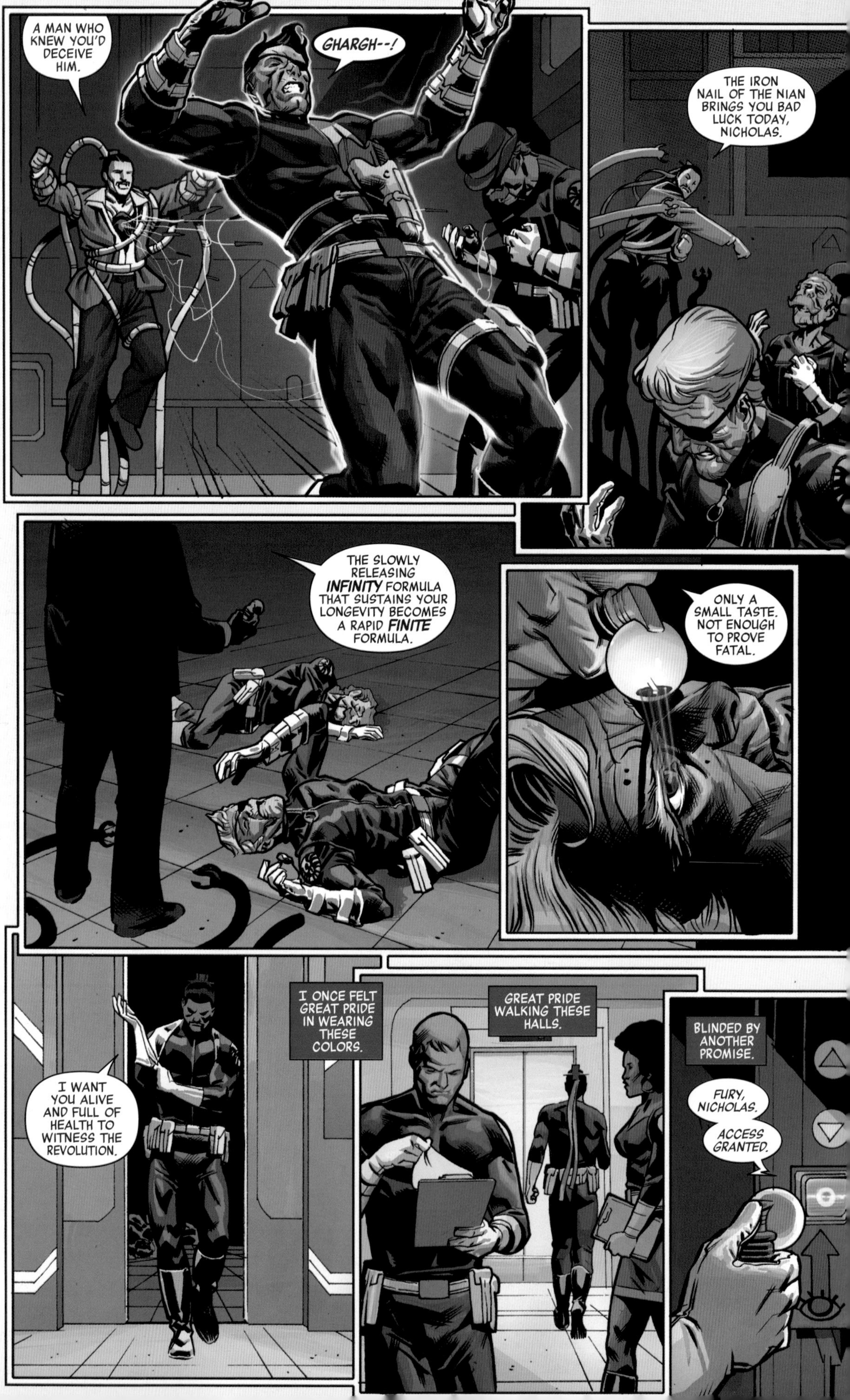
A MAN WHO KNEW YOU'D DECEIVE HIM.
GHARGH--!
THE IRON NAIL OF THE NIAN BRINGS YOU BAD LUCK TODAY, NICHOLAS.
THE SLOWLY RELEASING INFINITY FORMULA THAT SUSTAINS YOUR LONGEVITY BECOMES A RAPID FINITE FORMULA.
ONLY A SMALL TASTE. NOT ENOUGH TO PROVE FATAL.
I WANT YOU ALIVE AND FULL OF HEALTH TO WITNESS THE REVOLUTION.
I ONCE FELT GREAT PRIDE IN WEARING THESE COLORS.
GREAT PRIDE WALKING THESE HALLS.
BLINDED BY ANOTHER PROMISE.
FURY, NICHOLAS.
ACCESS GRANTED.

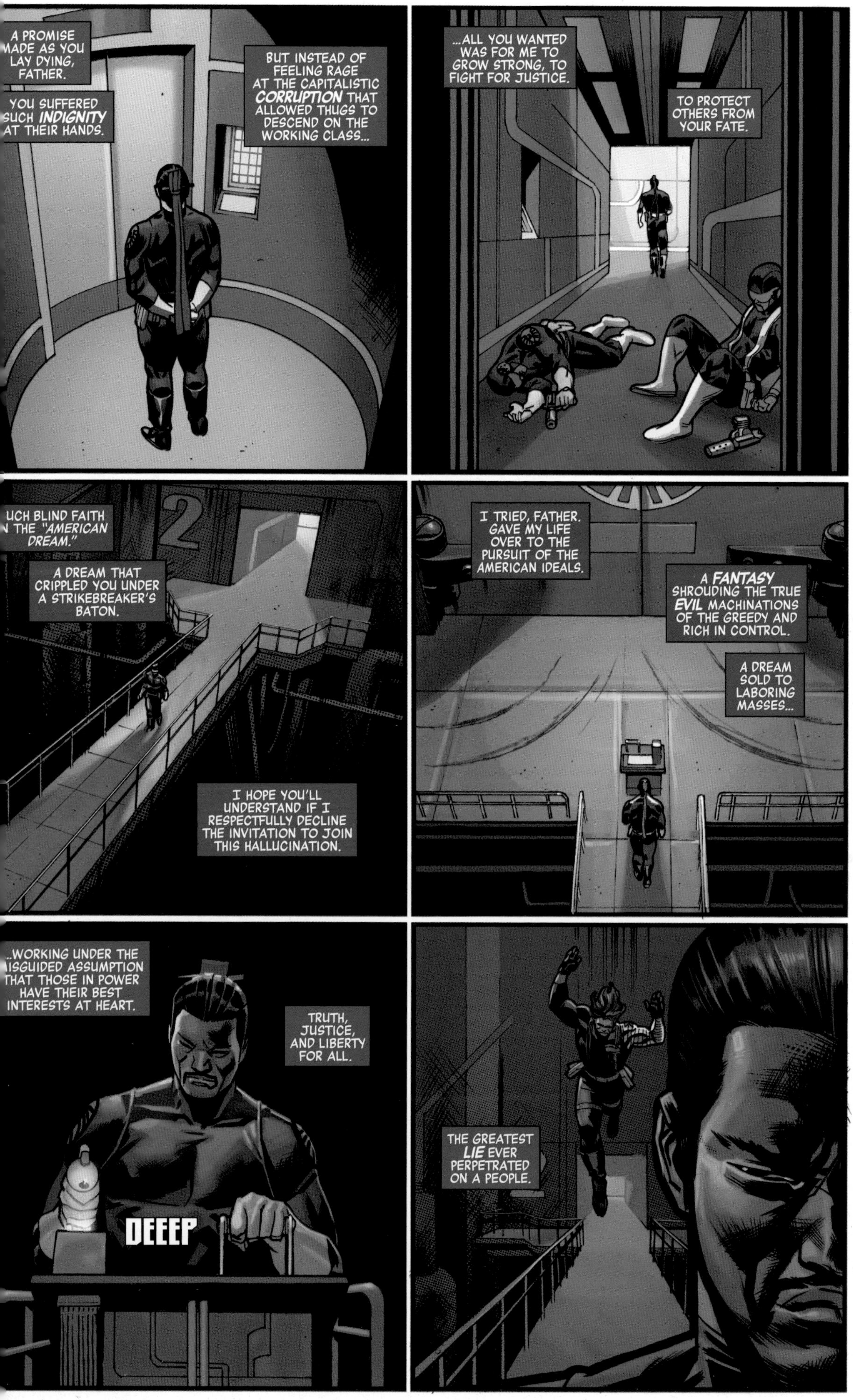
A PROMISE MADE AS YOU LAY DYING, FATHER.
YOU SUFFERED SUCH INDIGNITY AT THEIR HANDS.
BUT INSTEAD OF FEELING RAGE AT THE CAPITALISTIC CORRUPTION THAT ALLOWED THUGS TO DESCEND ON THE WORKING CLASS...
...ALL YOU WANTED WAS FOR ME TO GROW STRONG, TO FIGHT FOR JUSTICE.
TO PROTECT OTHERS FROM YOUR FATE.
UCH BLIND FAITH N THE "AMERICAN DREAM."
A DREAM THAT CRIPPLED YOU UNDER A STRIKEBREAKER'S BATON.
I HOPE YOU'LL UNDERSTAND IF I RESPECTFULLY DECLINE THE INVITATION TO JOIN THIS HALLUCINATION.
I TRIED, FATHER. GAVE MY LIFE OVER TO THE PURSUIT OF THE AMERICAN IDEALS.
A FANTASY SHROUDING THE TRUE EVIL MACHINATIONS OF THE GREEDY AND RICH IN CONTROL.
A DREAM SOLD TO LABORING MASSES...
..WORKING UNDER THE ISGUIDED ASSUMPTION THAT THOSE IN POWER HAVE THEIR BEST INTERESTS AT HEART.
TRUTH, JUSTICE, AND LIBERTY FOR ALL.
DEEEP
THE GREATEST LIE EVER PERPETRATED ON A PEOPLE.

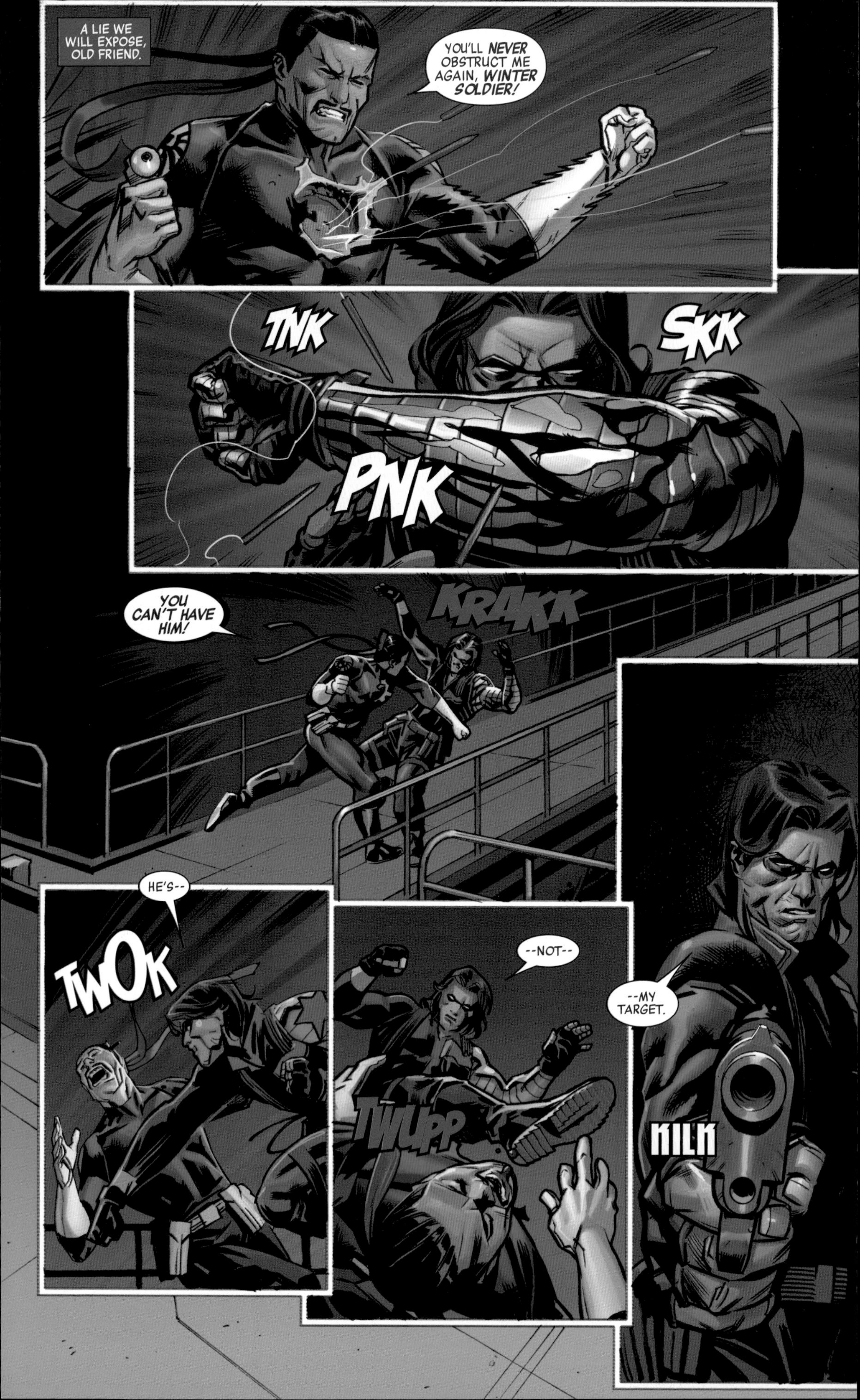
A LIE WE WILL EXPOSE, OLD FRIEND.
YOU'LL NEVER OBSTRUCT ME AGAIN, WINTER SOLDIER!
TNK
SKK
PNK
YOU CAN'T HAVE HIM!
KRAKK
HE'S--
TWOK
--NOT--
TWUPP
--MY TARGET.
KLIK

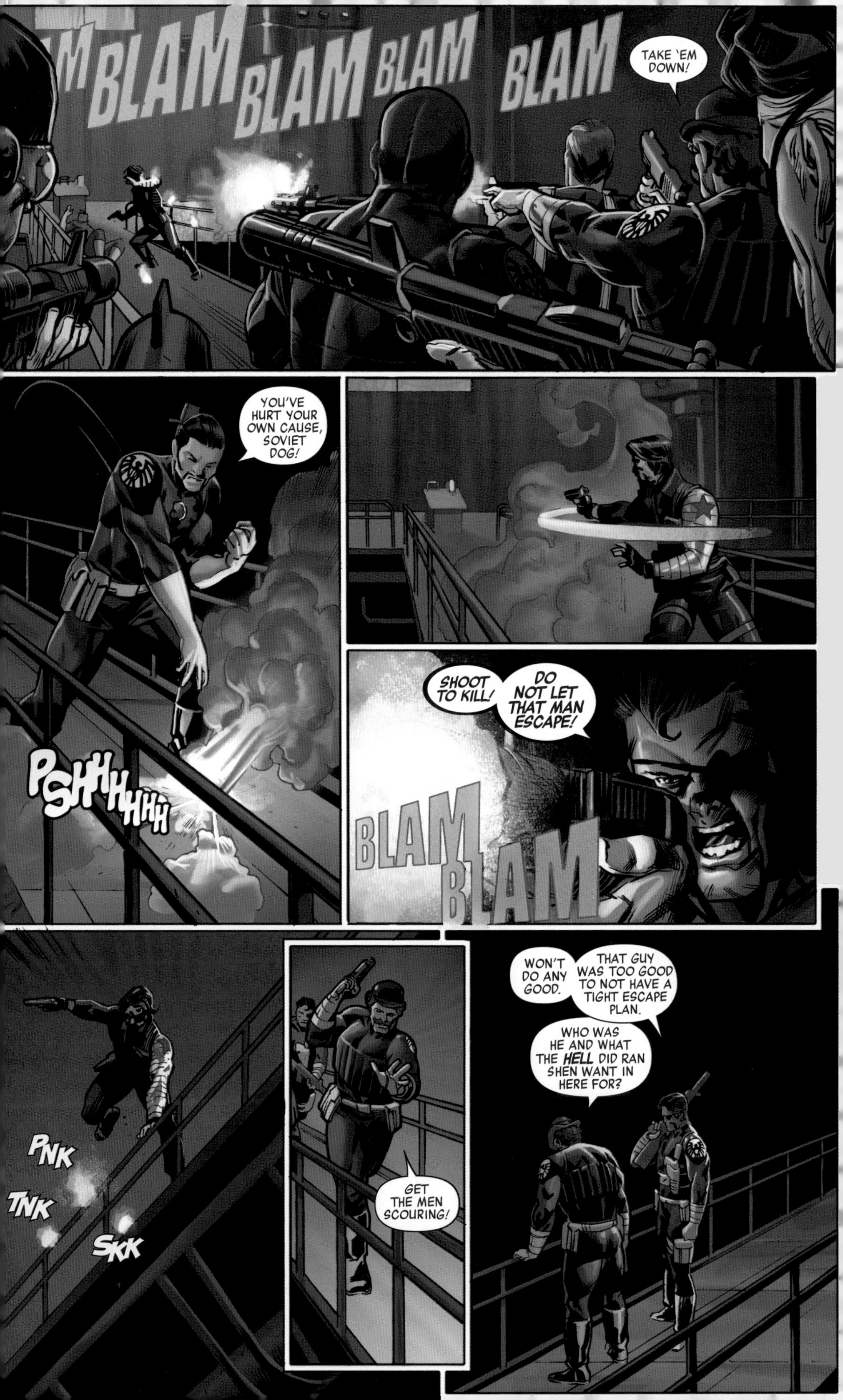

BLAM BLAM BLAM BLAM BLAM
TAKE 'EM DOWN!
YOU'VE HURT YOUR OWN CAUSE, SOVIET DOG!
PSHHHHHHH
SHOOT TO KILL!
DO NOT LET THAT MAN ESCAPE!
BLAM
BLAM
PNK
TNK
SKK
GET THE MEN SCOURING!
WON'T DO ANY GOOD.
THAT GUY WAS TOO GOOD TO NOT HAVE A TIGHT ESCAPE PLAN.
WHO WAS HE AND WHAT THE HELL DID RAN SHEN WANT IN HERE FOR?

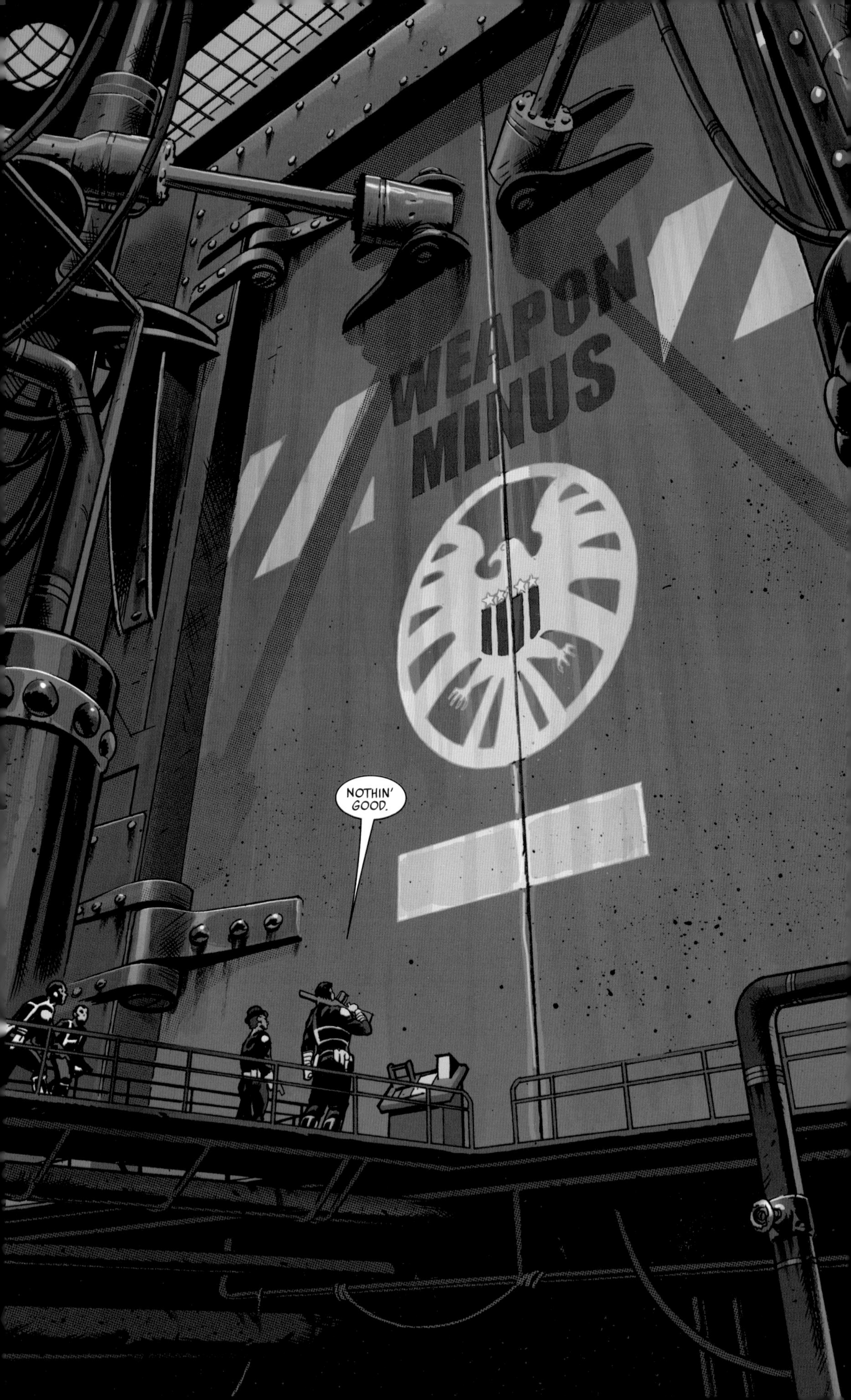
WEAPON
MINUS
NOTHIN' GOOD.

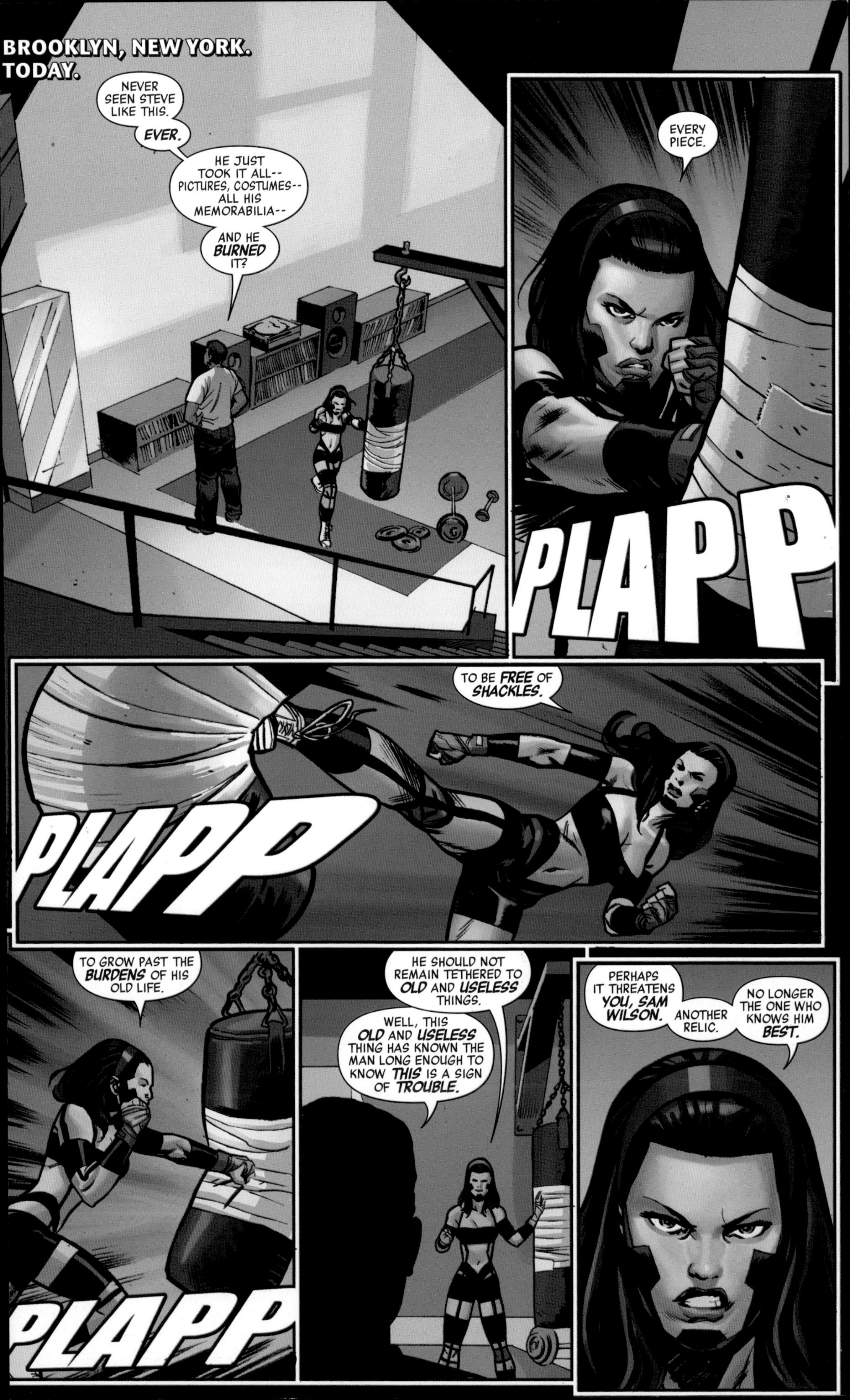
BROOKLYN, NEW YORK. TODAY.
NEVER SEEN STEVE LIKE THIS.
EVER.
HE JUST TOOK IT ALL-- PICTURES, COSTUMES-- ALL HIS MEMORABILIA--
AND HE BURNED IT?
EVERY PIECE.
PLAPP
TO BE FREE OF SHACKLES.
PLAPP
TO GROW PAST THE BURDENS OF HIS OLD LIFE.
PLAPP
HE SHOULD NOT REMAIN TETHERED TO OLD AND USELESS THINGS.
WELL, THIS OLD AND USELESS THING HAS KNOWN THE MAN LONG ENOUGH TO KNOW THIS IS A SIGN OF TROUBLE.
PERHAPS IT THREATENS YOU, SAM WILSON.
ANOTHER RELIC.
NO LONGER THE ONE WHO KNOWS HIM BEST.

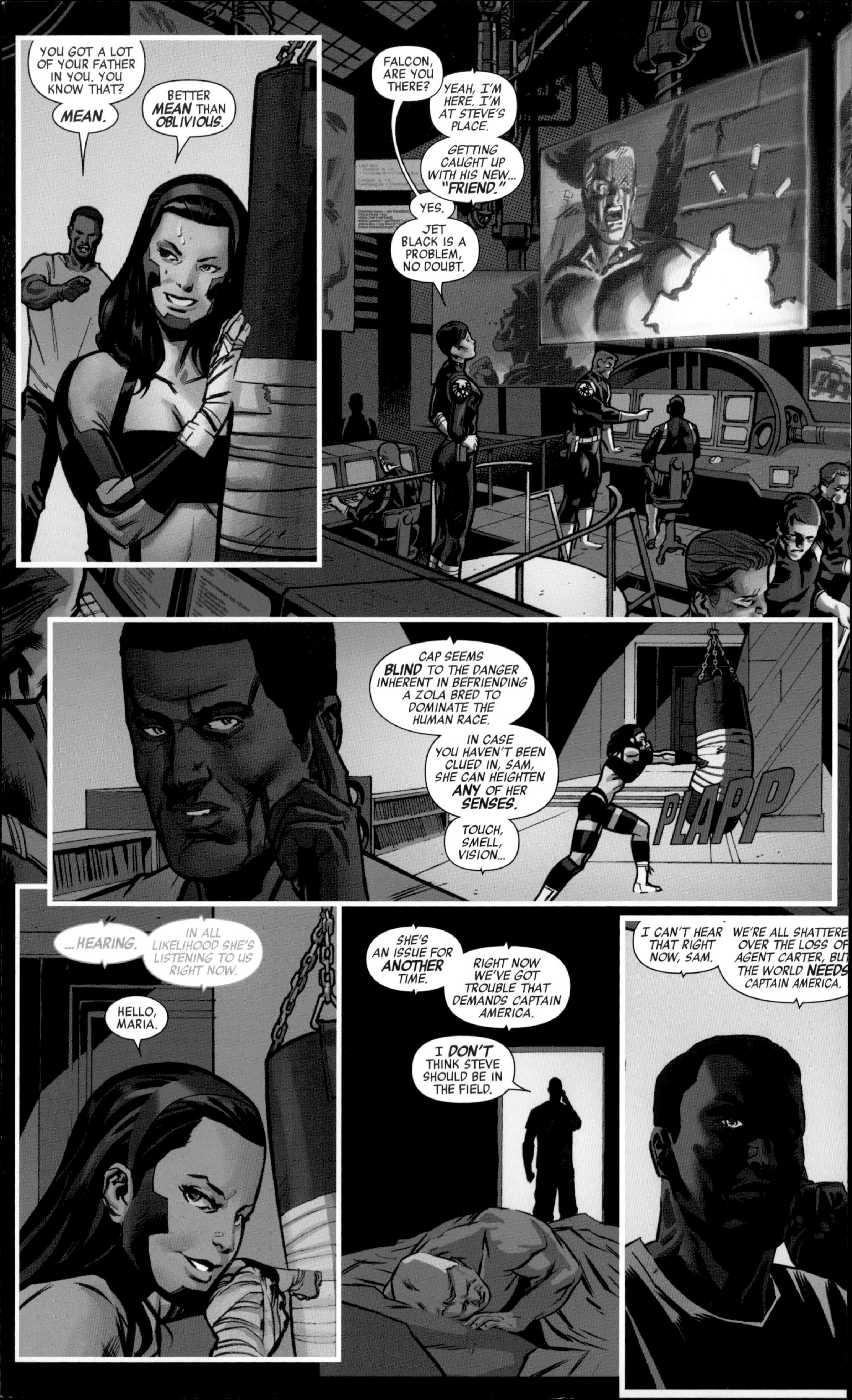
YOU GOT A LOT OF YOUR FATHER IN YOU. YOU KNOW THAT? **MEAN.**
BETTER **MEAN** THAN **OBLIVIOUS**.
FALCON, ARE YOU THERE?
YEAH, I'M HERE. I'M AT STEVE'S PLACE.
GETTING CAUGHT UP WITH HIS NEW... **"FRIEND."**
YES.
JET BLACK IS A PROBLEM, NO DOUBT.
CAP SEEMS **BLIND** TO THE DANGER INHERENT IN BEFRIENDING A ZOLA BRED TO DOMINATE THE HUMAN RACE.
IN CASE YOU HAVEN'T BEEN CLUED IN, SAM, SHE CAN HEIGHTEN **ANY** OF HER **SENSES**.
TOUCH, SMELL, VISION...
PLAPP
...HEARING.
IN ALL LIKELIHOOD SHE'S LISTENING TO US RIGHT NOW.
HELLO, MARIA.
SHE'S AN ISSUE FOR **ANOTHER** TIME.
RIGHT NOW WE'VE GOT TROUBLE THAT DEMANDS CAPTAIN AMERICA.
I **DON'T** THINK STEVE SHOULD BE IN THE FIELD.
I CAN'T HEAR THAT RIGHT NOW, SAM.
WE'RE ALL SHATTERE OVER THE LOSS OF AGENT CARTER, BUT THE WORLD **NEEDS** CAPTAIN AMERICA.

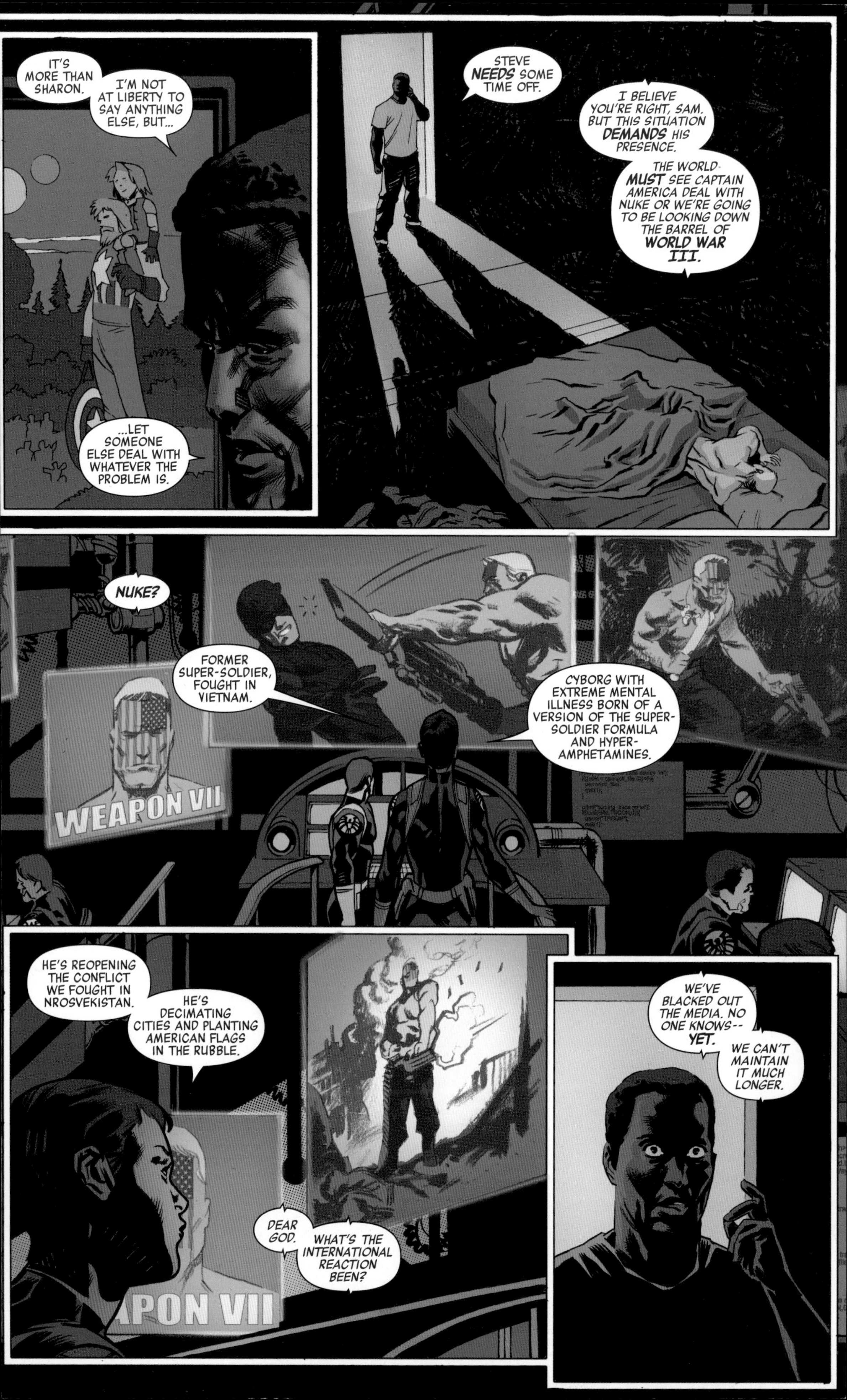
IT'S MORE THAN SHARON.
I'M NOT AT LIBERTY TO SAY ANYTHING ELSE, BUT...
...LET SOMEONE ELSE DEAL WITH WHATEVER THE PROBLEM IS.
STEVE NEEDS SOME TIME OFF.
I BELIEVE YOU'RE RIGHT, SAM. BUT THIS SITUATION DEMANDS HIS PRESENCE.
THE WORLD MUST SEE CAPTAIN AMERICA DEAL WITH NUKE OR WE'RE GOING TO BE LOOKING DOWN THE BARREL OF WORLD WAR III.
NUKE?
FORMER SUPER-SOLDIER, FOUGHT IN VIETNAM.
CYBORG WITH EXTREME MENTAL ILLNESS BORN OF A VERSION OF THE SUPER-SOLDIER FORMULA AND HYPER-AMPHETAMINES.
WEAPON VII
HE'S REOPENING THE CONFLICT WE FOUGHT IN NROSVEKISTAN.
HE'S DECIMATING CITIES AND PLANTING AMERICAN FLAGS IN THE RUBBLE.
DEAR GOD.
WHAT'S THE INTERNATIONAL REACTION BEEN?
APON VII
WE'VE BLACKED OUT THE MEDIA. NO ONE KNOWS-- YET.
WE CAN'T MAINTAIN IT MUCH LONGER.

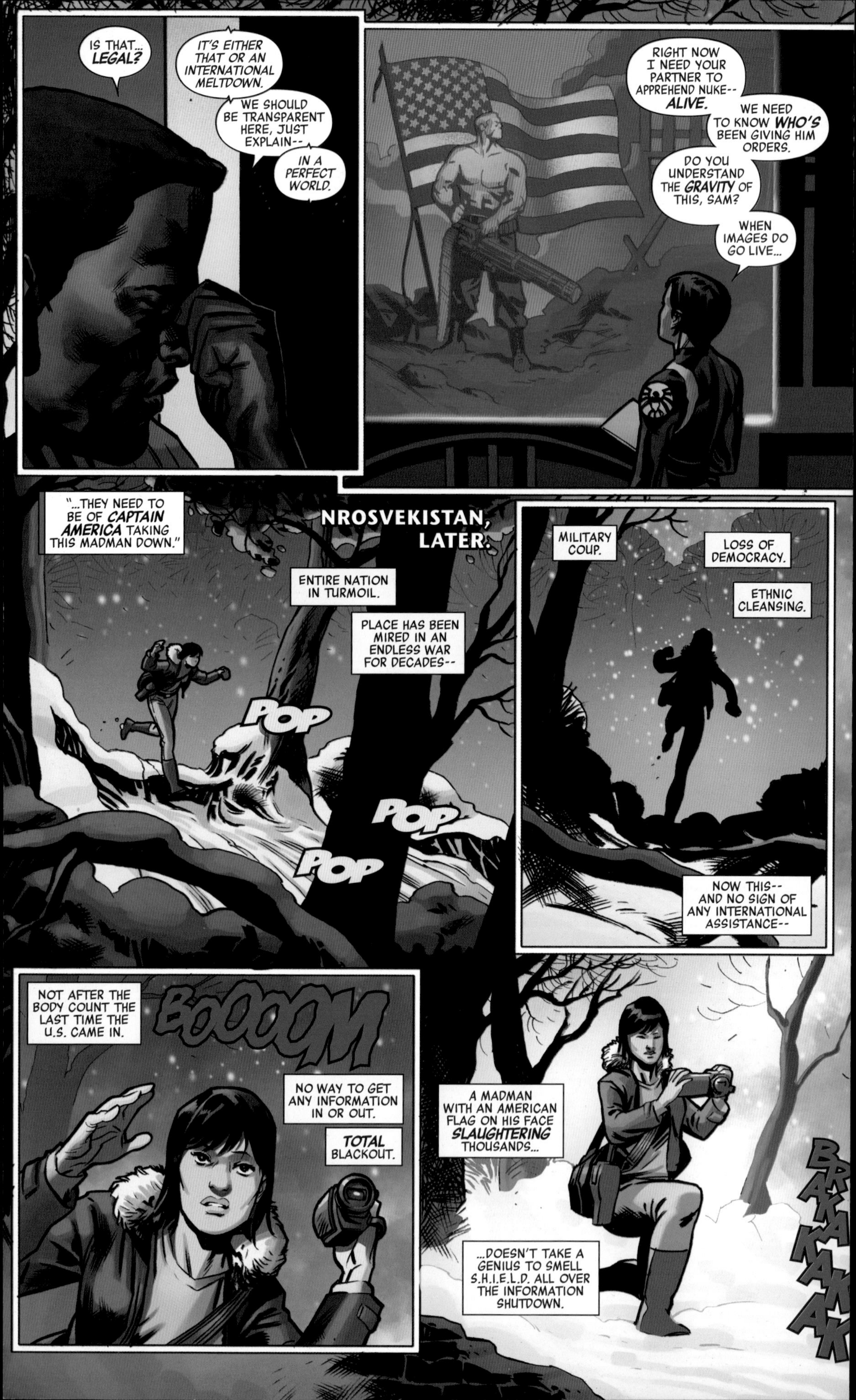
IS THAT... LEGAL?
IT'S EITHER THAT OR AN INTERNATIONAL MELTDOWN.
WE SHOULD BE TRANSPARENT HERE, JUST EXPLAIN--
IN A PERFECT WORLD.
RIGHT NOW I NEED YOUR PARTNER TO APPREHEND NUKE-- ALIVE.
WE NEED TO KNOW WHO'S BEEN GIVING HIM ORDERS.
DO YOU UNDERSTAND THE GRAVITY OF THIS, SAM?
WHEN IMAGES DO GO LIVE...
"...THEY NEED TO BE OF CAPTAIN AMERICA TAKING THIS MADMAN DOWN."
NROSVEKISTAN, LATER.
ENTIRE NATION IN TURMOIL.
PLACE HAS BEEN MIRED IN AN ENDLESS WAR FOR DECADES--
POP
POP
POP
MILITARY COUP.
LOSS OF DEMOCRACY.
ETHNIC CLEANSING.
NOW THIS-- AND NO SIGN OF ANY INTERNATIONAL ASSISTANCE--
NOT AFTER THE BODY COUNT THE LAST TIME THE U.S. CAME IN.
BOOOOM
NO WAY TO GET ANY INFORMATION IN OR OUT.
TOTAL BLACKOUT.
A MADMAN WITH AN AMERICAN FLAG ON HIS FACE SLAUGHTERING THOUSANDS...
...DOESN'T TAKE A GENIUS TO SMELL S.H.I.E.L.D. ALL OVER THE INFORMATION SHUTDOWN.
BRAKAKAKAK

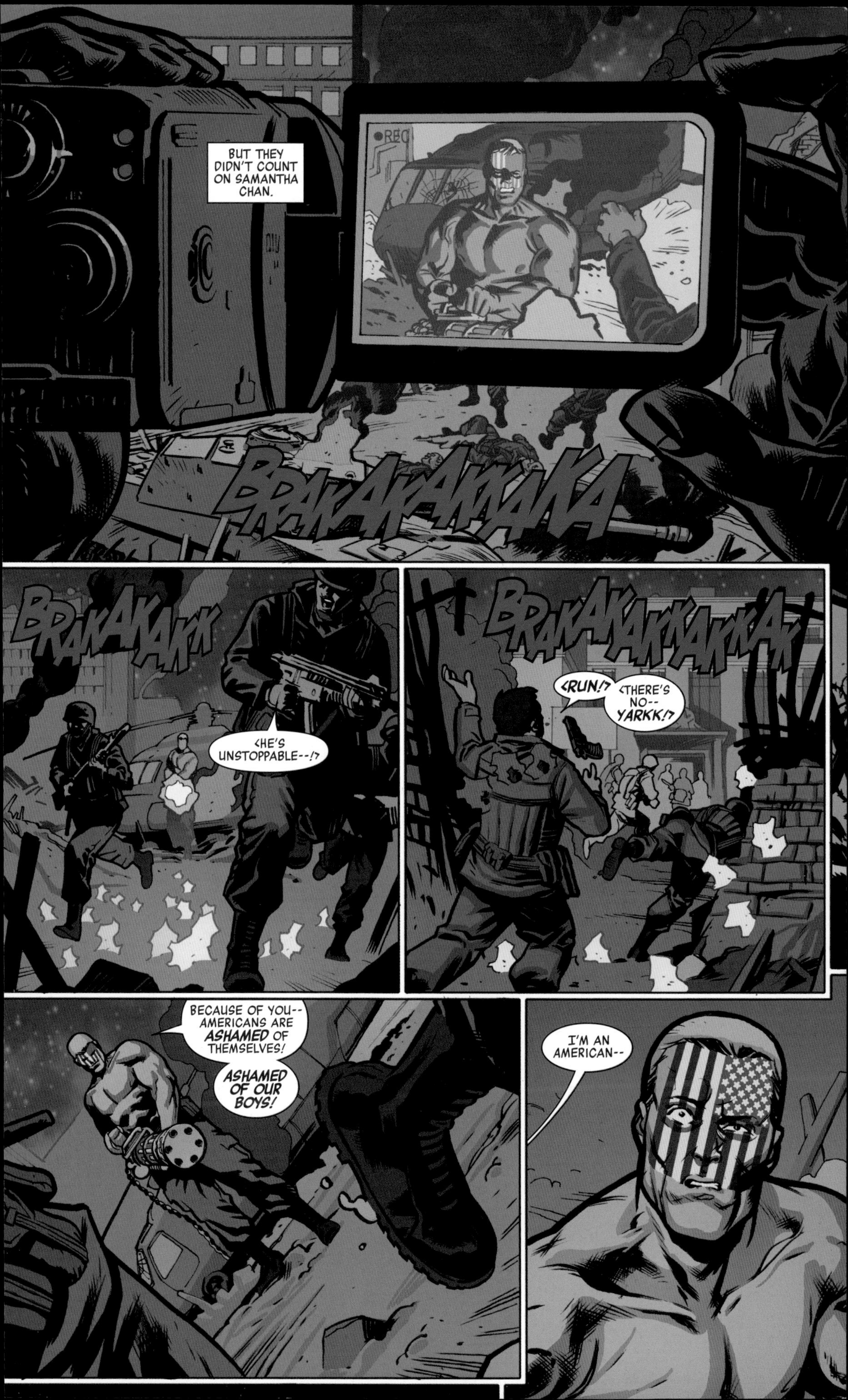

BUT THEY DIDN'T COUNT ON SAMANTHA CHAN.
REC
BRAKAKAKKAKA
BRAKAKAKK
<HE'S UNSTOPPABLE--!>
BRAKAKAKKAKKAK
<RUN!>
<THERE'S NO-- YARKK!>
BECAUSE OF YOU-- AMERICANS ARE ASHAMED OF THEMSELVES!
ASHAMED OF OUR BOYS!
I'M AN AMERICAN--

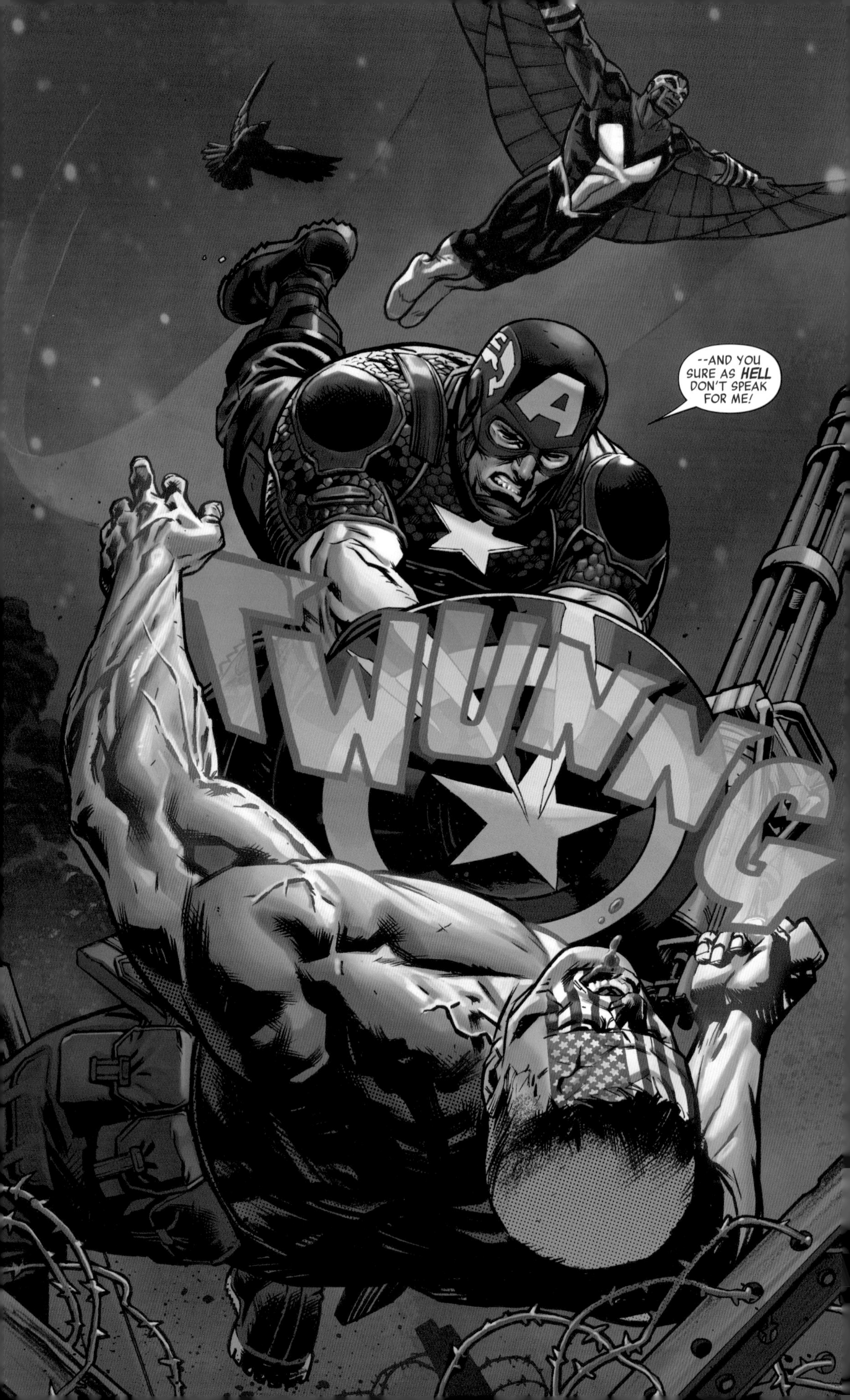
--AND YOU SURE AS HELL DON'T SPEAK FOR ME!
TWUNNG

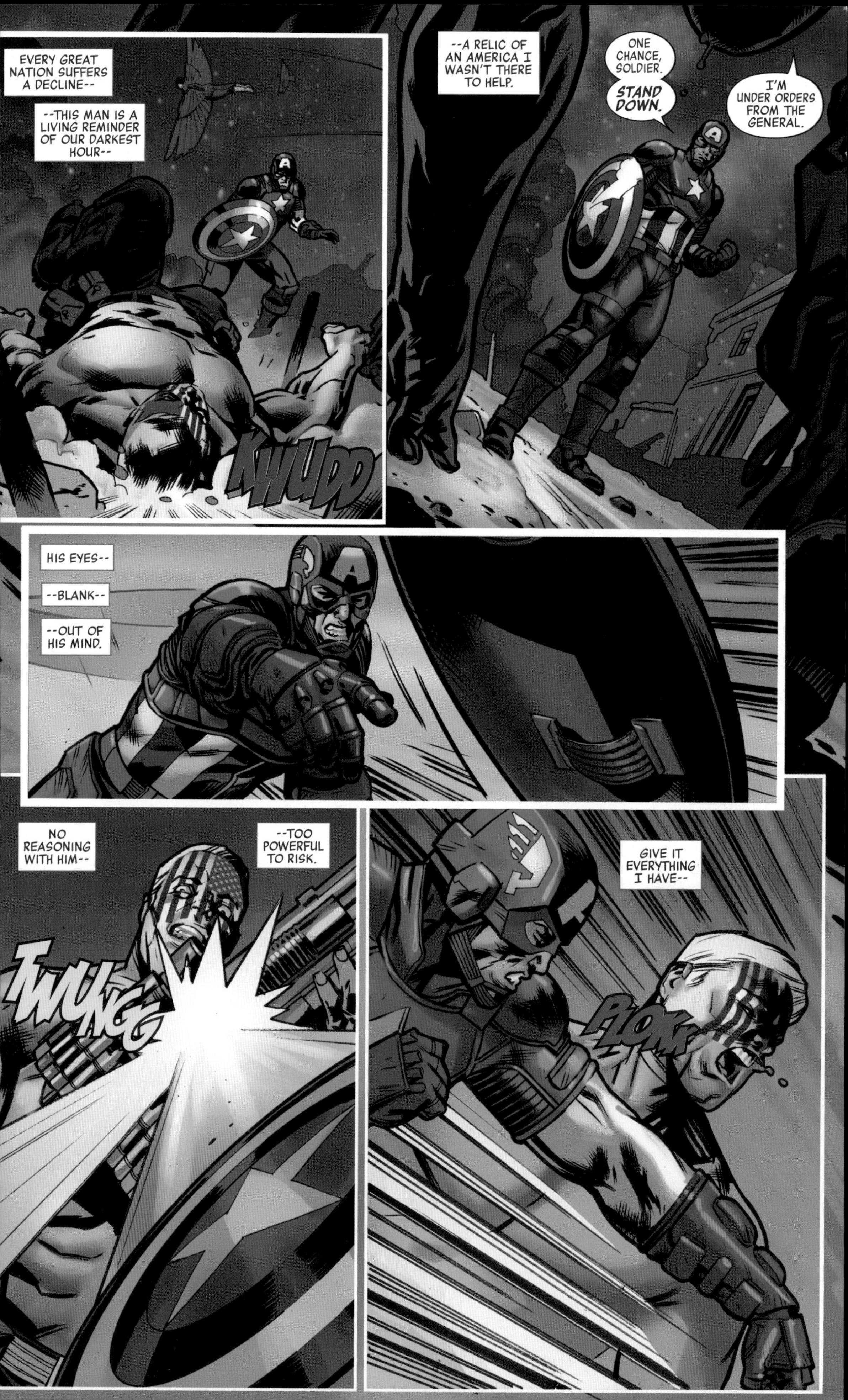
EVERY GREAT NATION SUFFERS A DECLINE--
--THIS MAN IS A LIVING REMINDER OF OUR DARKEST HOUR--
KWUDD
--A RELIC OF AN AMERICA I WASN'T THERE TO HELP.
ONE CHANCE, SOLDIER.
STAND DOWN.
I'M UNDER ORDERS FROM THE GENERAL.
HIS EYES--
--BLANK--
--OUT OF HIS MIND.
NO REASONING WITH HIM--
--TOO POWERFUL TO RISK.
TWUNGG
GIVE IT EVERYTHING I HAVE--
PLONK

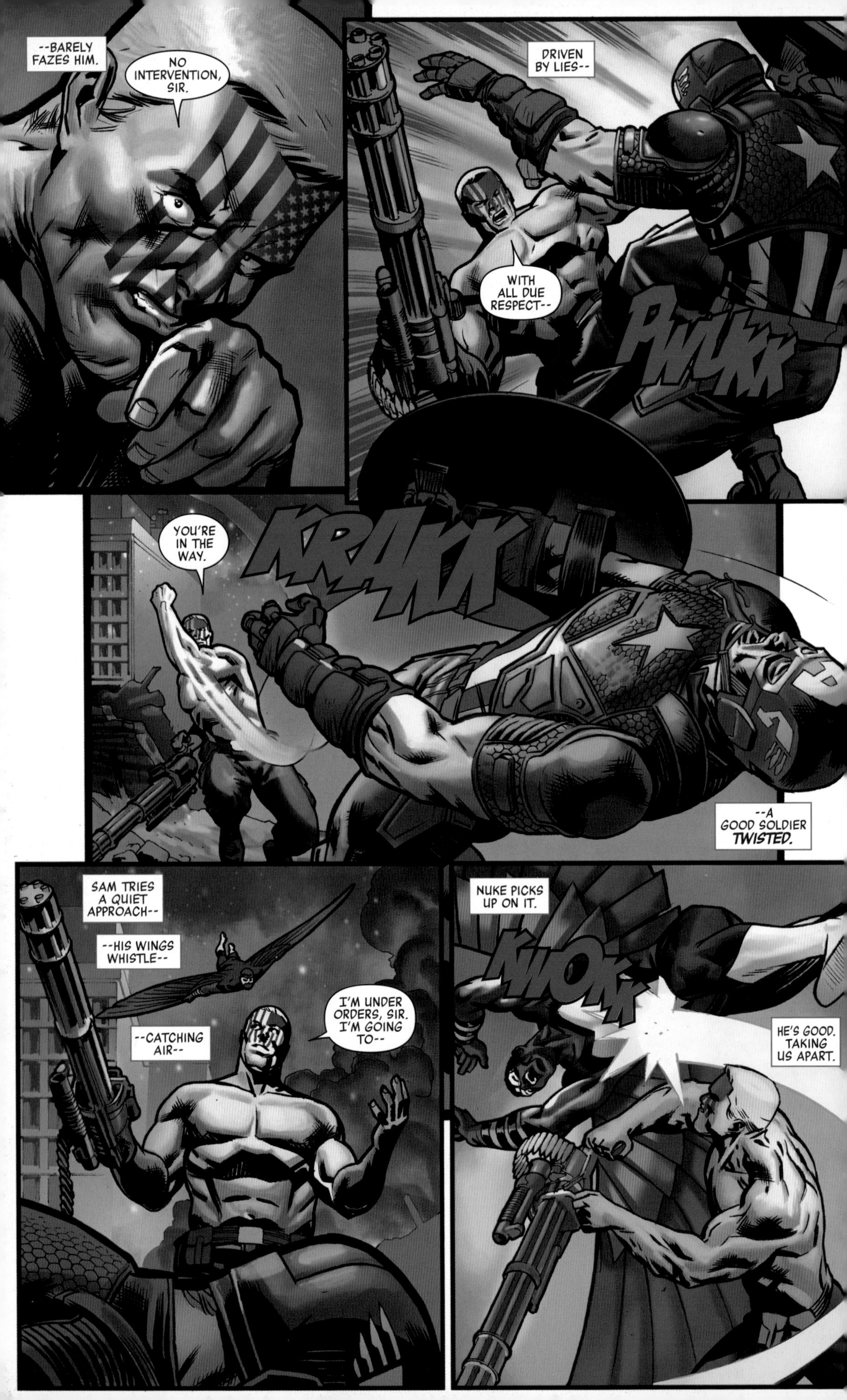
--BARELY FAZES HIM.
NO INTERVENTION, SIR.
DRIVEN BY LIES--
WITH ALL DUE RESPECT--
PWUKK
YOU'RE IN THE WAY.
KRAKK
--A GOOD SOLDIER TWISTED.
SAM TRIES A QUIET APPROACH--
--HIS WINGS WHISTLE--
--CATCHING AIR--
I'M UNDER ORDERS, SIR. I'M GOING TO--
NUKE PICKS UP ON IT.
KWOKK
HE'S GOOD. TAKING US APART.

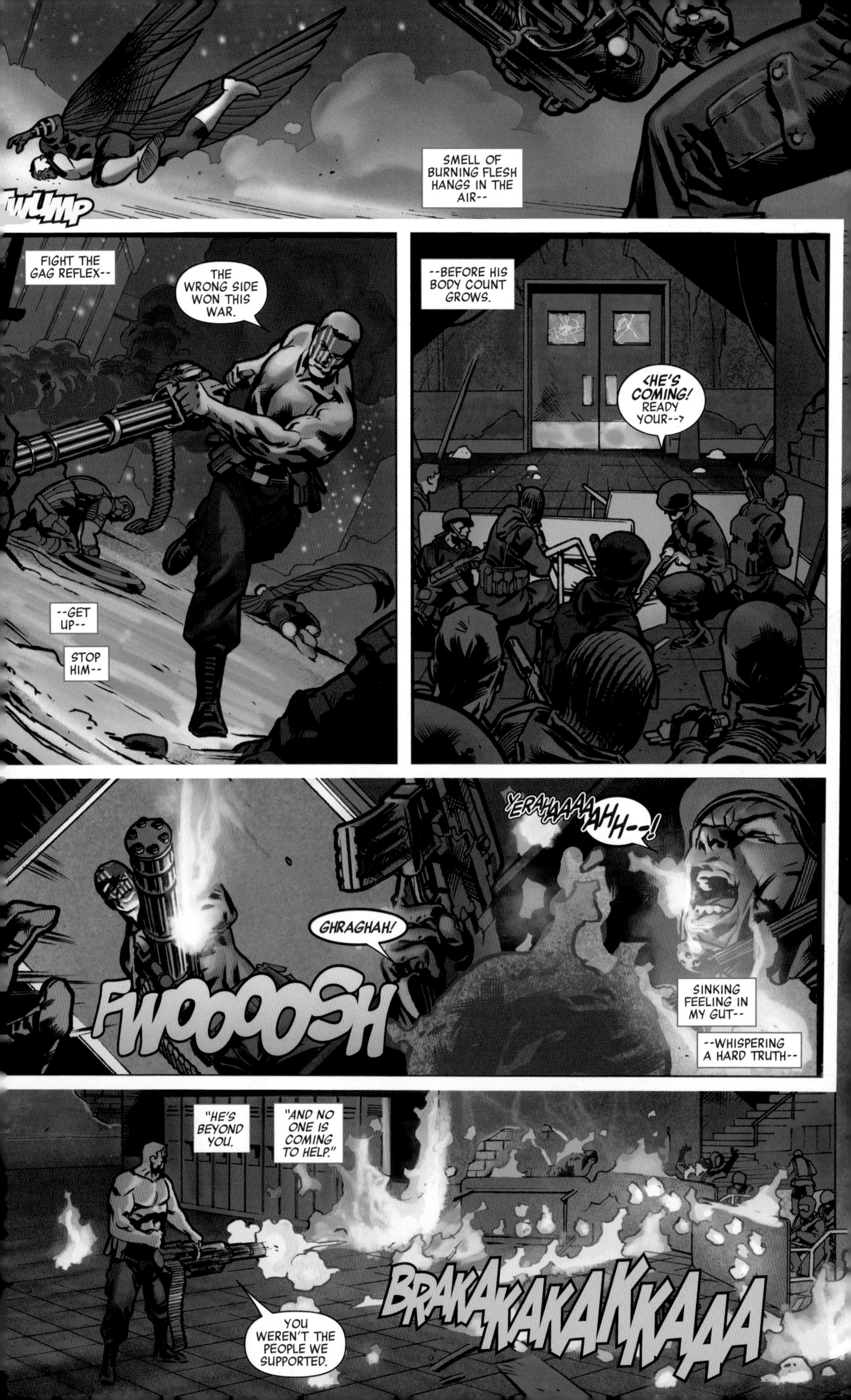
WUMP
SMELL OF BURNING FLESH HANGS IN THE AIR--
FIGHT THE GAG REFLEX--
THE WRONG SIDE WON THIS WAR.
--GET UP--
STOP HIM--
--BEFORE HIS BODY COUNT GROWS.
<HE'S COMING! READY YOUR-->
YERAHAAAAAAHH--!
GHRAGHAH!
FWOOOOSH
SINKING FEELING IN MY GUT--
--WHISPERING A HARD TRUTH--
"HE'S BEYOND YOU.
"AND NO ONE IS COMING TO HELP."
YOU WEREN'T THE PEOPLE WE SUPPORTED.
BRAKAKAKAKAKKAAA

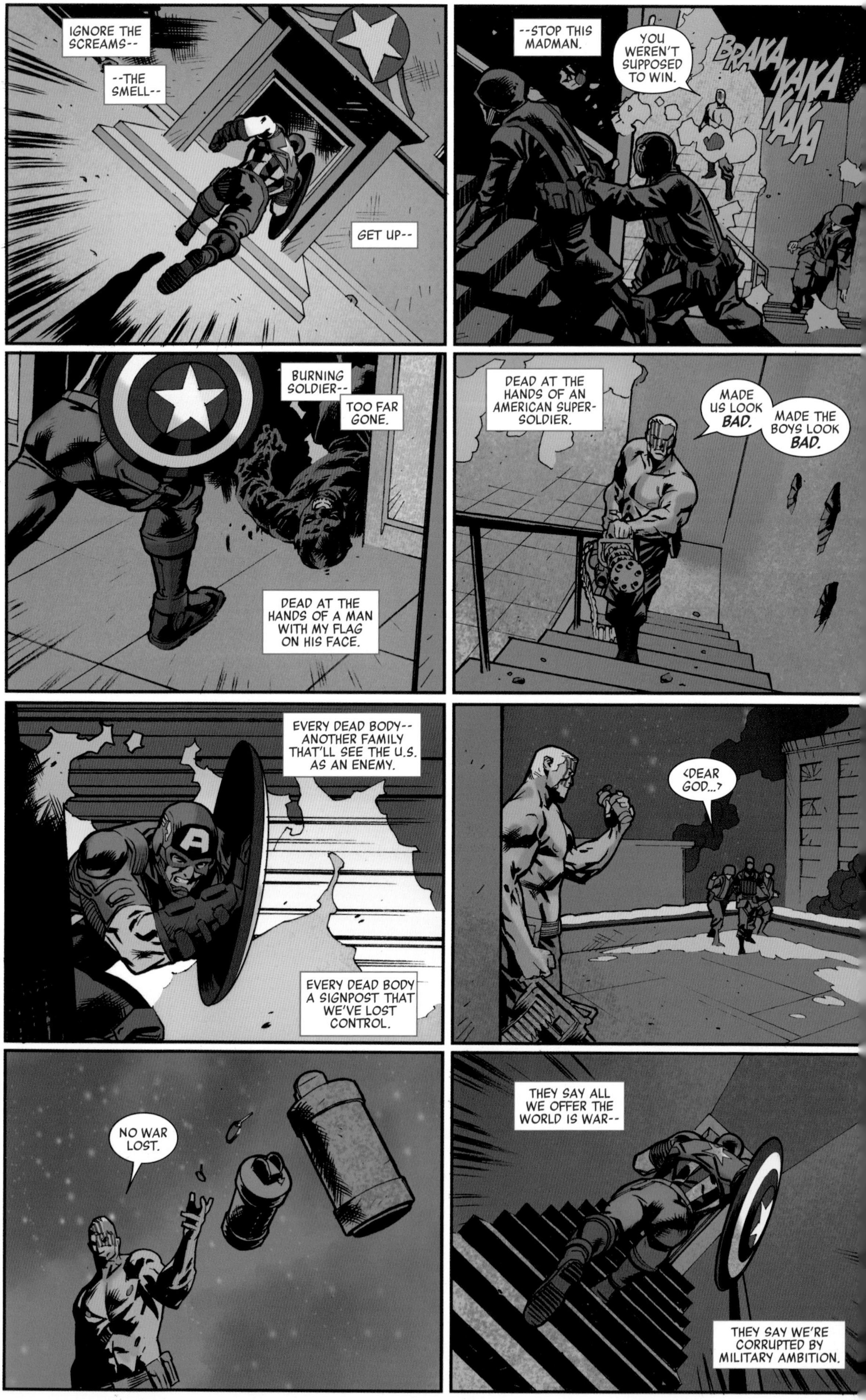
IGNORE THE SCREAMS--
--THE SMELL--
GET UP--
--STOP THIS MADMAN.
YOU WEREN'T SUPPOSED TO WIN.
BRAKAKAKAKAKA
BURNING SOLDIER--
TOO FAR GONE.
DEAD AT THE HANDS OF A MAN WITH MY FLAG ON HIS FACE.
DEAD AT THE HANDS OF AN AMERICAN SUPER-SOLDIER.
MADE US LOOK BAD.
MADE THE BOYS LOOK BAD.
EVERY DEAD BODY-- ANOTHER FAMILY THAT'LL SEE THE U.S. AS AN ENEMY.
EVERY DEAD BODY A SIGNPOST THAT WE'VE LOST CONTROL.
<DEAR GOD...>
NO WAR LOST.
THEY SAY ALL WE OFFER THE WORLD IS WAR--
THEY SAY WE'RE CORRUPTED BY MILITARY AMBITION.

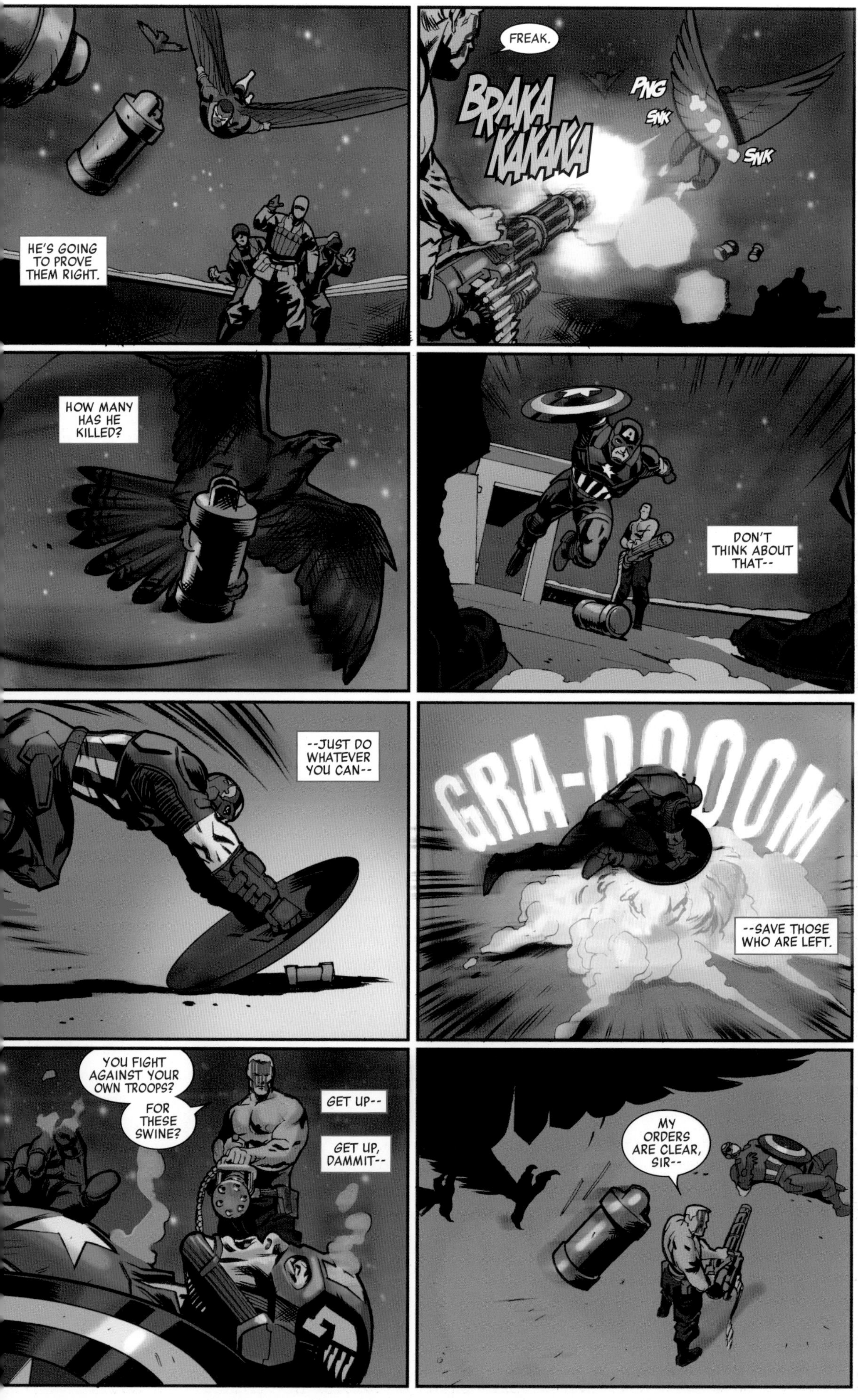
HE'S GOING TO PROVE THEM RIGHT.
FREAK.
BRAKA KAKAKA
PNG
SNK
SNK
HOW MANY HAS HE KILLED?
DON'T THINK ABOUT THAT--
--JUST DO WHATEVER YOU CAN--
GRA-DOOOM
--SAVE THOSE WHO ARE LEFT.
YOU FIGHT AGAINST YOUR OWN TROOPS?
FOR THESE SWINE?
GET UP--
GET UP, DAMMIT--
MY ORDERS ARE CLEAR, SIR--

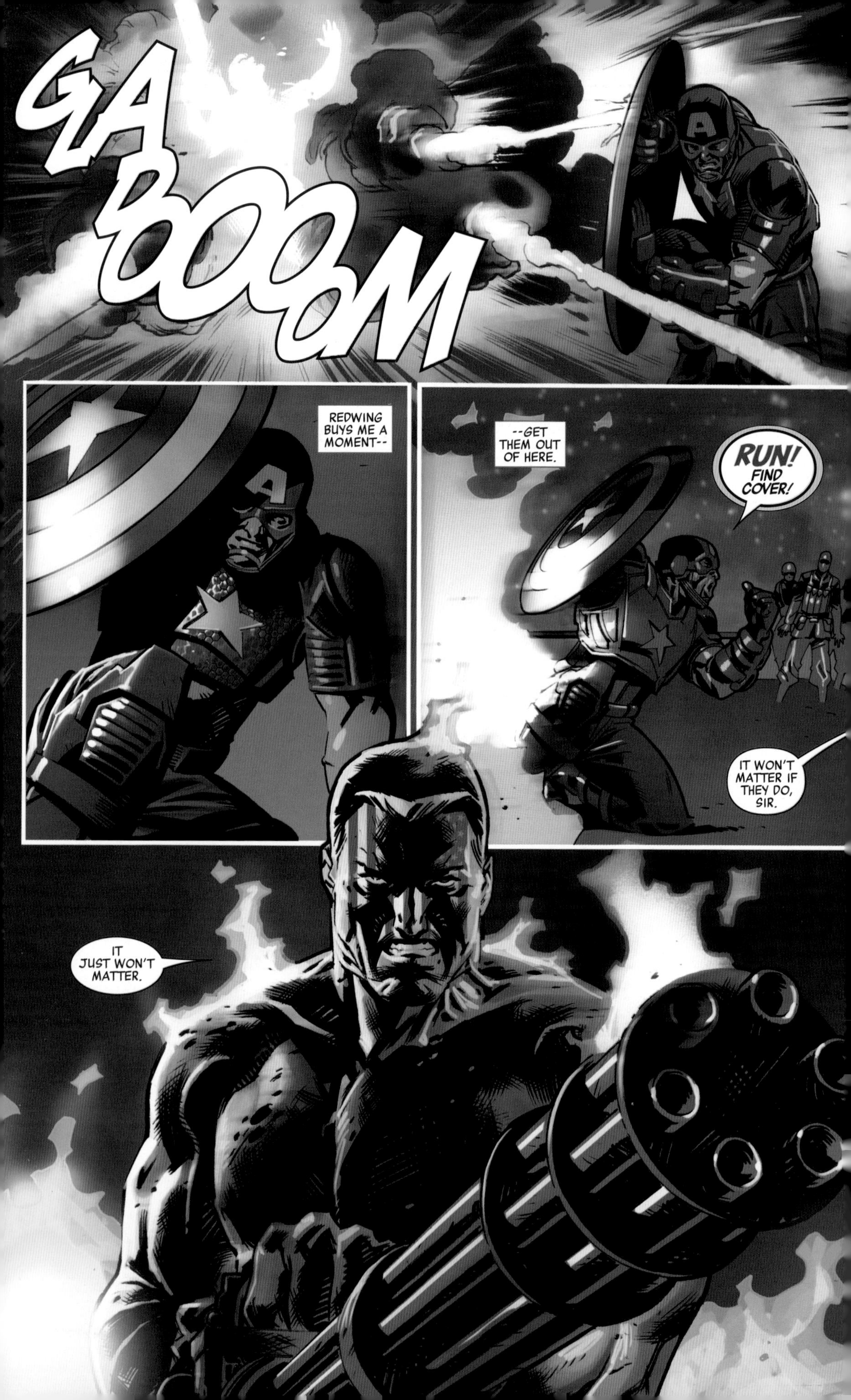
GA BOOOOM
REDWING BUYS ME A MOMENT--
--GET THEM OUT OF HERE.
RUN! FIND COVER!
IT WON'T MATTER IF THEY DO, SIR.
IT JUST WON'T MATTER.

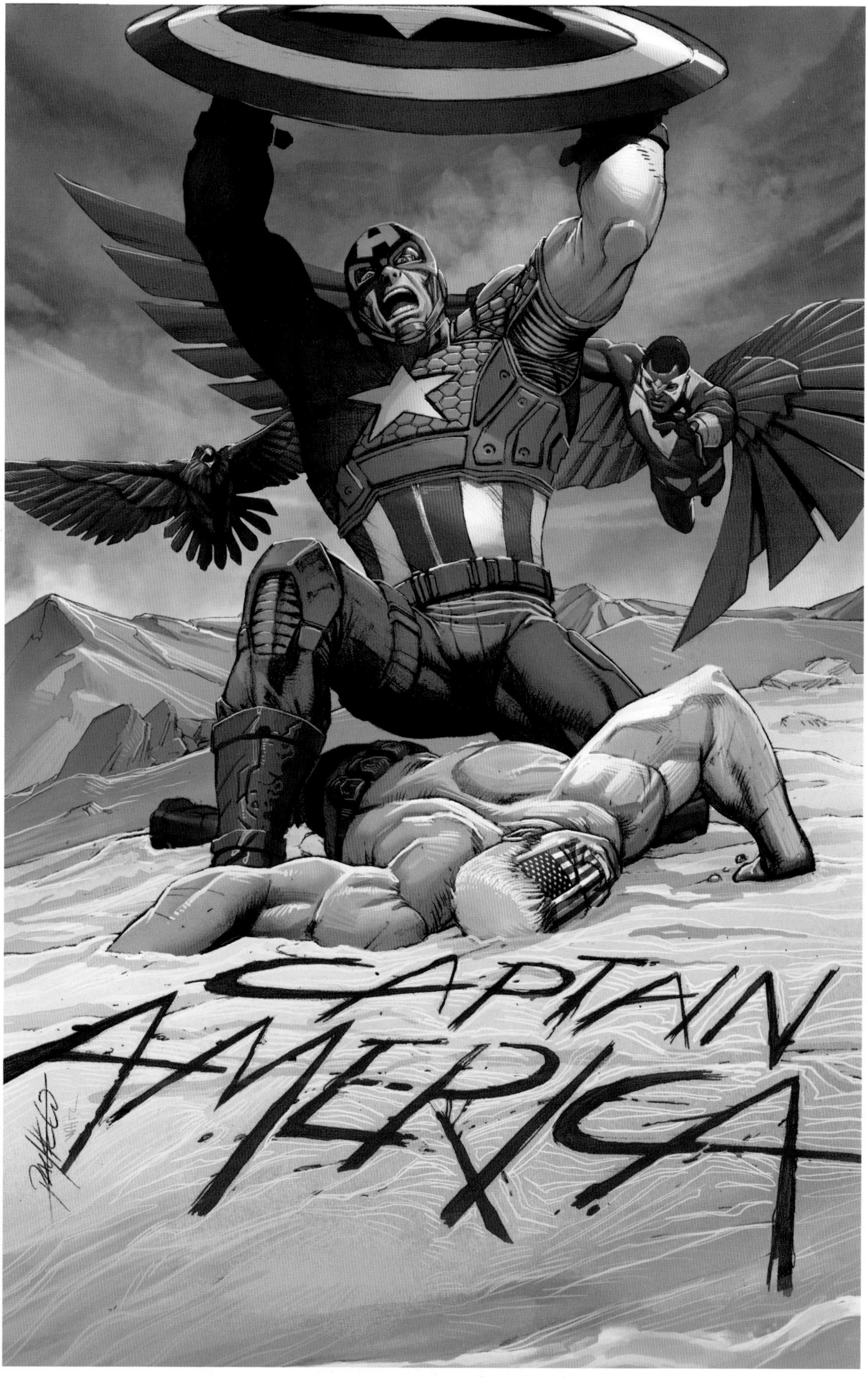
CAPTAIN AMERICA

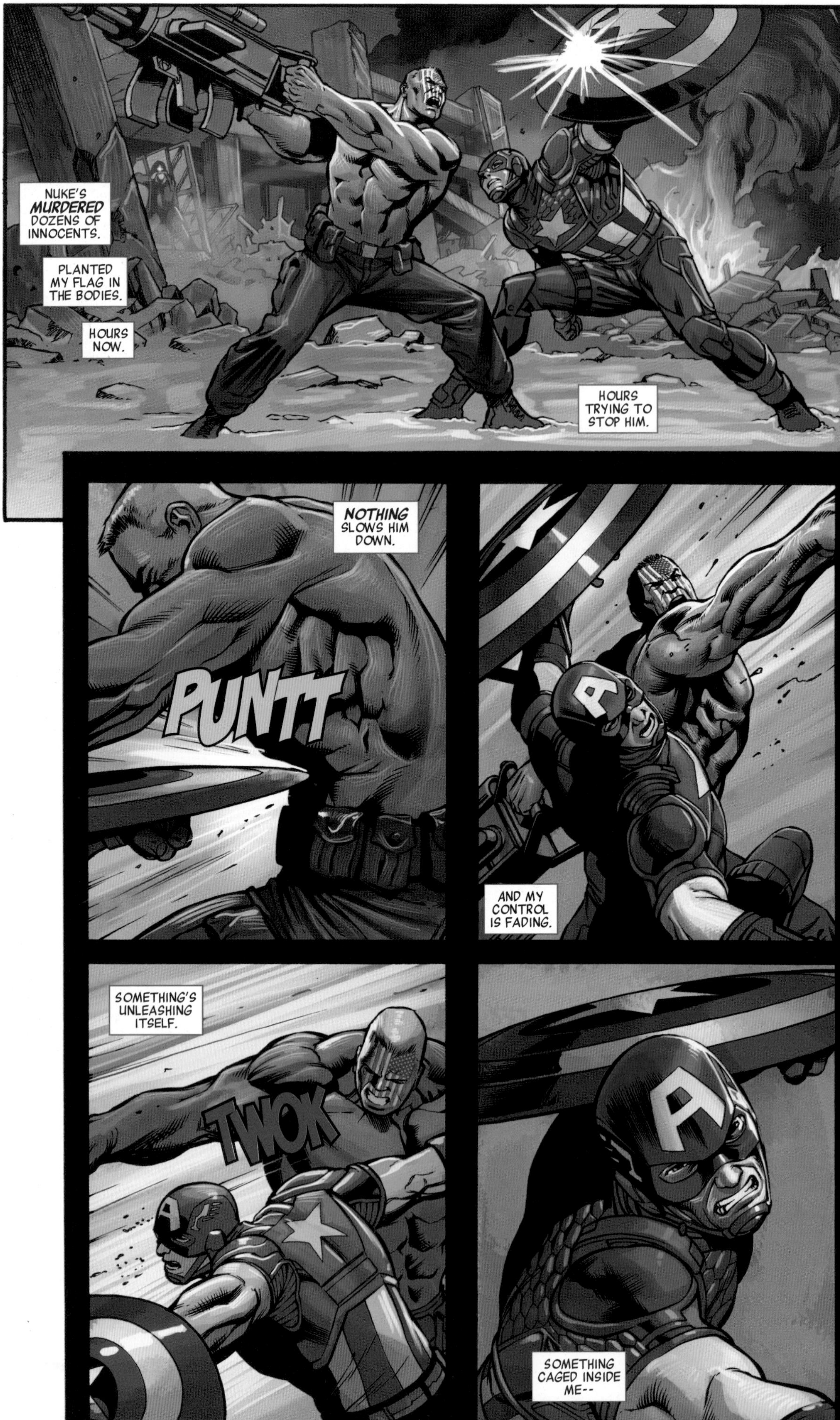
NUKE'S *MURDERED* DOZENS OF INNOCENTS.
PLANTED MY FLAG IN THE BODIES.
HOURS NOW.
HOURS TRYING TO STOP HIM.
NOTHING SLOWS HIM DOWN.
PUNTT
AND MY CONTROL IS FADING.
SOMETHING'S UNLEASHING ITSELF.
TWOK
SOMETHING CAGED INSIDE ME--

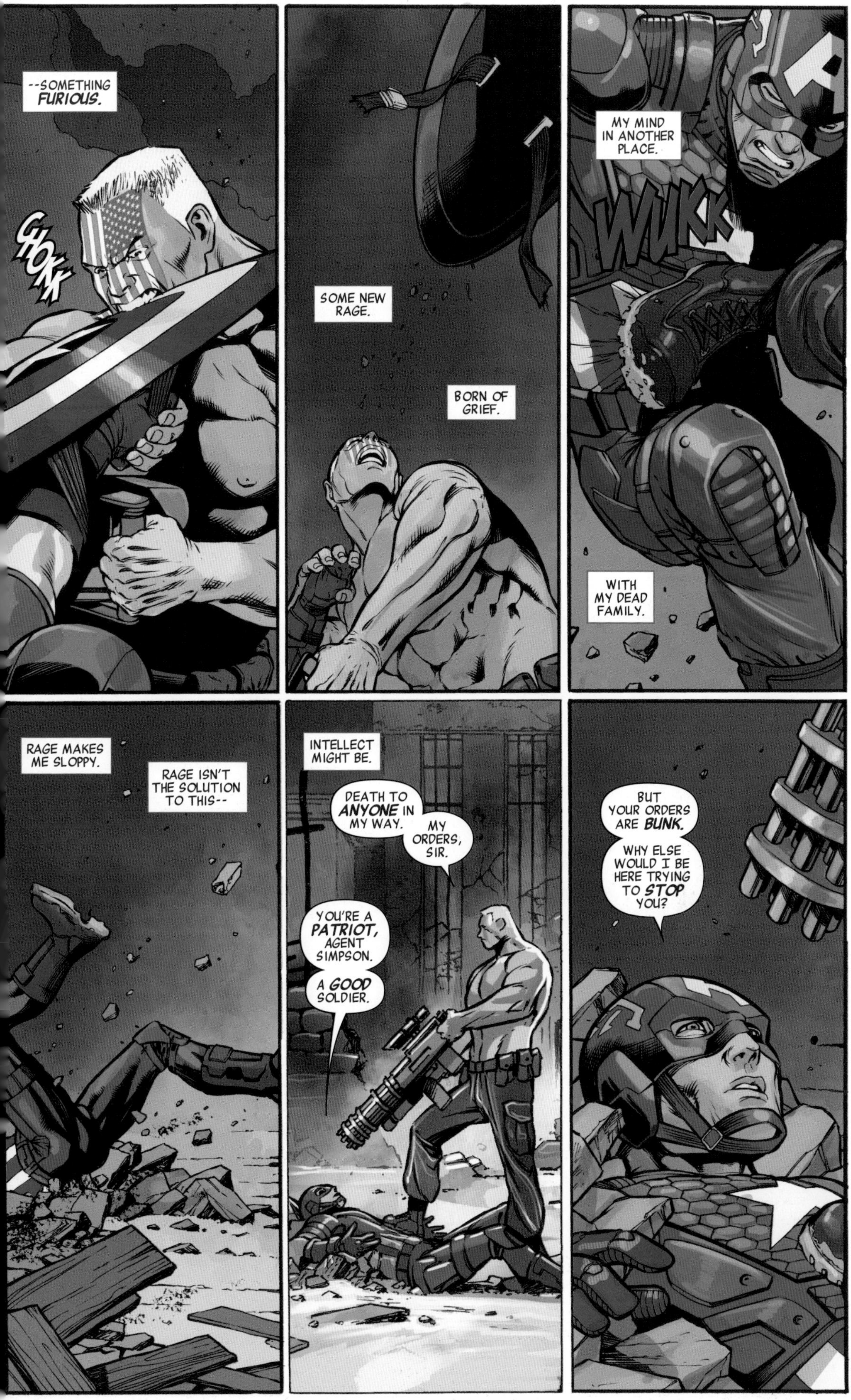
--SOMETHING FURIOUS.
CHOKK
SOME NEW RAGE.
BORN OF GRIEF.
MY MIND IN ANOTHER PLACE.
WUKK
WITH MY DEAD FAMILY.
RAGE MAKES ME SLOPPY.
RAGE ISN'T THE SOLUTION TO THIS--
INTELLECT MIGHT BE.
DEATH TO ANYONE IN MY WAY.
MY ORDERS, SIR.
YOU'RE A PATRIOT, AGENT SIMPSON.
A GOOD SOLDIER.
BUT YOUR ORDERS ARE BUNK.
WHY ELSE WOULD I BE HERE TRYING TO STOP YOU?

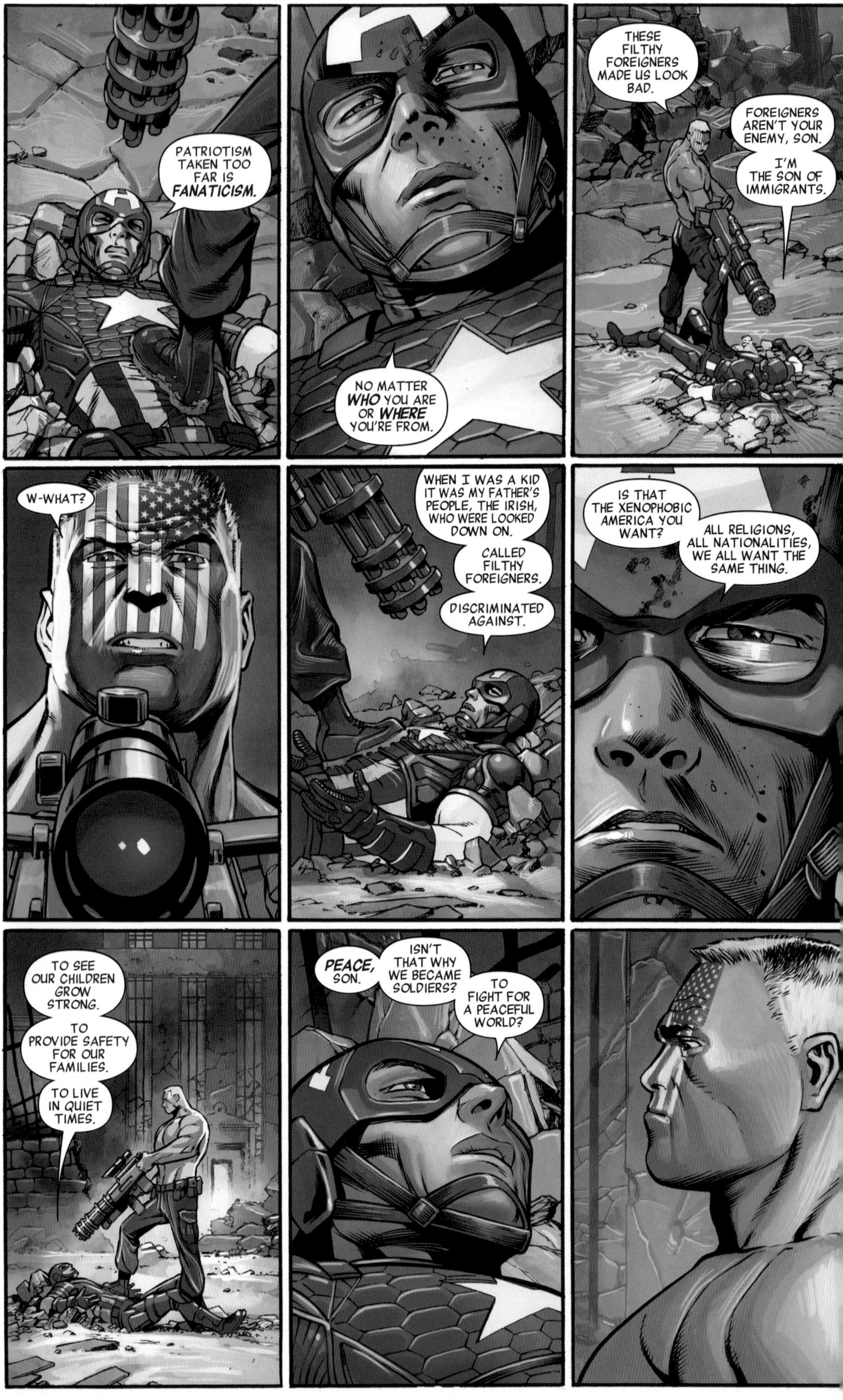
PATRIOTISM TAKEN TOO FAR IS FANATICISM.
NO MATTER WHO YOU ARE OR WHERE YOU'RE FROM.
THESE FILTHY FOREIGNERS MADE US LOOK BAD.
FOREIGNERS AREN'T YOUR ENEMY, SON.
I'M THE SON OF IMMIGRANTS.
W-WHAT?
WHEN I WAS A KID IT WAS MY FATHER'S PEOPLE, THE IRISH, WHO WERE LOOKED DOWN ON.
CALLED FILTHY FOREIGNERS.
DISCRIMINATED AGAINST.
IS THAT THE XENOPHOBIC AMERICA YOU WANT?
ALL RELIGIONS, ALL NATIONALITIES, WE ALL WANT THE SAME THING.
TO SEE OUR CHILDREN GROW STRONG.
TO PROVIDE SAFETY FOR OUR FAMILIES.
TO LIVE IN QUIET TIMES.
PEACE, SON.
ISN'T THAT WHY WE BECAME SOLDIERS?
TO FIGHT FOR A PEACEFUL WORLD?

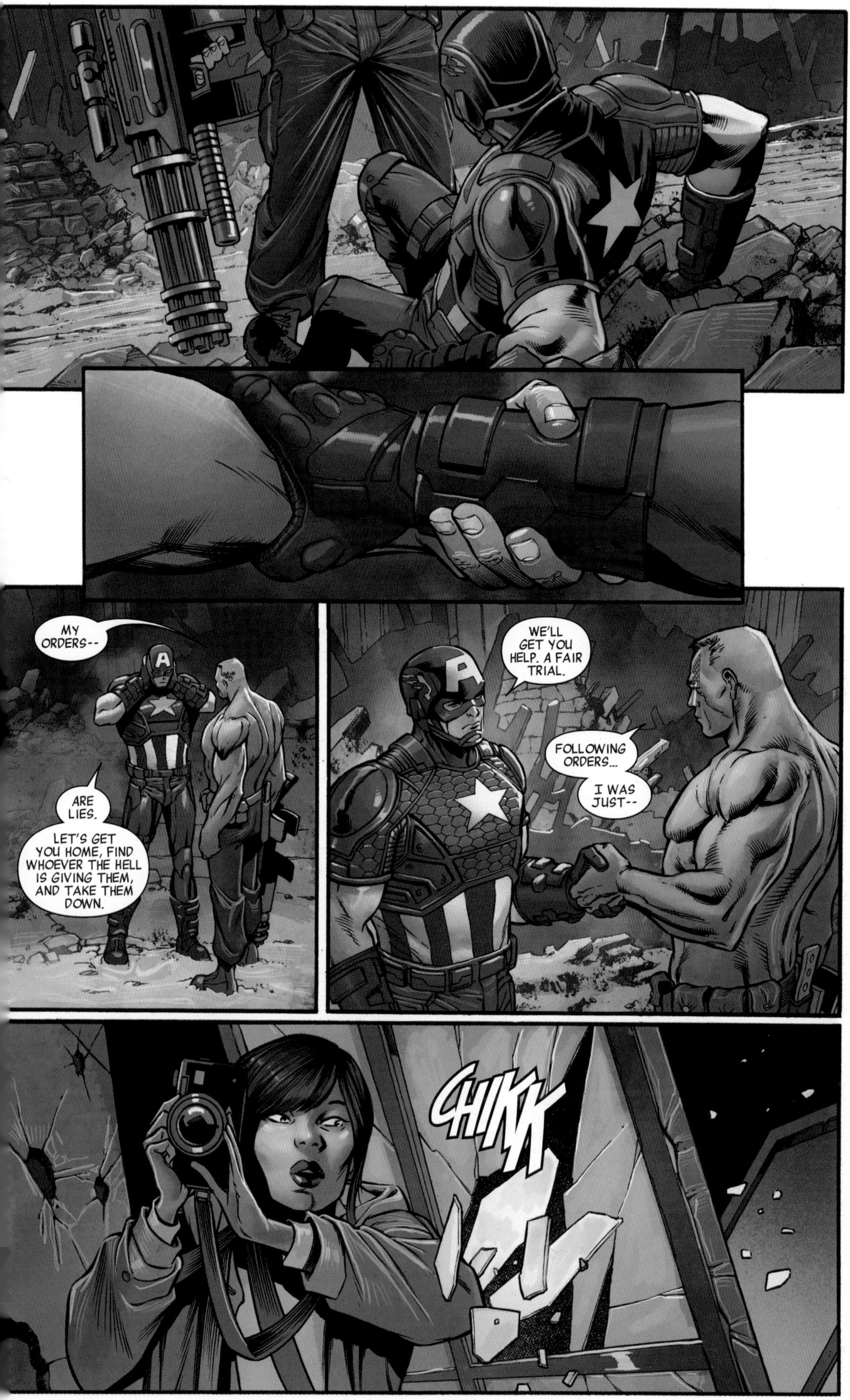
MY ORDERS--
ARE LIES.
LET'S GET YOU HOME, FIND WHOEVER THE HELL IS GIVING THEM, AND TAKE THEM DOWN.
WE'LL GET YOU HELP. A FAIR TRIAL.
FOLLOWING ORDERS...
I WAS JUST--
CHIKK

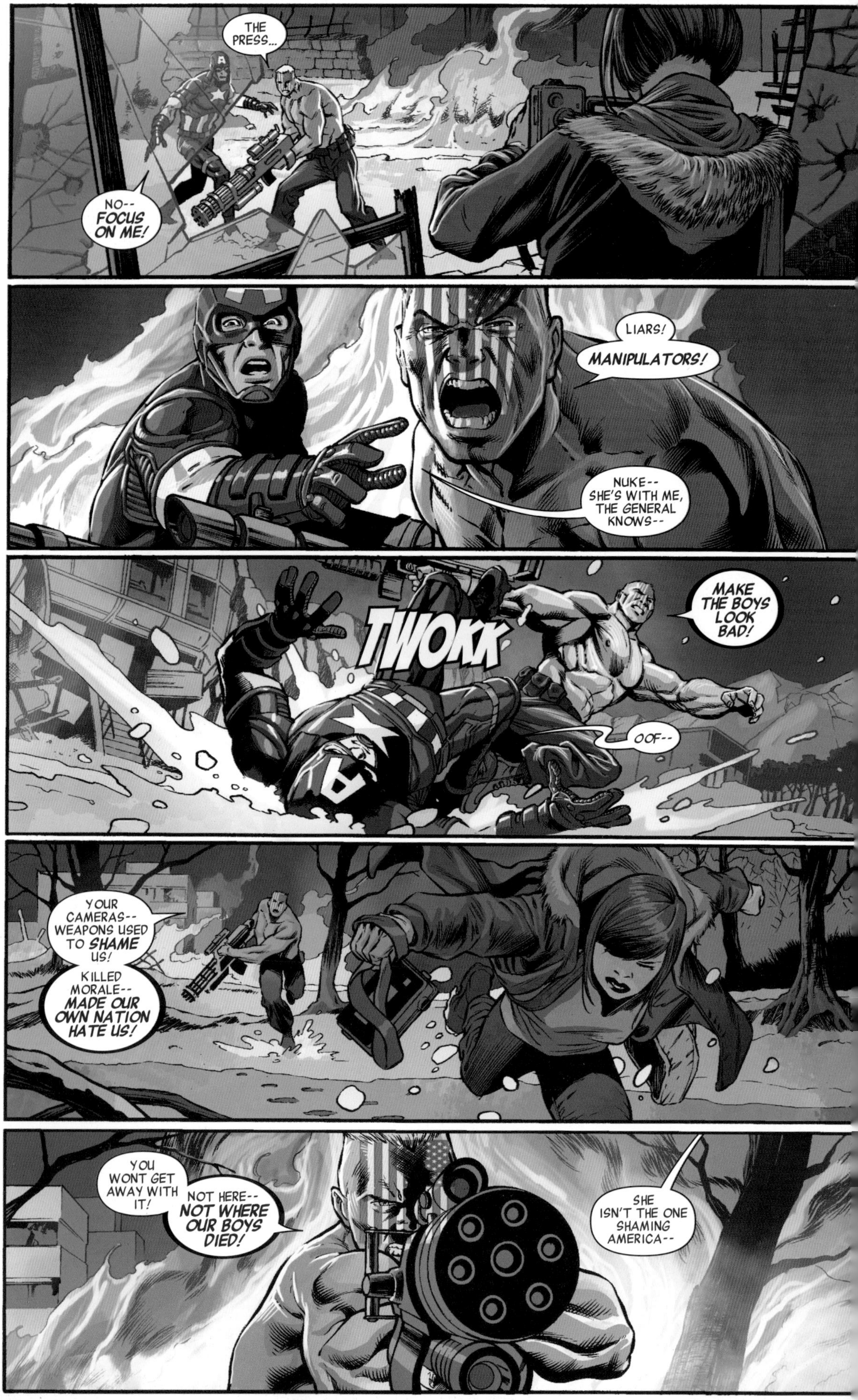
THE PRESS...
NO-- FOCUS ON ME!
LIARS!
MANIPULATORS!
NUKE-- SHE'S WITH ME, THE GENERAL KNOWS--
MAKE THE BOYS LOOK BAD!
TWOKK
OOF--
YOUR CAMERAS-- WEAPONS USED TO SHAME US!
KILLED MORALE-- MADE OUR OWN NATION HATE US!
YOU WONT GET AWAY WITH IT!
NOT HERE-- NOT WHERE OUR BOYS DIED!
SHE ISN'T THE ONE SHAMING AMERICA--

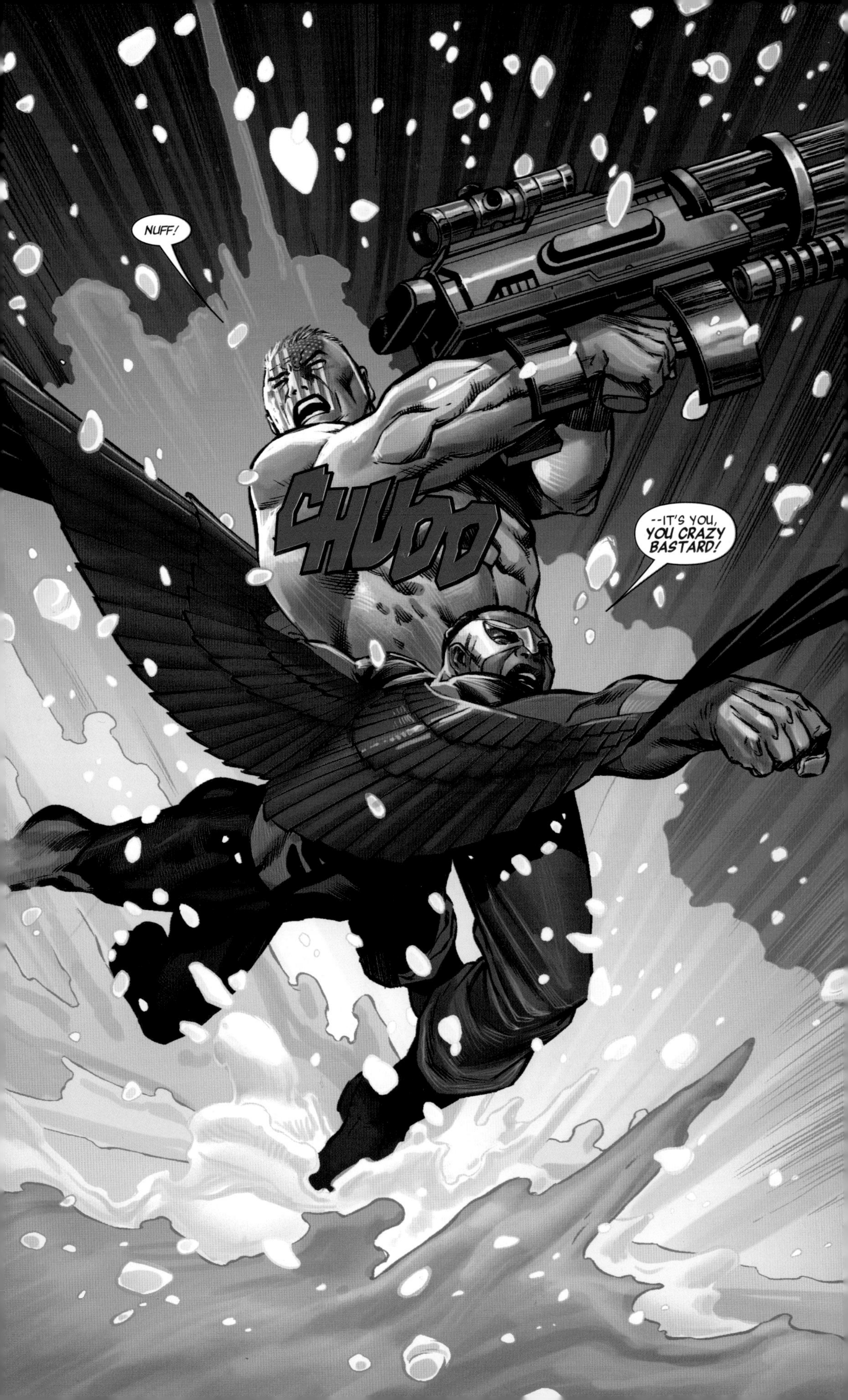
NUFF!
CHUDD
--IT'S YOU, YOU CRAZY BASTARD!

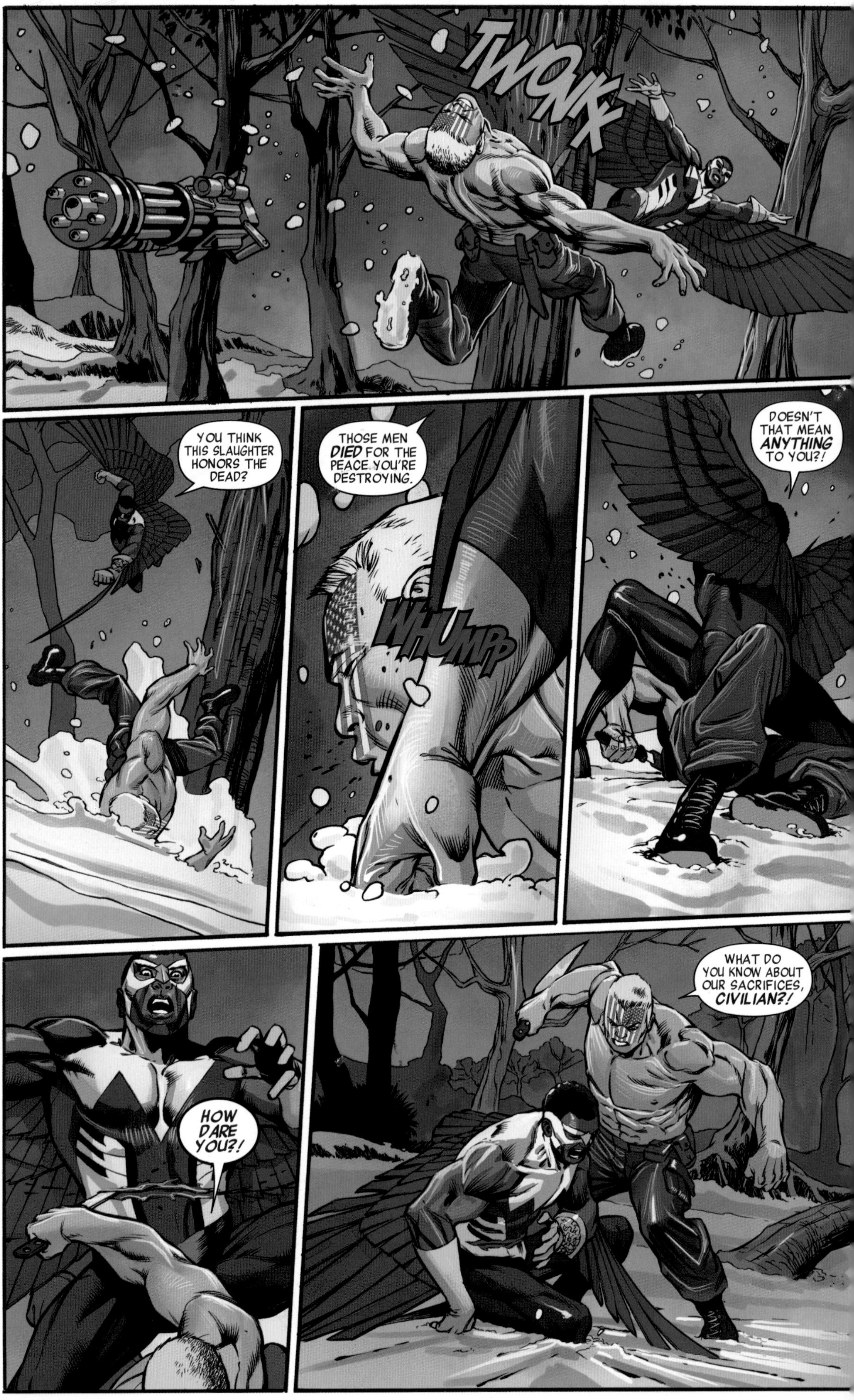
TWONKK
YOU THINK THIS SLAUGHTER HONORS THE DEAD?
THOSE MEN DIED FOR THE PEACE YOU'RE DESTROYING.
WHUMPP
DOESN'T THAT MEAN ANYTHING TO YOU?!
HOW DARE YOU?!
WHAT DO YOU KNOW ABOUT OUR SACRIFICES, CIVILIAN?!

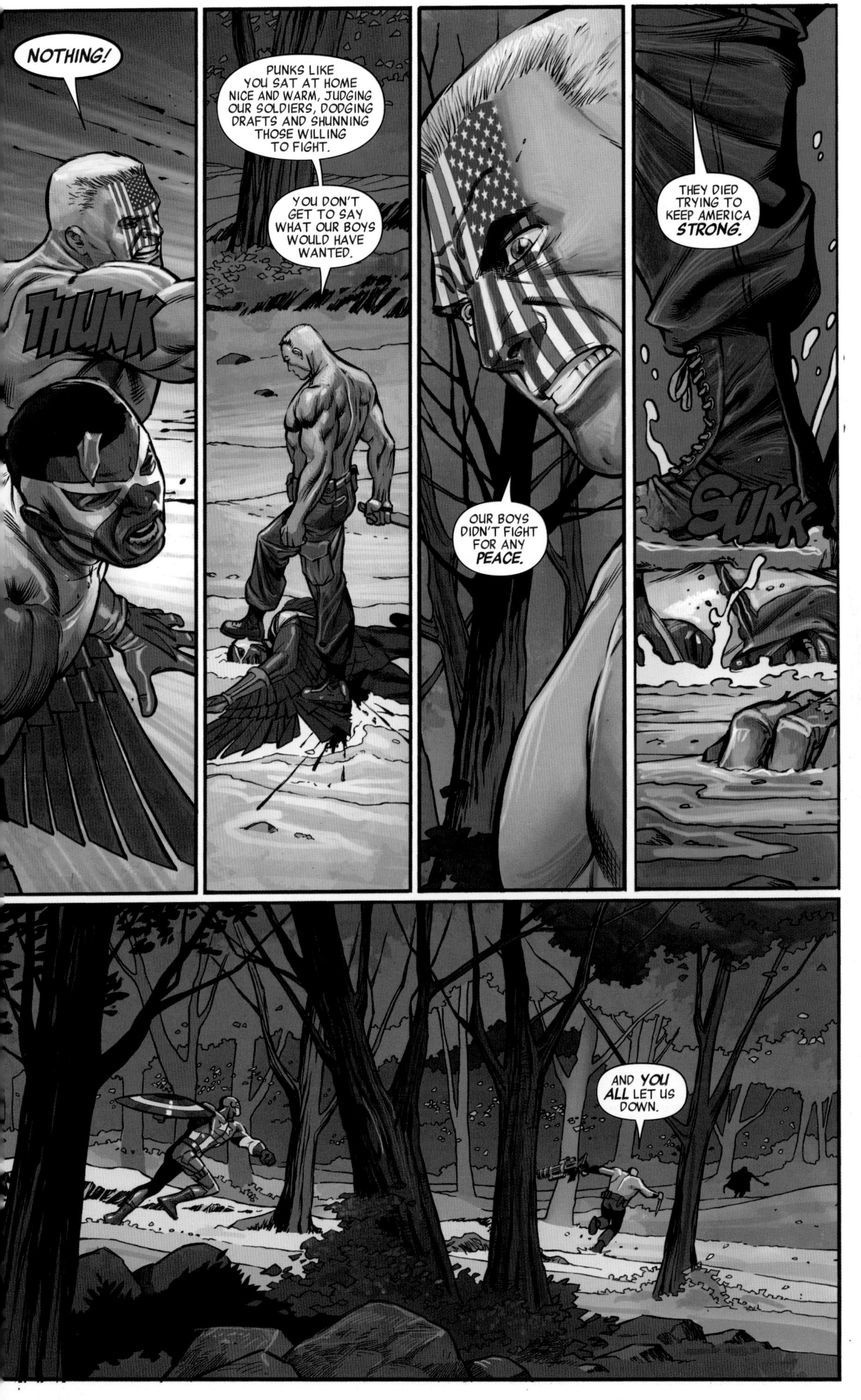
NOTHING!
THUNK
PUNKS LIKE YOU SAT AT HOME NICE AND WARM, JUDGING OUR SOLDIERS, DODGING DRAFTS AND SHUNNING THOSE WILLING TO FIGHT.
YOU DON'T GET TO SAY WHAT OUR BOYS WOULD HAVE WANTED.
OUR BOYS DIDN'T FIGHT FOR ANY PEACE.
THEY DIED TRYING TO KEEP AMERICA STRONG.
SUKK
AND YOU ALL LET US DOWN.

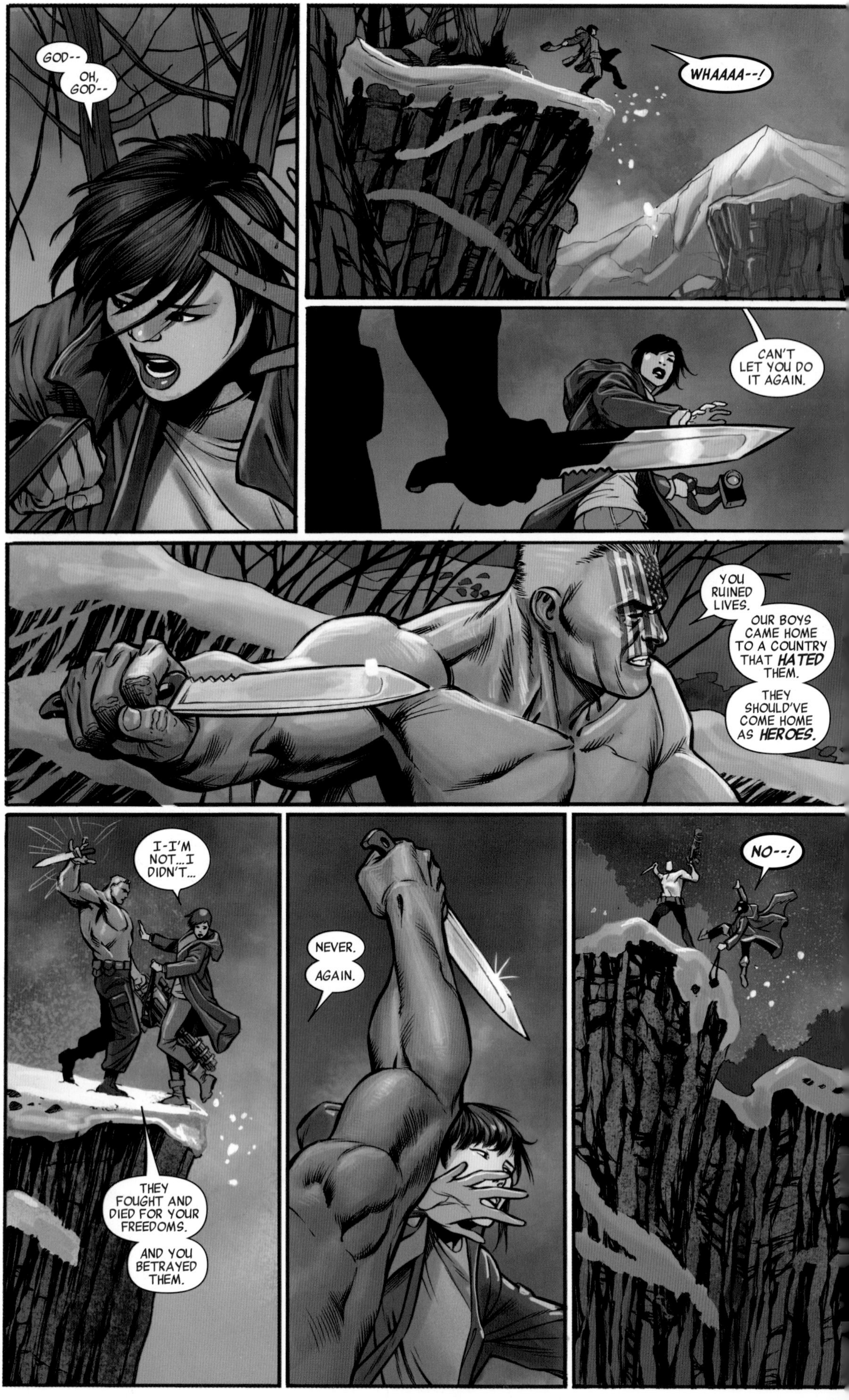
GOD--
OH, GOD--
WHAAAA--!
CAN'T LET YOU DO IT AGAIN.
YOU RUINED LIVES.
OUR BOYS CAME HOME TO A COUNTRY THAT HATED THEM.
THEY SHOULD'VE COME HOME AS HEROES.
I-I'M NOT...I DIDN'T...
THEY FOUGHT AND DIED FOR YOUR FREEDOMS.
AND YOU BETRAYED THEM.
NEVER.
AGAIN.
NO--!

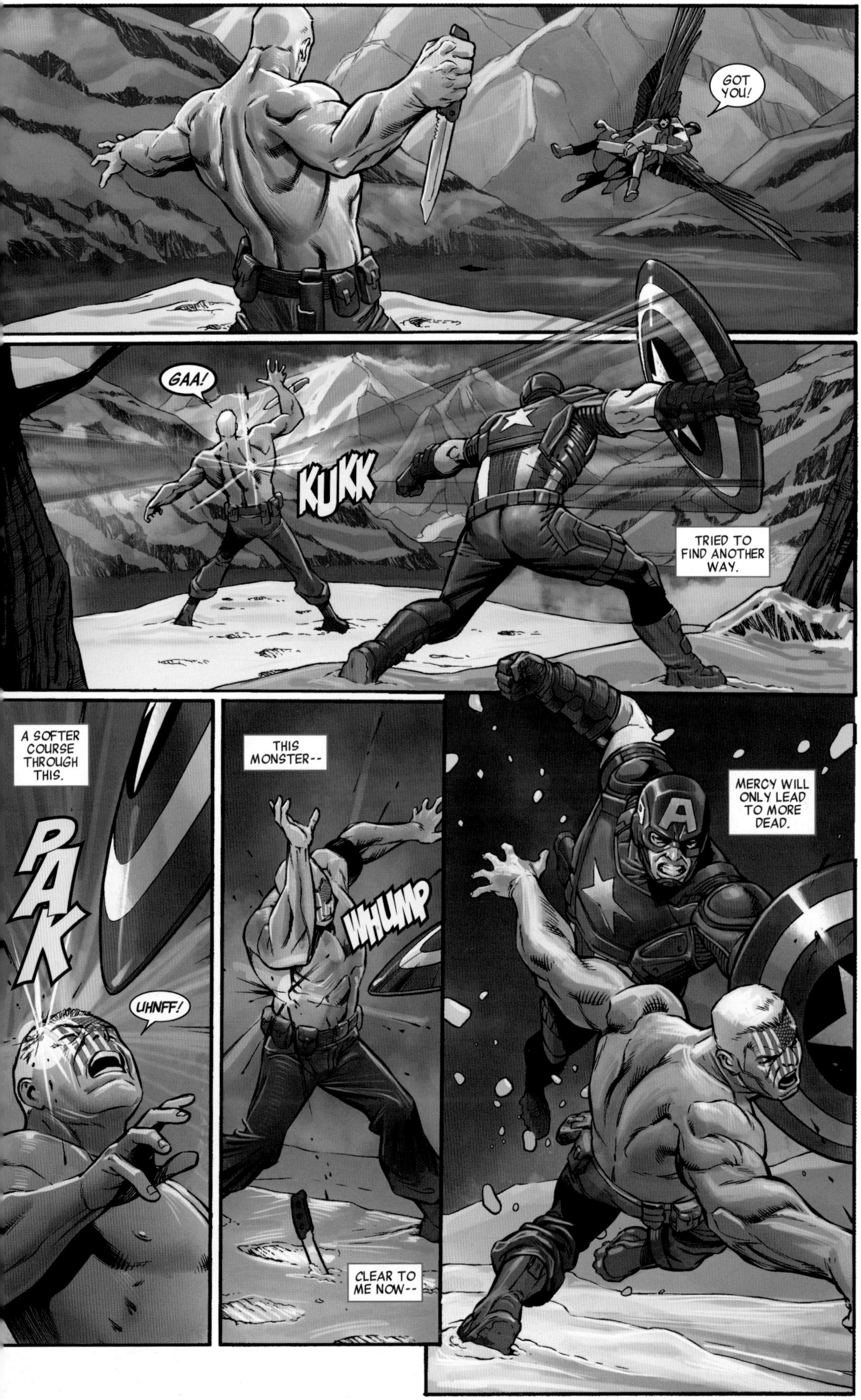

GOT YOU!
GAA!
KUKK
TRIED TO FIND ANOTHER WAY.
A SOFTER COURSE THROUGH THIS.
PAK
UHNFF!
THIS MONSTER--
WHUMP
CLEAR TO ME NOW--
MERCY WILL ONLY LEAD TO MORE DEAD.

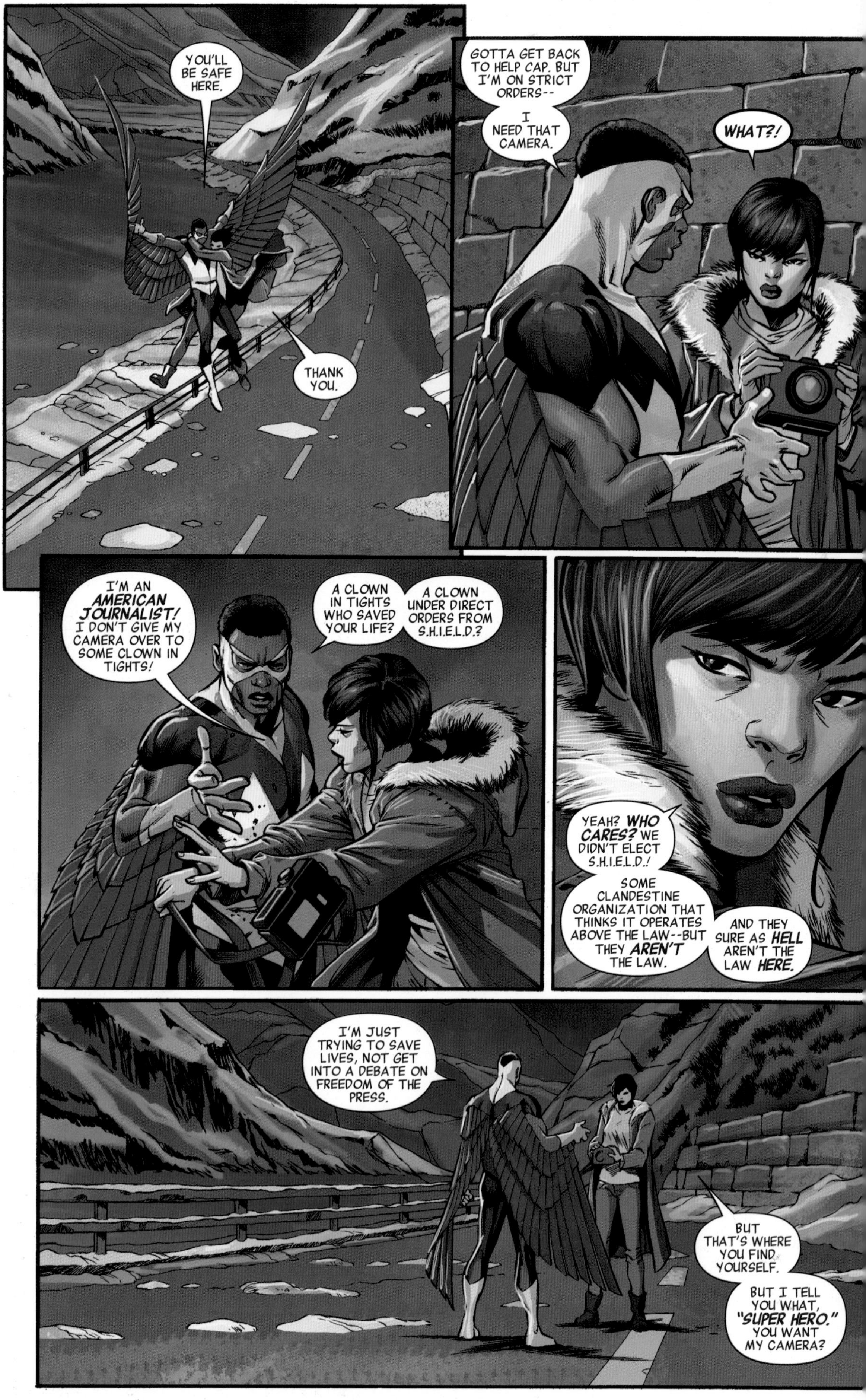
YOU'LL BE SAFE HERE.
THANK YOU.
GOTTA GET BACK TO HELP CAP. BUT I'M ON STRICT ORDERS--
I NEED THAT CAMERA.
WHAT?!
I'M AN AMERICAN JOURNALIST! I DON'T GIVE MY CAMERA OVER TO SOME CLOWN IN TIGHTS!
A CLOWN IN TIGHTS WHO SAVED YOUR LIFE?
A CLOWN UNDER DIRECT ORDERS FROM S.H.I.E.L.D.?
YEAH? WHO CARES? WE DIDN'T ELECT S.H.I.E.L.D.!
SOME CLANDESTINE ORGANIZATION THAT THINKS IT OPERATES ABOVE THE LAW--BUT THEY AREN'T THE LAW.
AND THEY SURE AS HELL AREN'T THE LAW HERE.
I'M JUST TRYING TO SAVE LIVES, NOT GET INTO A DEBATE ON FREEDOM OF THE PRESS.
BUT THAT'S WHERE YOU FIND YOURSELF.
BUT I TELL YOU WHAT, "SUPER HERO." YOU WANT MY CAMERA?

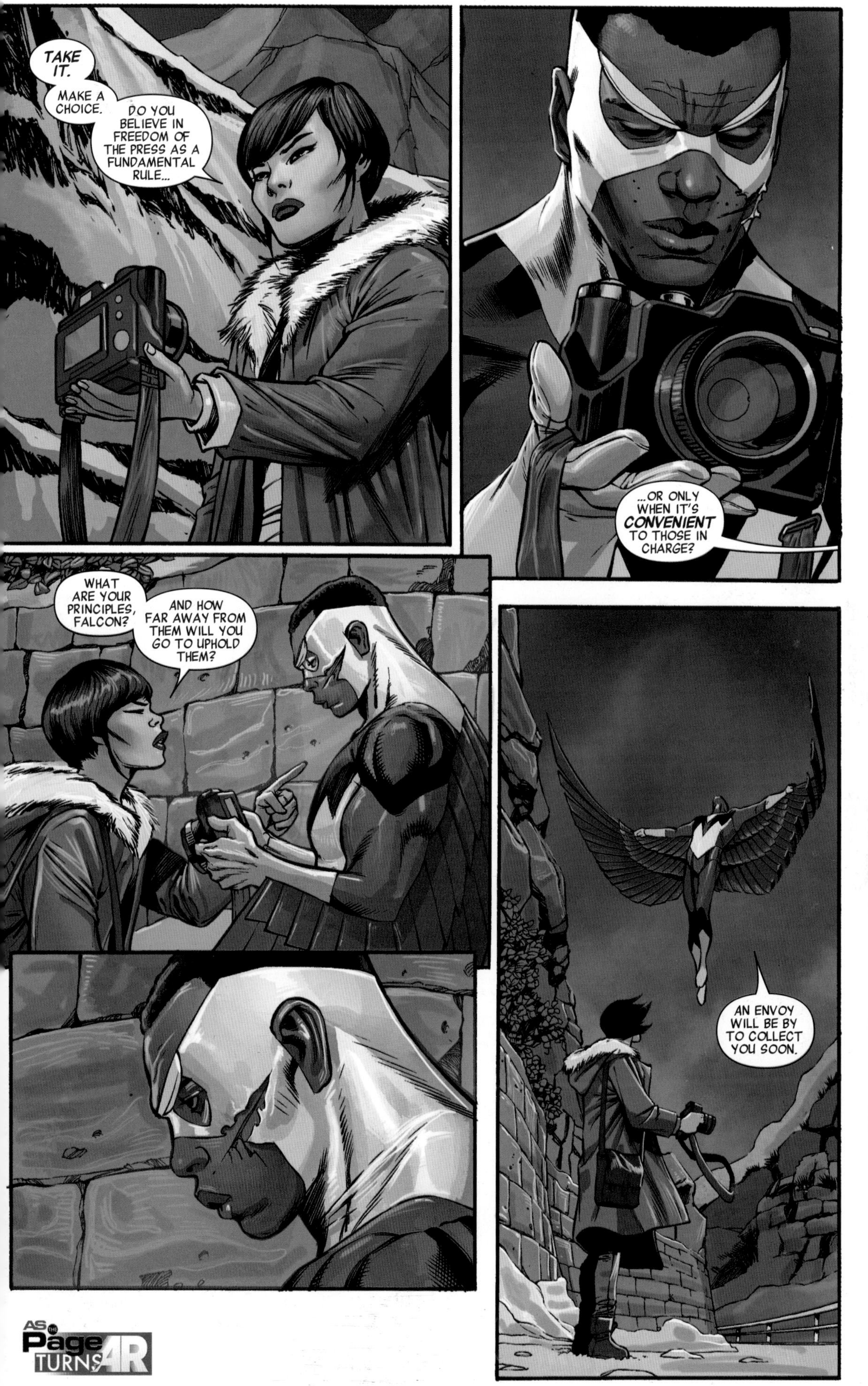
TAKE IT.
MAKE A CHOICE.
DO YOU BELIEVE IN FREEDOM OF THE PRESS AS A FUNDAMENTAL RULE...
...OR ONLY WHEN IT'S CONVENIENT TO THOSE IN CHARGE?
WHAT ARE YOUR PRINCIPLES, FALCON?
AND HOW FAR AWAY FROM THEM WILL YOU GO TO UPHOLD THEM?
AN ENVOY WILL BE BY TO COLLECT YOU SOON.

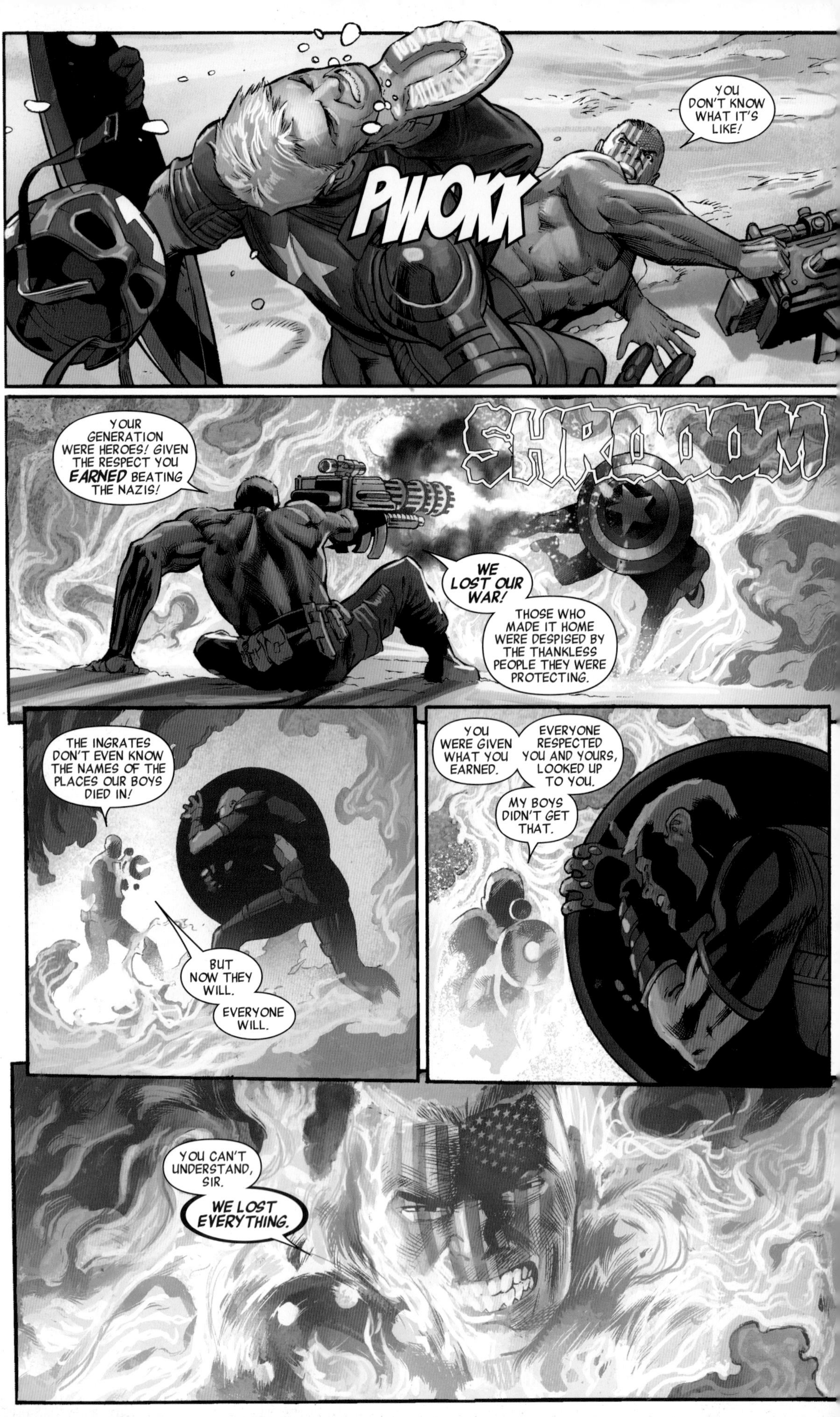
PWOKK
YOU DON'T KNOW WHAT IT'S LIKE!
YOUR GENERATION WERE HEROES! GIVEN THE RESPECT YOU EARNED BEATING THE NAZIS!
SHROOOOM
WE LOST OUR WAR!
THOSE WHO MADE IT HOME WERE DESPISED BY THE THANKLESS PEOPLE THEY WERE PROTECTING.
THE INGRATES DON'T EVEN KNOW THE NAMES OF THE PLACES OUR BOYS DIED IN!
BUT NOW THEY WILL.
EVERYONE WILL.
YOU WERE GIVEN WHAT YOU EARNED.
EVERYONE RESPECTED YOU AND YOURS, LOOKED UP TO YOU.
MY BOYS DIDN'T GET THAT.
YOU CAN'T UNDERSTAND, SIR.
WE LOST EVERYTHING.

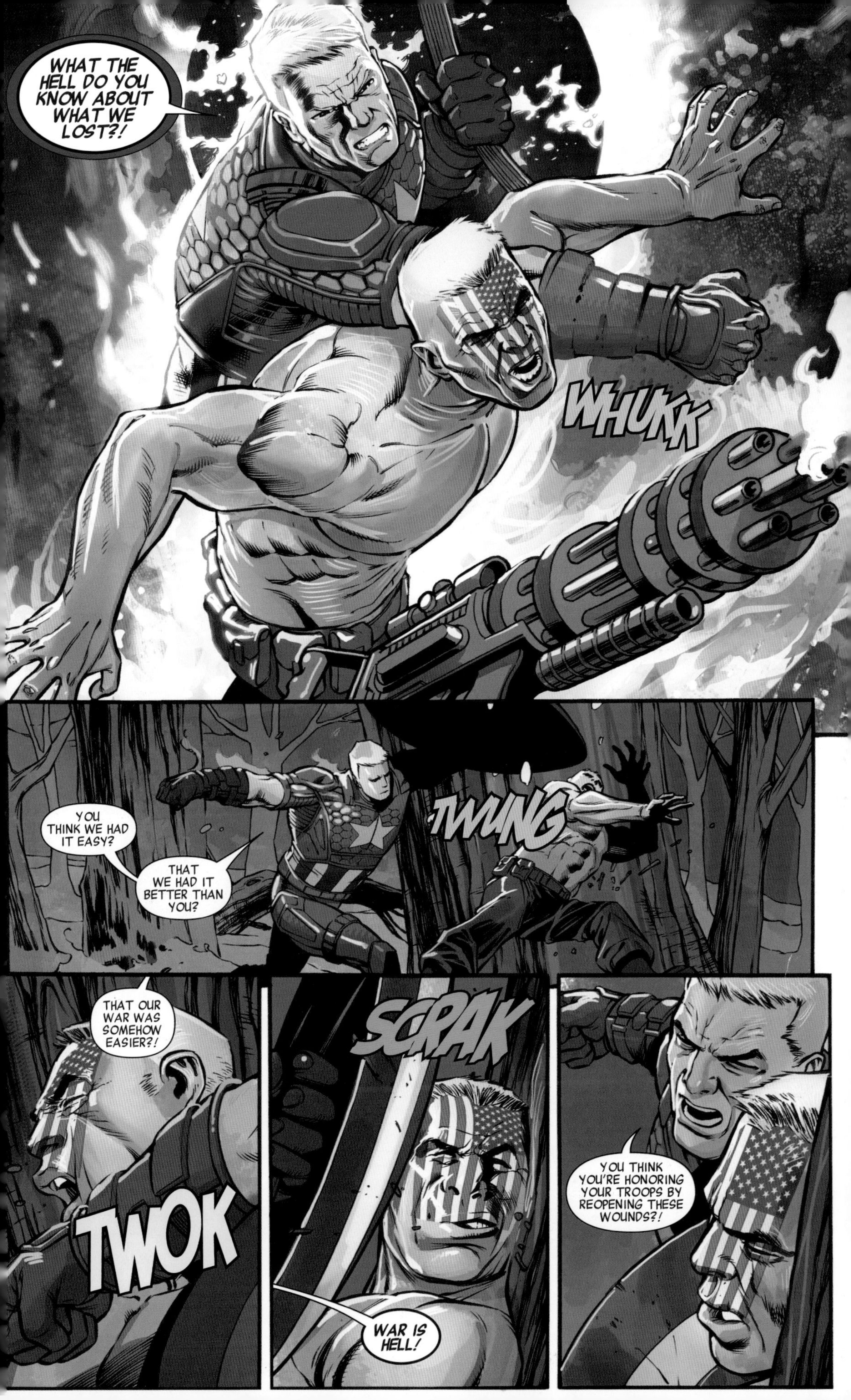
WHAT THE HELL DO YOU KNOW ABOUT WHAT WE LOST?!
WHUKK
YOU THINK WE HAD IT EASY?
TWUNG
THAT WE HAD IT BETTER THAN YOU?
THAT OUR WAR WAS SOMEHOW EASIER?!
TWOK
SCRAK
WAR IS HELL!
YOU THINK YOU'RE HONORING YOUR TROOPS BY REOPENING THESE WOUNDS?!

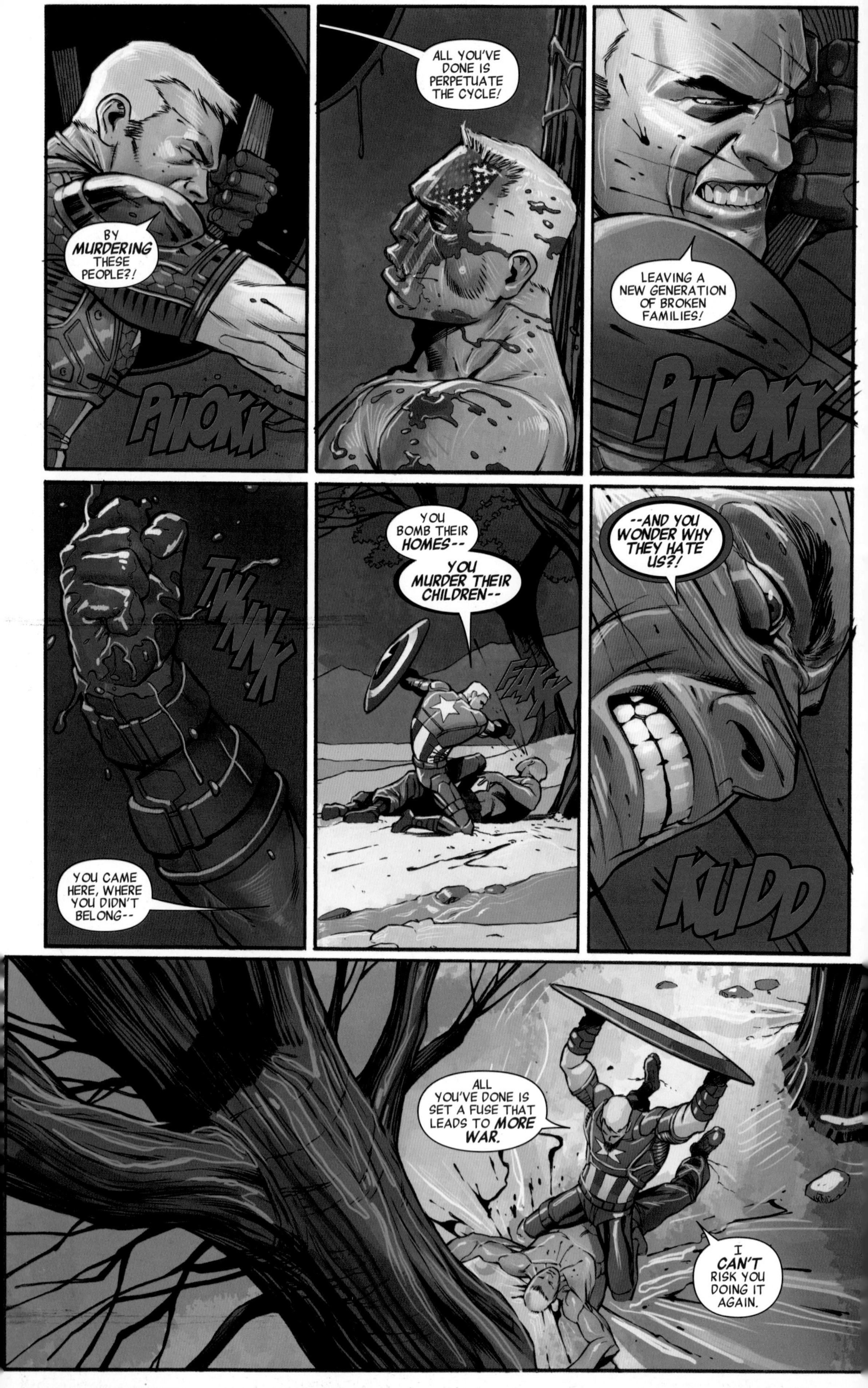

BY MURDERING THESE PEOPLE?!
PWOKK
ALL YOU'VE DONE IS PERPETUATE THE CYCLE!
LEAVING A NEW GENERATION OF BROKEN FAMILIES!
PWOKK
TWINK
YOU CAME HERE, WHERE YOU DIDN'T BELONG--
YOU BOMB THEIR HOMES--
YOU MURDER THEIR CHILDREN--
--AND YOU WONDER WHY THEY HATE US?!
KUDD
ALL YOU'VE DONE IS SET A FUSE THAT LEADS TO MORE WAR.
I CAN'T RISK YOU DOING IT AGAIN.

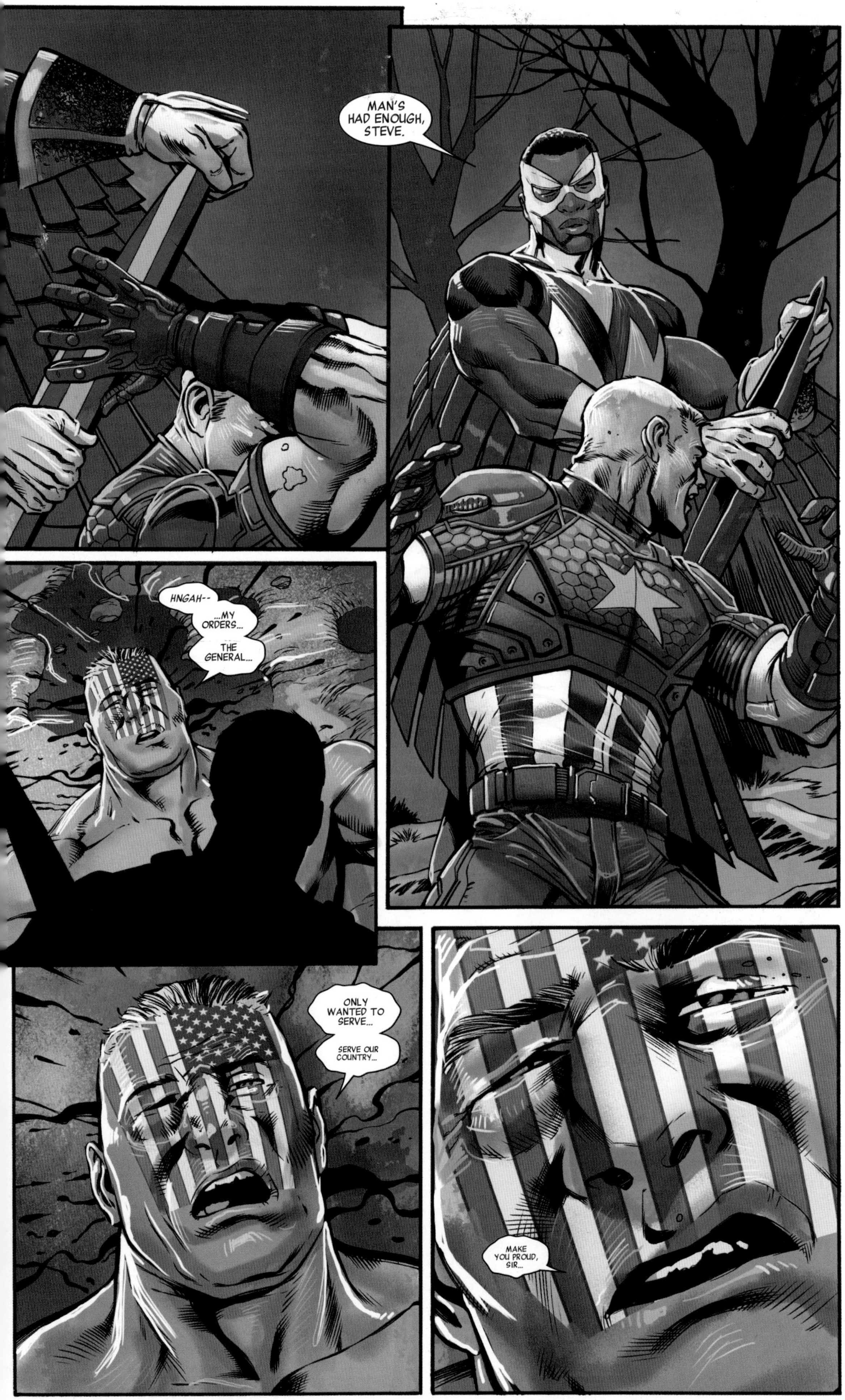
MAN'S HAD ENOUGH, STEVE.
HNGAH--
...MY ORDERS...
THE GENERAL...
ONLY WANTED TO SERVE...
SERVE OUR COUNTRY...
MAKE YOU PROUD, SIR...

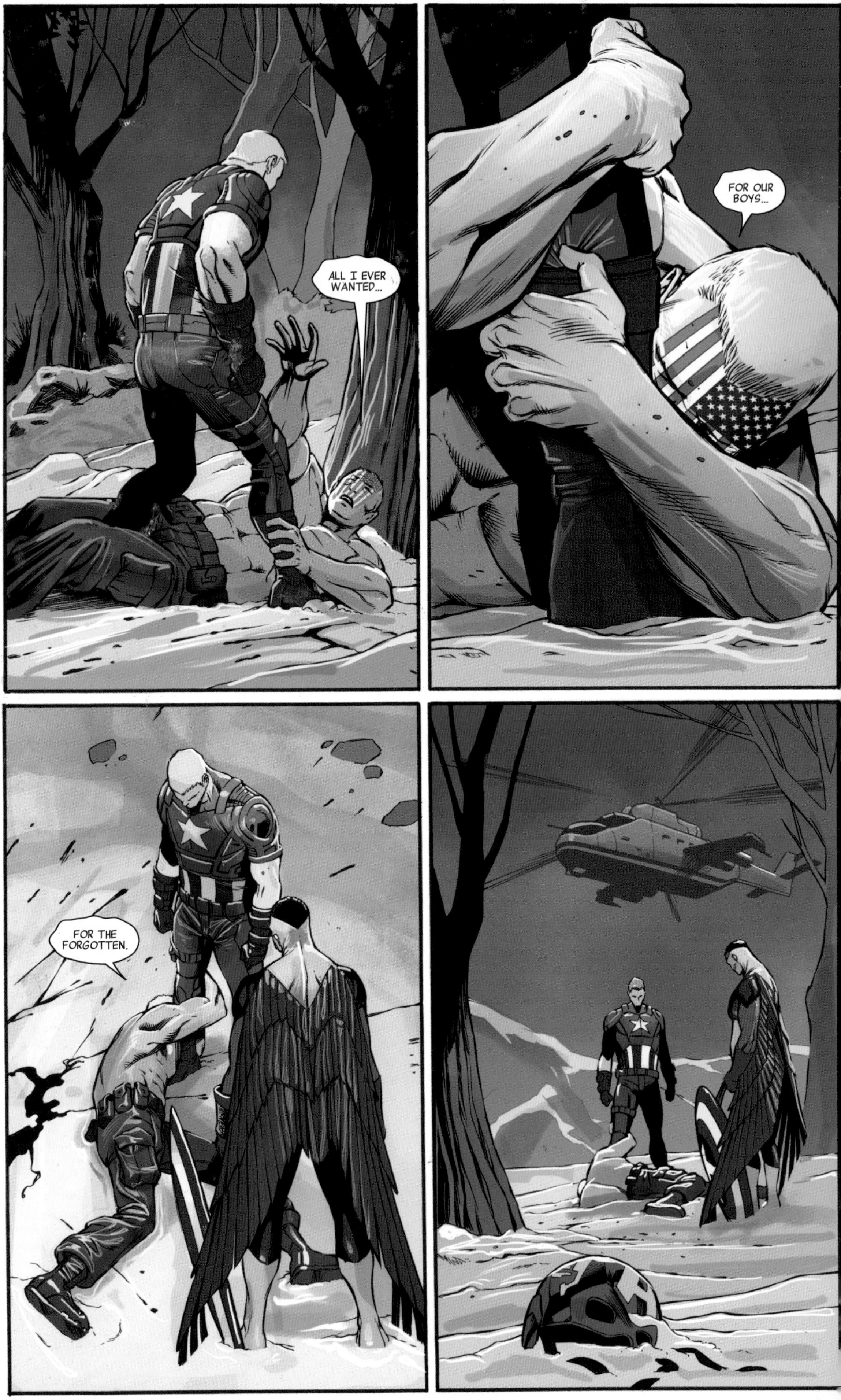
ALL I EVER WANTED...
FOR OUR BOYS...
FOR THE FORGOTTEN.

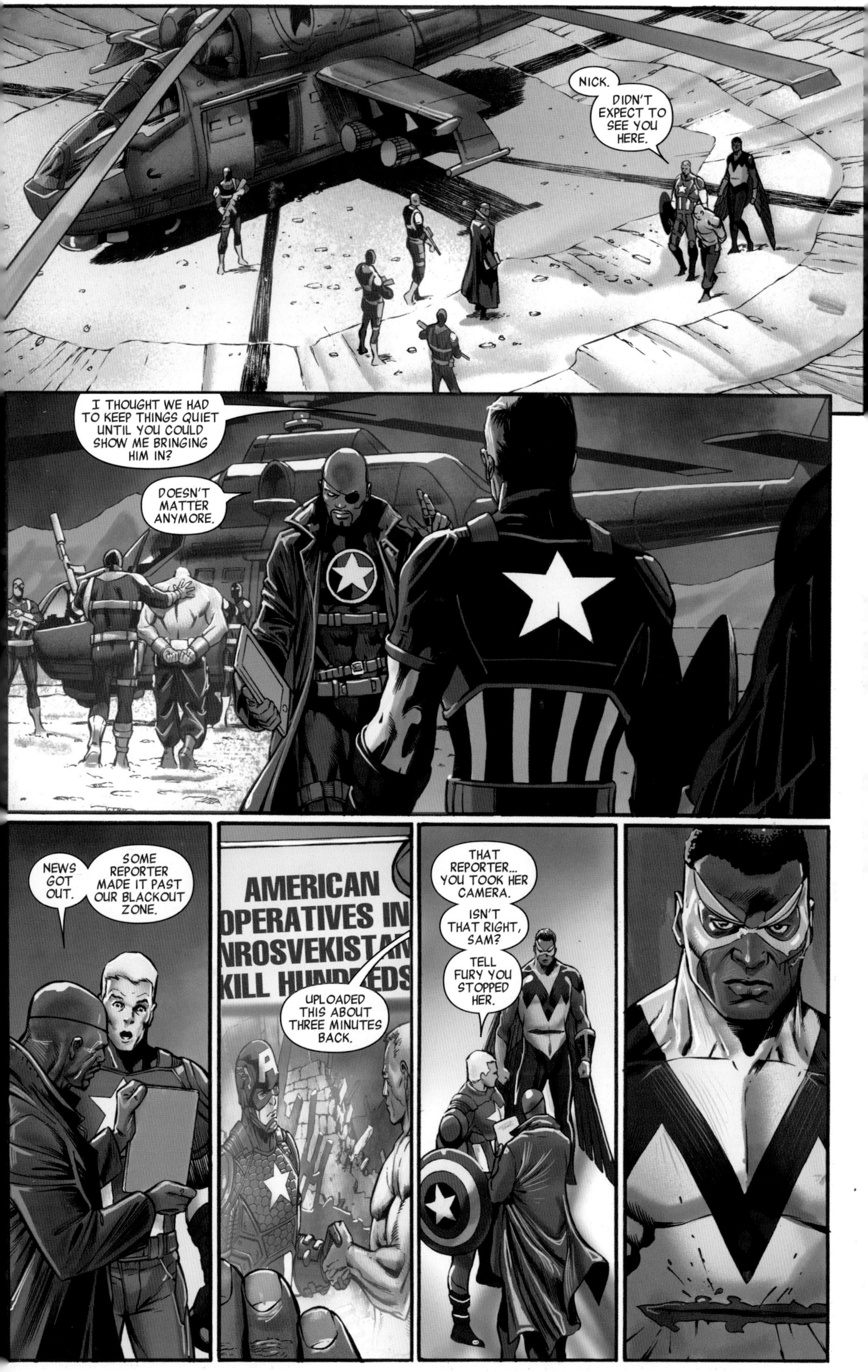

NICK. DIDN'T EXPECT TO SEE YOU HERE.
I THOUGHT WE HAD TO KEEP THINGS QUIET UNTIL YOU COULD SHOW ME BRINGING HIM IN?
DOESN'T MATTER ANYMORE.
NEWS GOT OUT.
SOME REPORTER MADE IT PAST OUR BLACKOUT ZONE.
AMERICAN OPERATIVES IN NROSVEKISTAN KILL HUN
UPLOADED THIS ABOUT THREE MINUTES BACK.
THAT REPORTER... YOU TOOK HER CAMERA.
ISN'T THAT RIGHT, SAM?
TELL FURY YOU STOPPED HER.

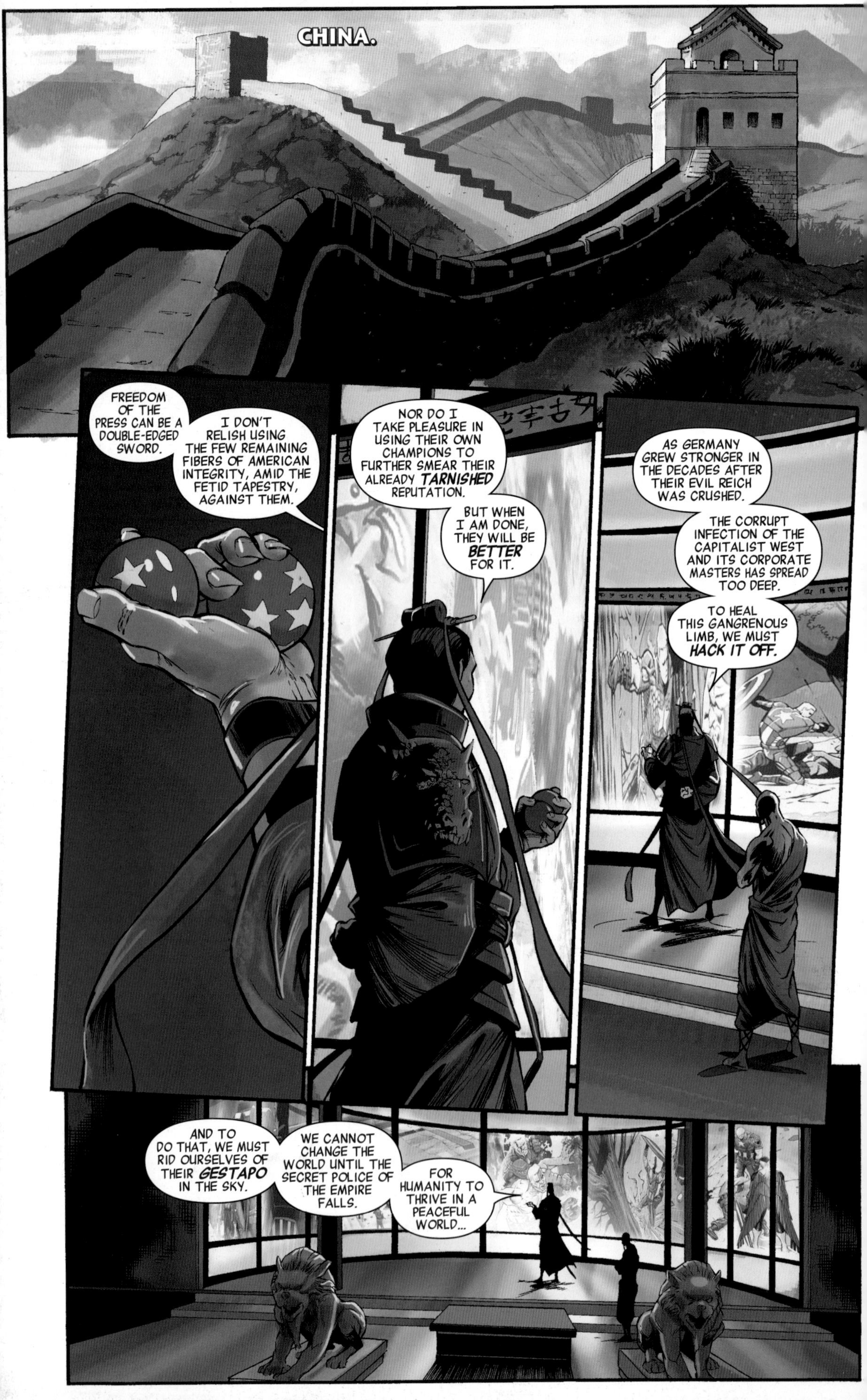
CHINA.
FREEDOM OF THE PRESS CAN BE A DOUBLE-EDGED SWORD.
I DON'T RELISH USING THE FEW REMAINING FIBERS OF AMERICAN INTEGRITY, AMID THE FETID TAPESTRY, AGAINST THEM.
NOR DO I TAKE PLEASURE IN USING THEIR OWN CHAMPIONS TO FURTHER SMEAR THEIR ALREADY TARNISHED REPUTATION.
BUT WHEN I AM DONE, THEY WILL BE BETTER FOR IT.
AS GERMANY GREW STRONGER IN THE DECADES AFTER THEIR EVIL REICH WAS CRUSHED.
THE CORRUPT INFECTION OF THE CAPITALIST WEST AND ITS CORPORATE MASTERS HAS SPREAD TOO DEEP.
TO HEAL THIS GANGRENOUS LIMB, WE MUST HACK IT OFF.
AND TO DO THAT, WE MUST RID OURSELVES OF THEIR GESTAPO IN THE SKY.
WE CANNOT CHANGE THE WORLD UNTIL THE SECRET POLICE OF THE EMPIRE FALLS.
FOR HUMANITY TO THRIVE IN A PEACEFUL WORLD...

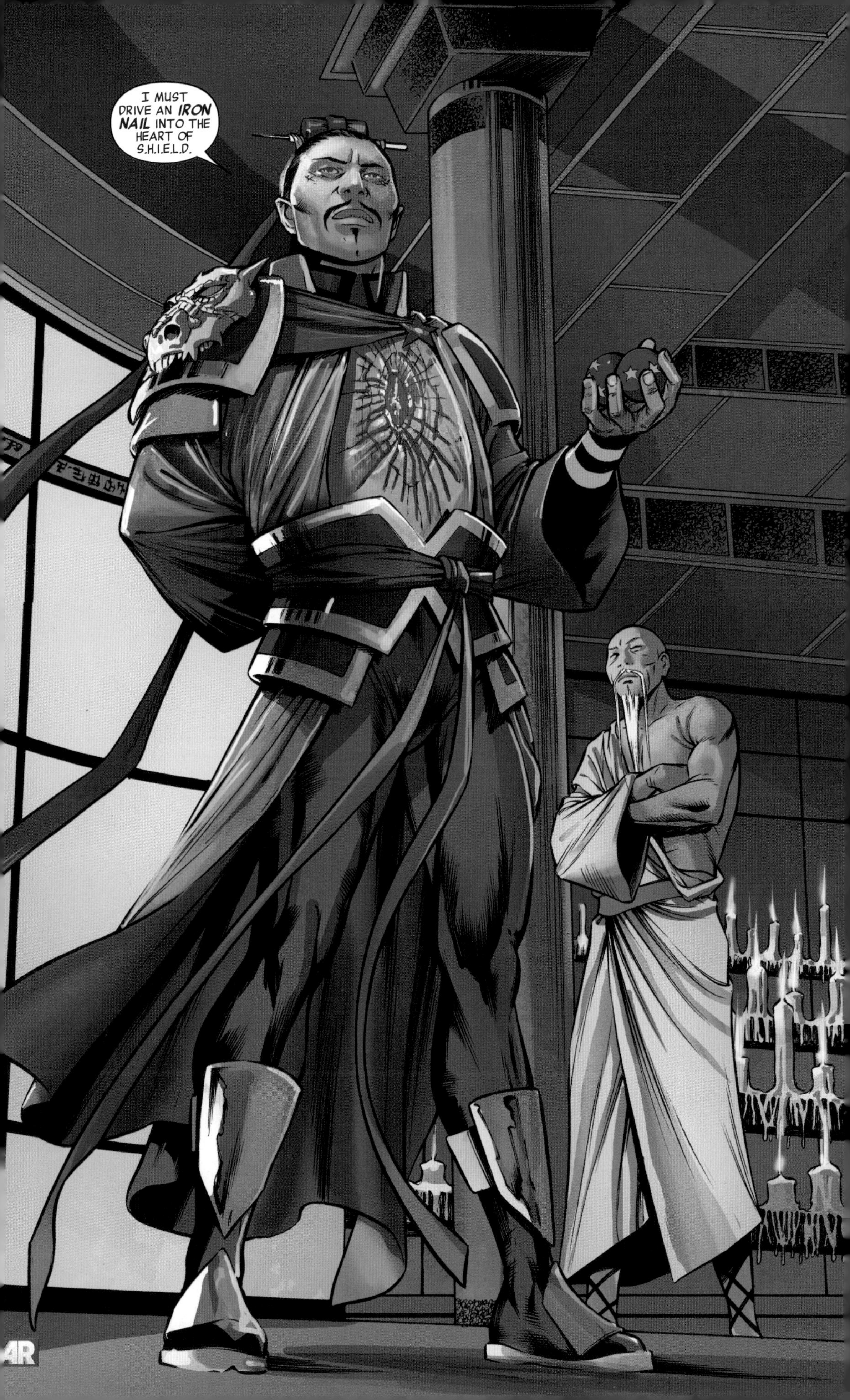
I MUST DRIVE AN IRON NAIL INTO THE HEART OF S.H.I.E.L.D.

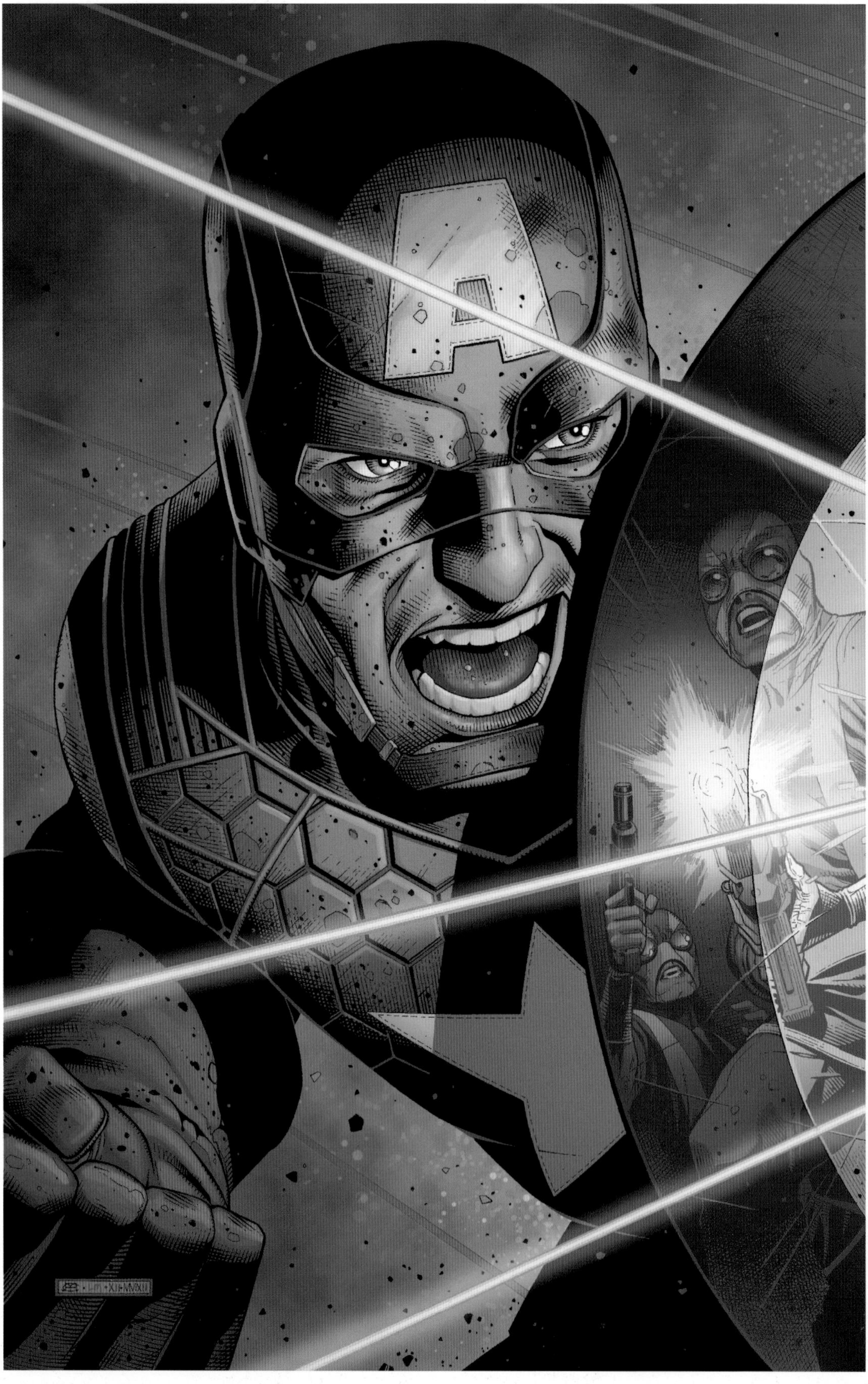

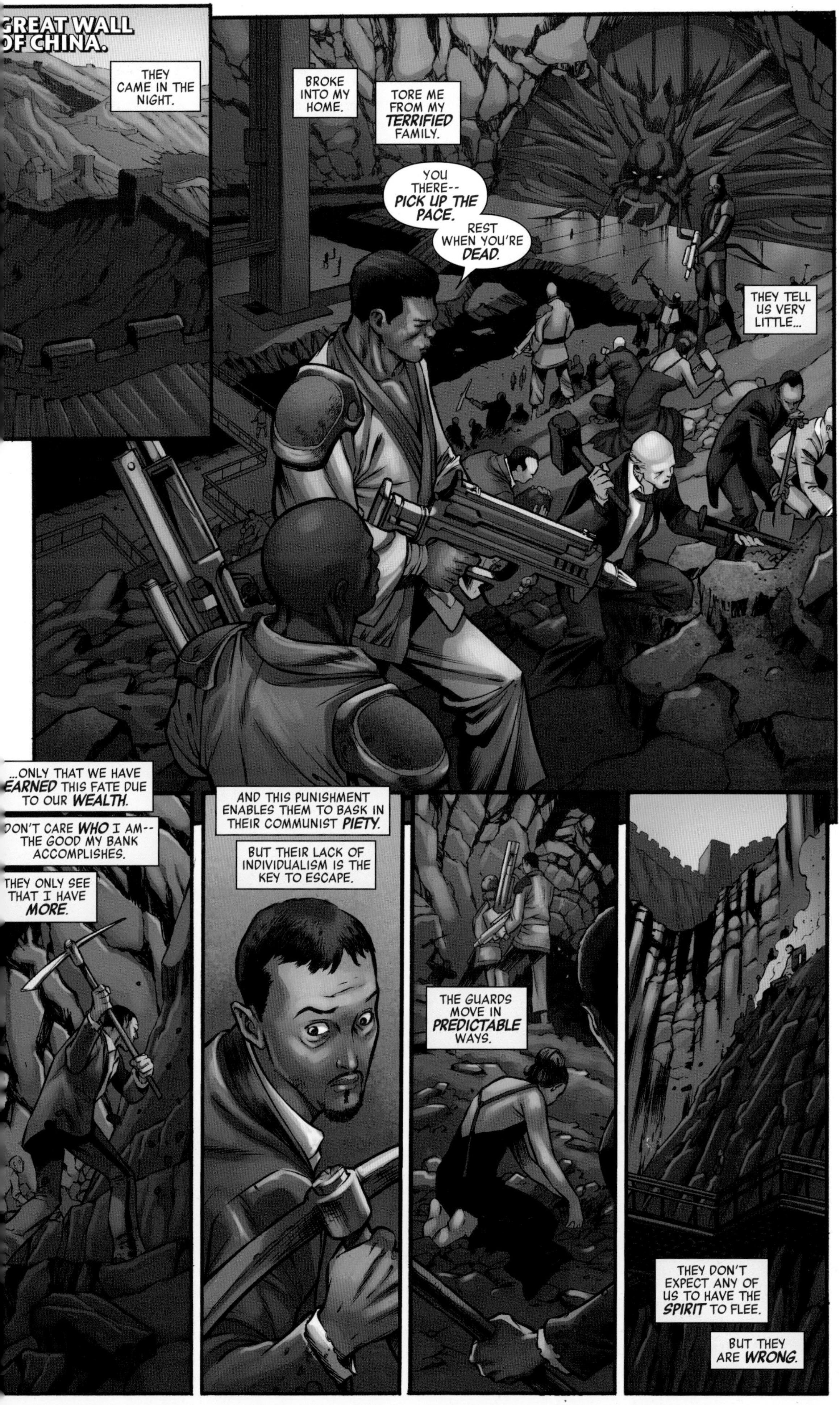
GREAT WALL OF CHINA.
THEY CAME IN THE NIGHT.
BROKE INTO MY HOME.
TORE ME FROM MY TERRIFIED FAMILY.
YOU THERE-- PICK UP THE PACE.
REST WHEN YOU'RE DEAD.
THEY TELL US VERY LITTLE...
...ONLY THAT WE HAVE EARNED THIS FATE DUE TO OUR WEALTH.
DON'T CARE WHO I AM-- THE GOOD MY BANK ACCOMPLISHES.
THEY ONLY SEE THAT I HAVE MORE.
AND THIS PUNISHMENT ENABLES THEM TO BASK IN THEIR COMMUNIST PIETY.
BUT THEIR LACK OF INDIVIDUALISM IS THE KEY TO ESCAPE.
THE GUARDS MOVE IN PREDICTABLE WAYS.
THEY DON'T EXPECT ANY OF US TO HAVE THE SPIRIT TO FLEE.
BUT THEY ARE WRONG.

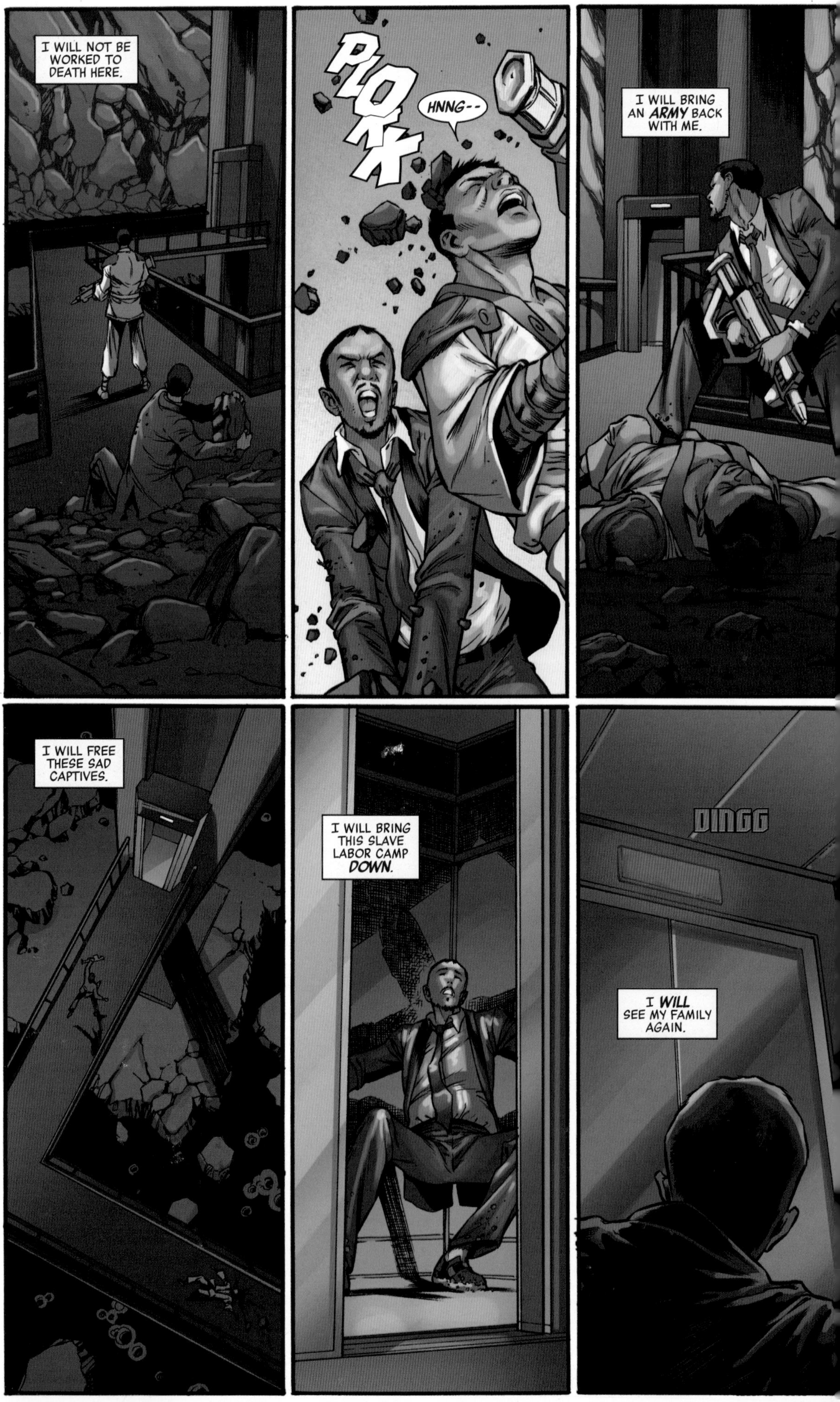

I WILL NOT BE WORKED TO DEATH HERE.
PLOKK
HNNG--
I WILL BRING AN ARMY BACK WITH ME.
I WILL FREE THESE SAD CAPTIVES.
I WILL BRING THIS SLAVE LABOR CAMP DOWN.
DINGG
I WILL SEE MY FAMILY AGAIN.

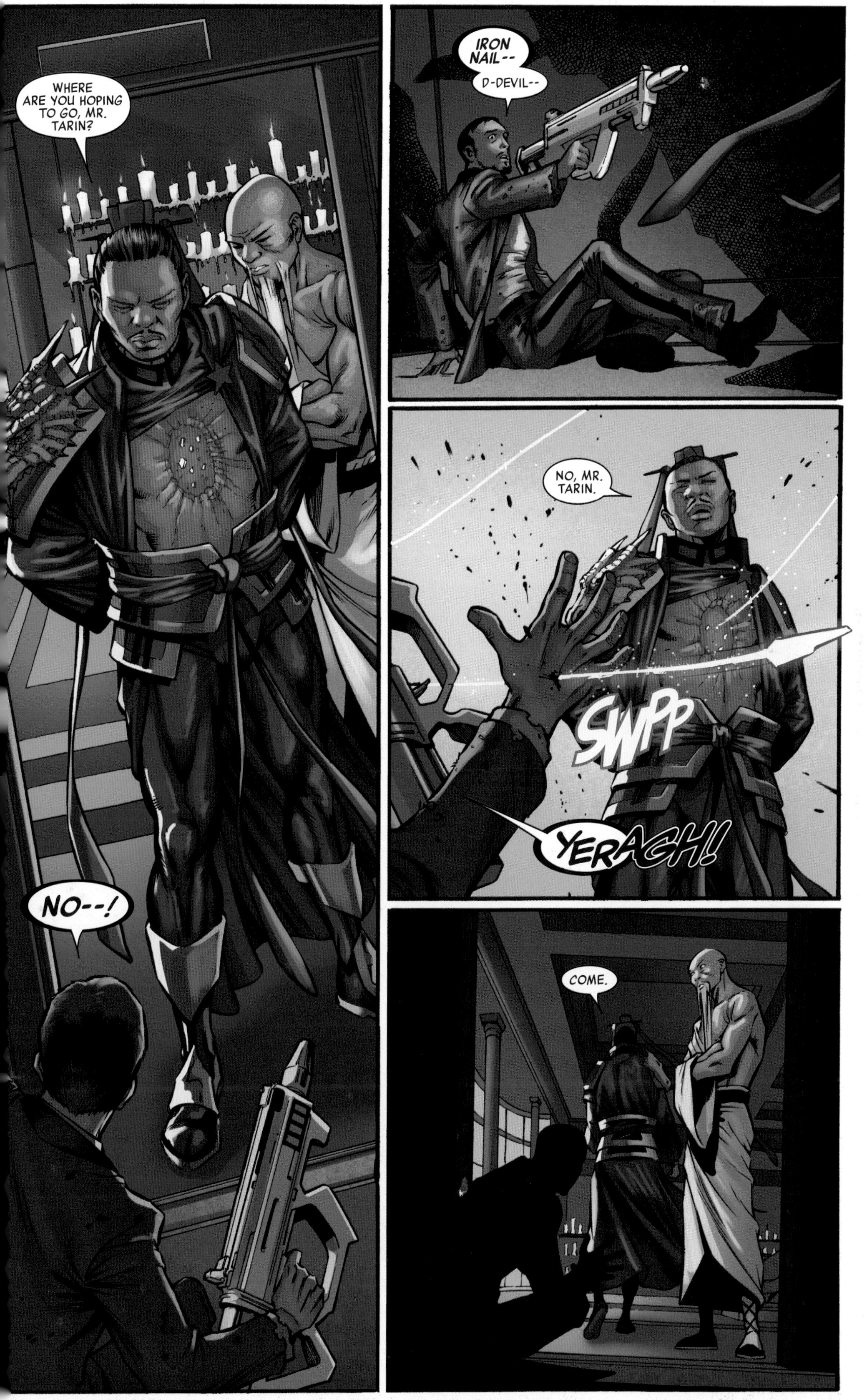
WHERE ARE YOU HOPING TO GO, MR. TARIN?
NO--!
IRON NAIL--
D-DEVIL--
NO, MR. TARIN.
SWPP
YERAGH!
COME.

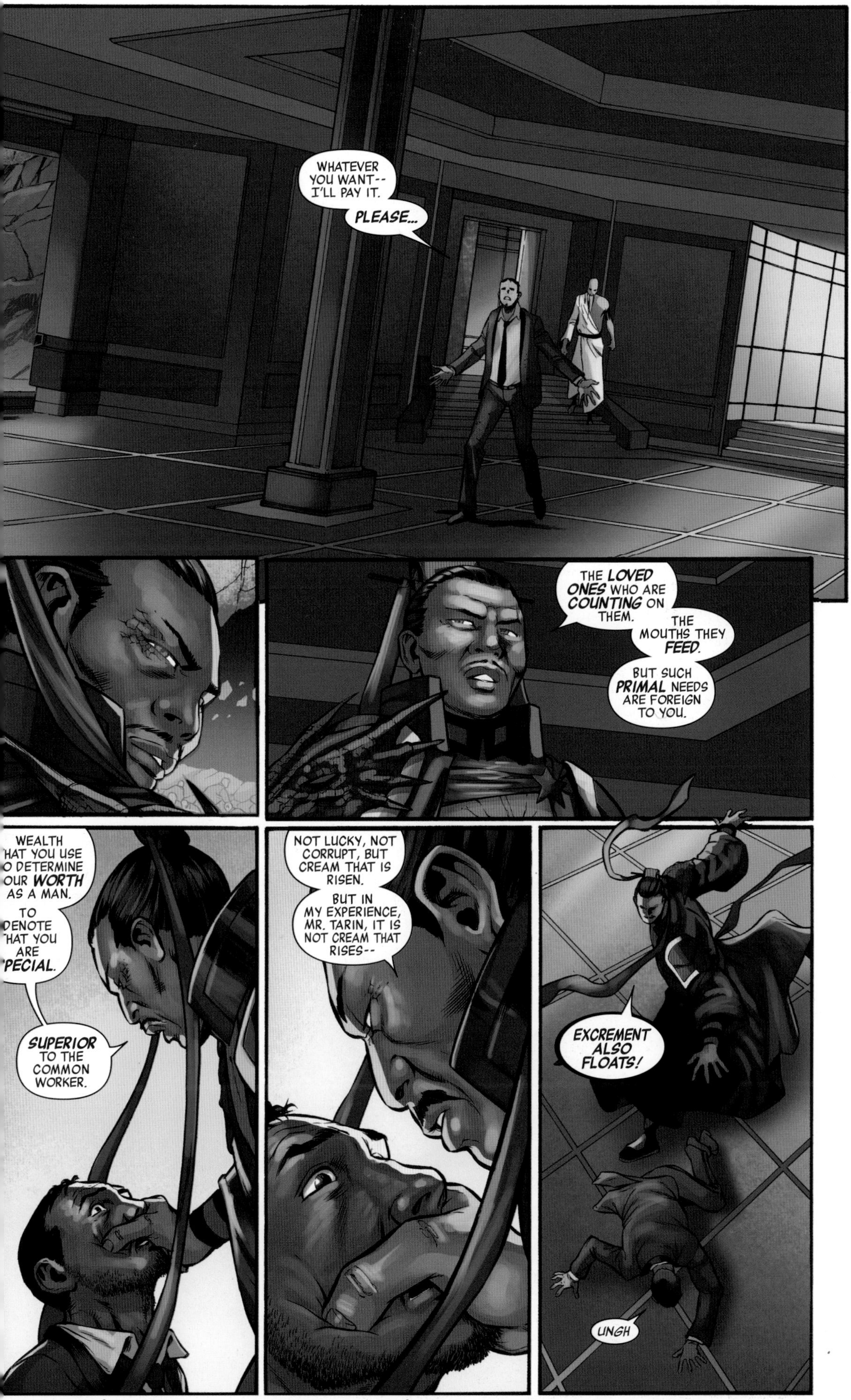
WHATEVER YOU WANT-- I'LL PAY IT.
PLEASE...
THE LOVED ONES WHO ARE COUNTING ON THEM.
THE MOUTHS THEY FEED.
BUT SUCH PRIMAL NEEDS ARE FOREIGN TO YOU.
WEALTH THAT YOU USE TO DETERMINE YOUR WORTH AS A MAN.
TO DENOTE THAT YOU ARE SPECIAL.
SUPERIOR TO THE COMMON WORKER.
NOT LUCKY, NOT CORRUPT, BUT CREAM THAT IS RISEN.
BUT IN MY EXPERIENCE, MR. TARIN, IT IS NOT CREAM THAT RISES--
EXCREMENT ALSO FLOATS!
UNGH

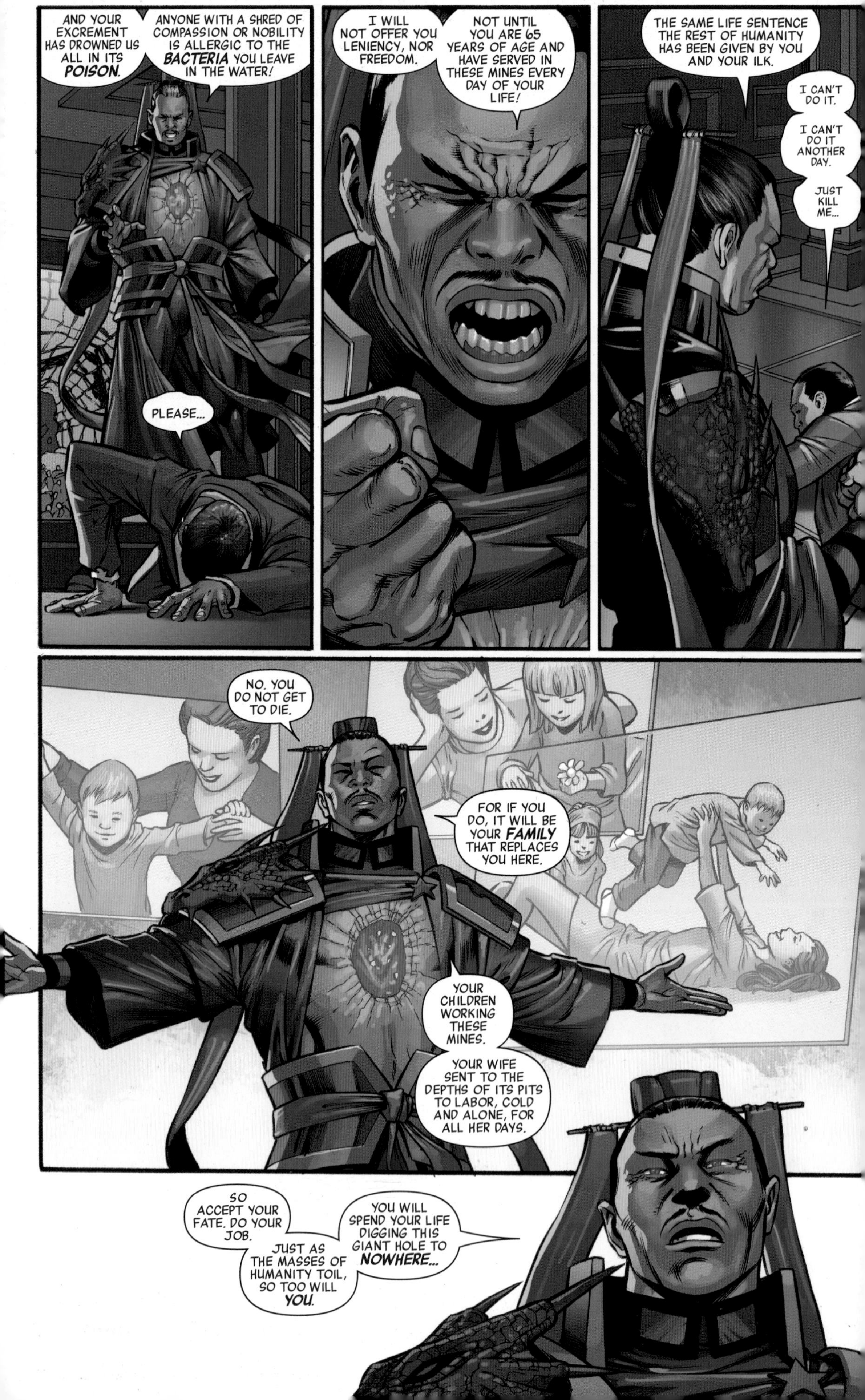
AND YOUR EXCREMENT HAS DROWNED US ALL IN ITS POISON.
ANYONE WITH A SHRED OF COMPASSION OR NOBILITY IS ALLERGIC TO THE BACTERIA YOU LEAVE IN THE WATER!
PLEASE...
I WILL NOT OFFER YOU LENIENCY, NOR FREEDOM.
NOT UNTIL YOU ARE 65 YEARS OF AGE AND HAVE SERVED IN THESE MINES EVERY DAY OF YOUR LIFE!
THE SAME LIFE SENTENCE THE REST OF HUMANITY HAS BEEN GIVEN BY YOU AND YOUR ILK.
I CAN'T DO IT.
I CAN'T DO IT ANOTHER DAY.
JUST KILL ME...
NO. YOU DO NOT GET TO DIE.
FOR IF YOU DO, IT WILL BE YOUR FAMILY THAT REPLACES YOU HERE.
YOUR CHILDREN WORKING THESE MINES.
YOUR WIFE SENT TO THE DEPTHS OF ITS PITS TO LABOR, COLD AND ALONE, FOR ALL HER DAYS.
SO ACCEPT YOUR FATE. DO YOUR JOB.
JUST AS THE MASSES OF HUMANITY TOIL, SO TOO WILL YOU.
YOU WILL SPEND YOUR LIFE DIGGING THIS GIANT HOLE TO NOWHERE...

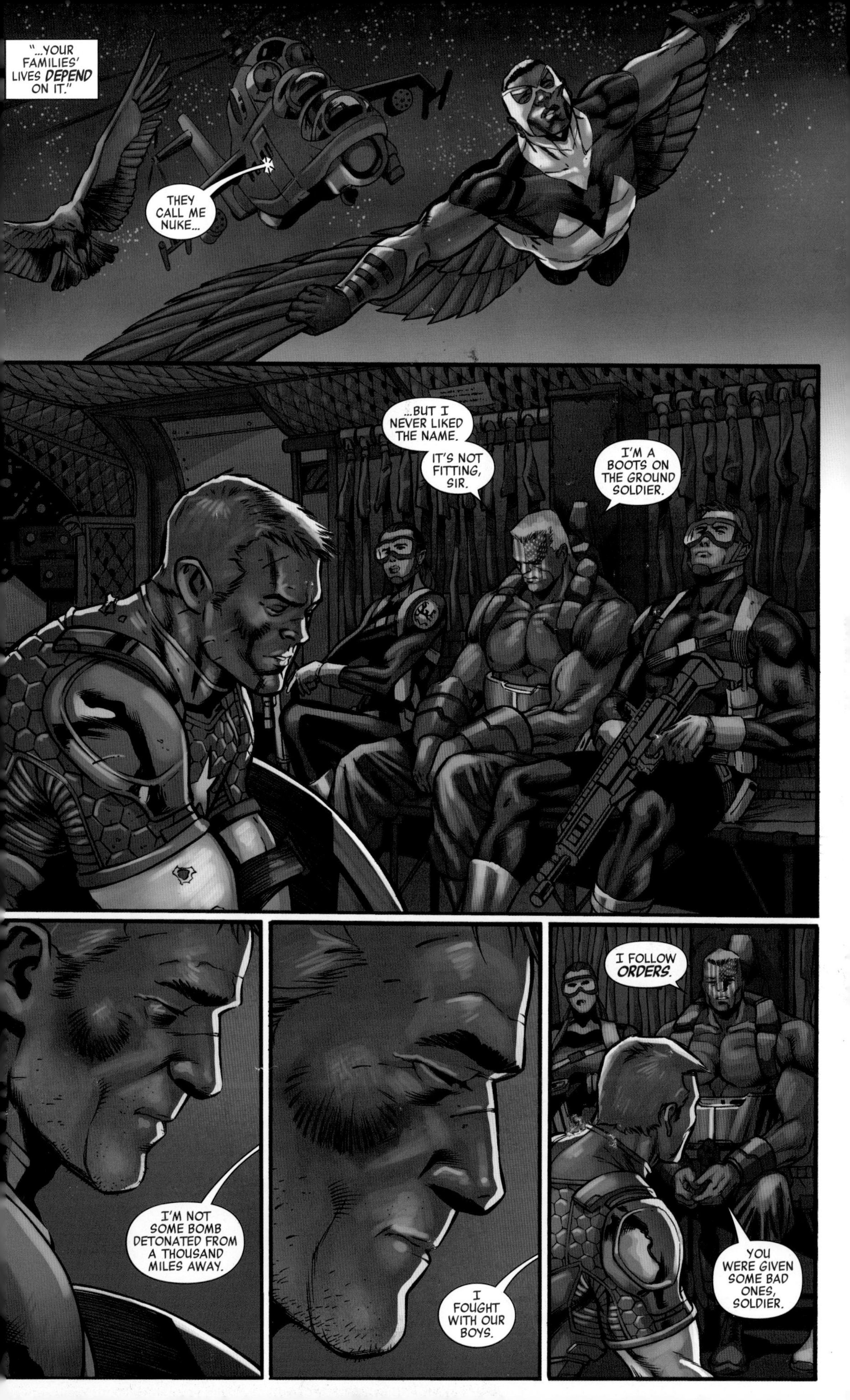
"...YOUR FAMILIES' LIVES **DEPEND** ON IT."
THEY CALL ME NUKE...
...BUT I NEVER LIKED THE NAME.
IT'S NOT FITTING, SIR.
I'M A BOOTS ON THE GROUND SOLDIER.
I'M NOT SOME BOMB DETONATED FROM A THOUSAND MILES AWAY.
I FOUGHT WITH OUR BOYS.
I FOLLOW **ORDERS**.
YOU WERE GIVEN SOME BAD ONES, SOLDIER.

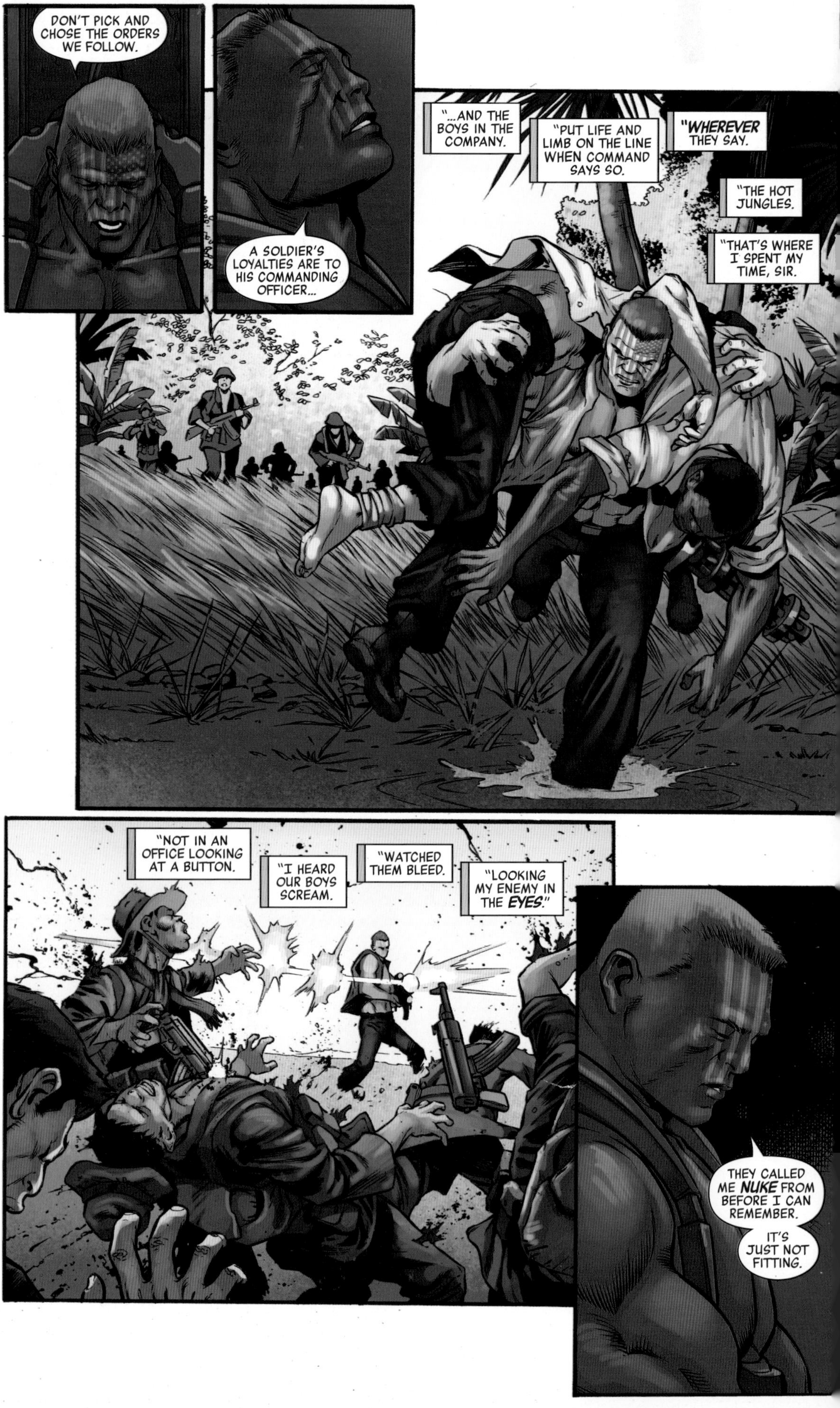
DON'T PICK AND CHOSE THE ORDERS WE FOLLOW.
A SOLDIER'S LOYALTIES ARE TO HIS COMMANDING OFFICER...
"...AND THE BOYS IN THE COMPANY.
"PUT LIFE AND LIMB ON THE LINE WHEN COMMAND SAYS SO.
"WHEREVER THEY SAY.
"THE HOT JUNGLES.
"THAT'S WHERE I SPENT MY TIME, SIR.
"NOT IN AN OFFICE LOOKING AT A BUTTON.
"I HEARD OUR BOYS SCREAM.
"WATCHED THEM BLEED.
"LOOKING MY ENEMY IN THE EYES."
THEY CALLED ME NUKE FROM BEFORE I CAN REMEMBER.
IT'S JUST NOT FITTING.

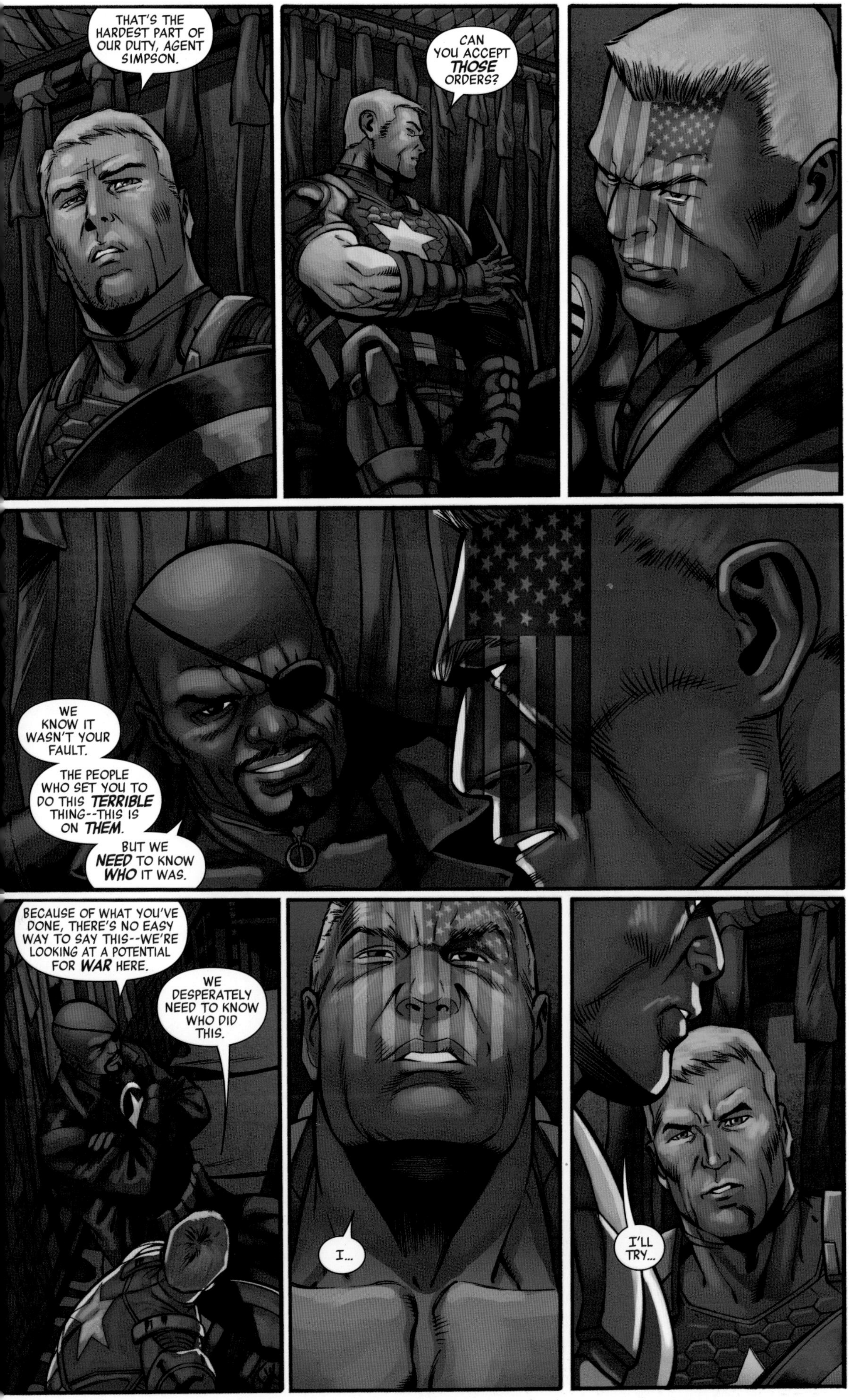
THAT'S THE HARDEST PART OF OUR DUTY, AGENT SIMPSON.
CAN YOU ACCEPT THOSE ORDERS?
WE KNOW IT WASN'T YOUR FAULT.
THE PEOPLE WHO SET YOU TO DO THIS TERRIBLE THING--THIS IS ON THEM.
BUT WE NEED TO KNOW WHO IT WAS.
BECAUSE OF WHAT YOU'VE DONE, THERE'S NO EASY WAY TO SAY THIS--WE'RE LOOKING AT A POTENTIAL FOR WAR HERE.
WE DESPERATELY NEED TO KNOW WHO DID THIS.
I...
I'LL TRY...

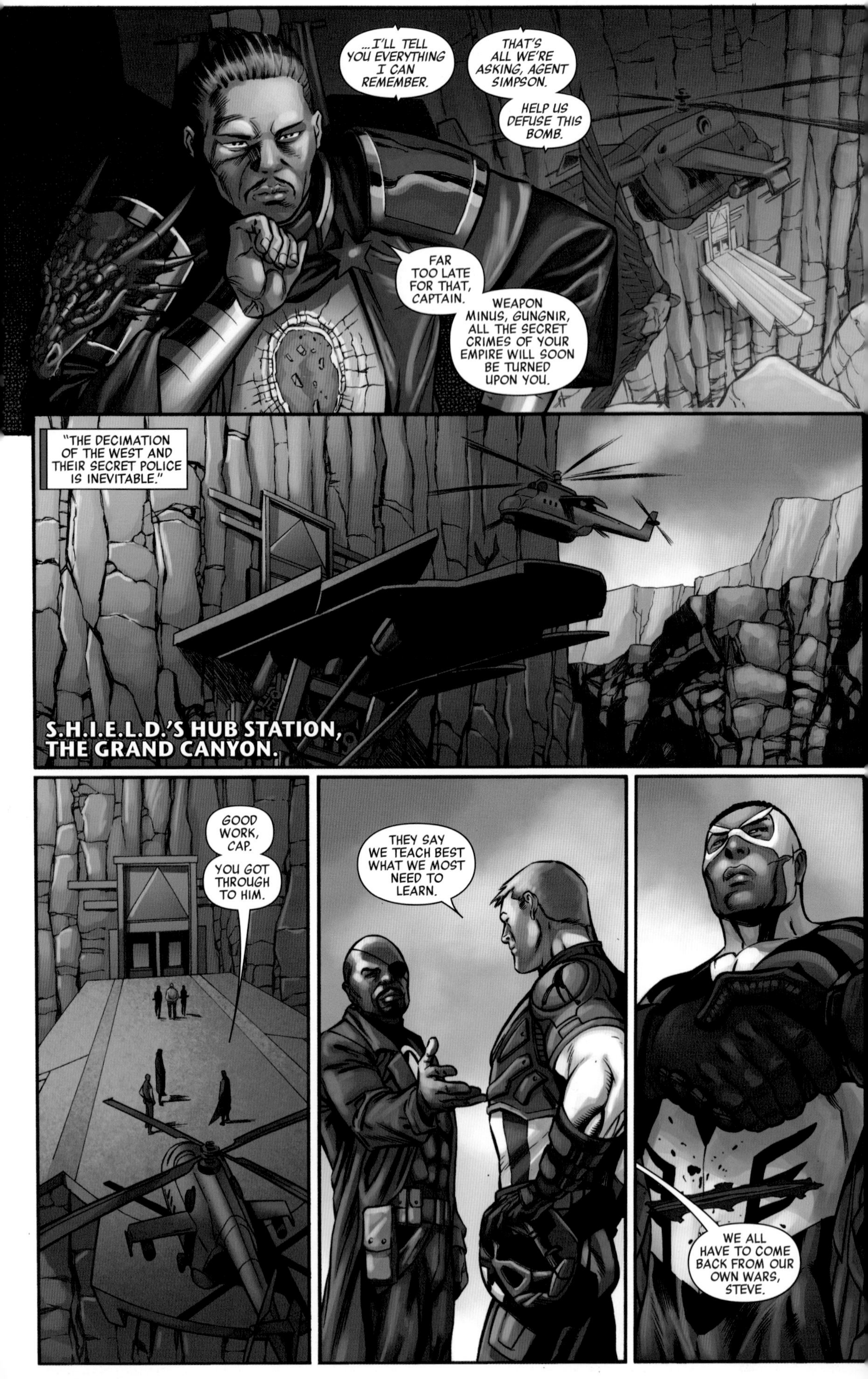
...I'LL TELL YOU EVERYTHING I CAN REMEMBER.
THAT'S ALL WE'RE ASKING, AGENT SIMPSON.
HELP US DEFUSE THIS BOMB.
FAR TOO LATE FOR THAT, CAPTAIN.
WEAPON MINUS, GUNGNIR, ALL THE SECRET CRIMES OF YOUR EMPIRE WILL SOON BE TURNED UPON YOU.
"THE DECIMATION OF THE WEST AND THEIR SECRET POLICE IS INEVITABLE."
S.H.I.E.L.D.'S HUB STATION, THE GRAND CANYON.
GOOD WORK, CAP.
YOU GOT THROUGH TO HIM.
THEY SAY WE TEACH BEST WHAT WE MOST NEED TO LEARN.
WE ALL HAVE TO COME BACK FROM OUR OWN WARS, STEVE.

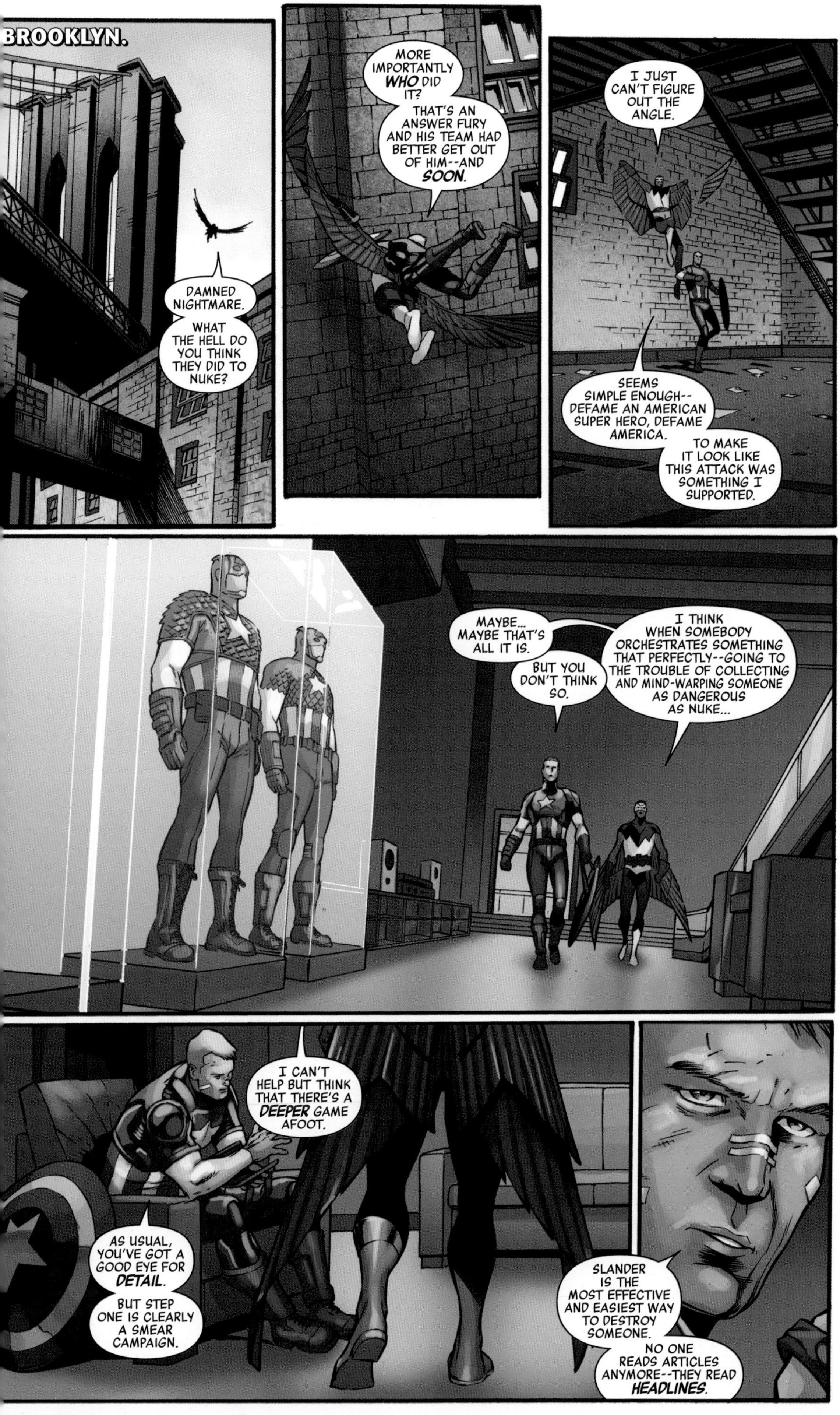
BROOKLYN.
DAMNED NIGHTMARE.
WHAT THE HELL DO YOU THINK THEY DID TO NUKE?
MORE IMPORTANTLY WHO DID IT?
THAT'S AN ANSWER FURY AND HIS TEAM HAD BETTER GET OUT OF HIM--AND SOON.
I JUST CAN'T FIGURE OUT THE ANGLE.
SEEMS SIMPLE ENOUGH--DEFAME AN AMERICAN SUPER HERO, DEFAME AMERICA.
TO MAKE IT LOOK LIKE THIS ATTACK WAS SOMETHING I SUPPORTED.
MAYBE... MAYBE THAT'S ALL IT IS.
BUT YOU DON'T THINK SO.
I THINK WHEN SOMEBODY ORCHESTRATES SOMETHING THAT PERFECTLY--GOING TO THE TROUBLE OF COLLECTING AND MIND-WARPING SOMEONE AS DANGEROUS AS NUKE...
I CAN'T HELP BUT THINK THAT THERE'S A DEEPER GAME AFOOT.
AS USUAL, YOU'VE GOT A GOOD EYE FOR DETAIL.
BUT STEP ONE IS CLEARLY A SMEAR CAMPAIGN.
SLANDER IS THE MOST EFFECTIVE AND EASIEST WAY TO DESTROY SOMEONE.
NO ONE READS ARTICLES ANYMORE--THEY READ HEADLINES.

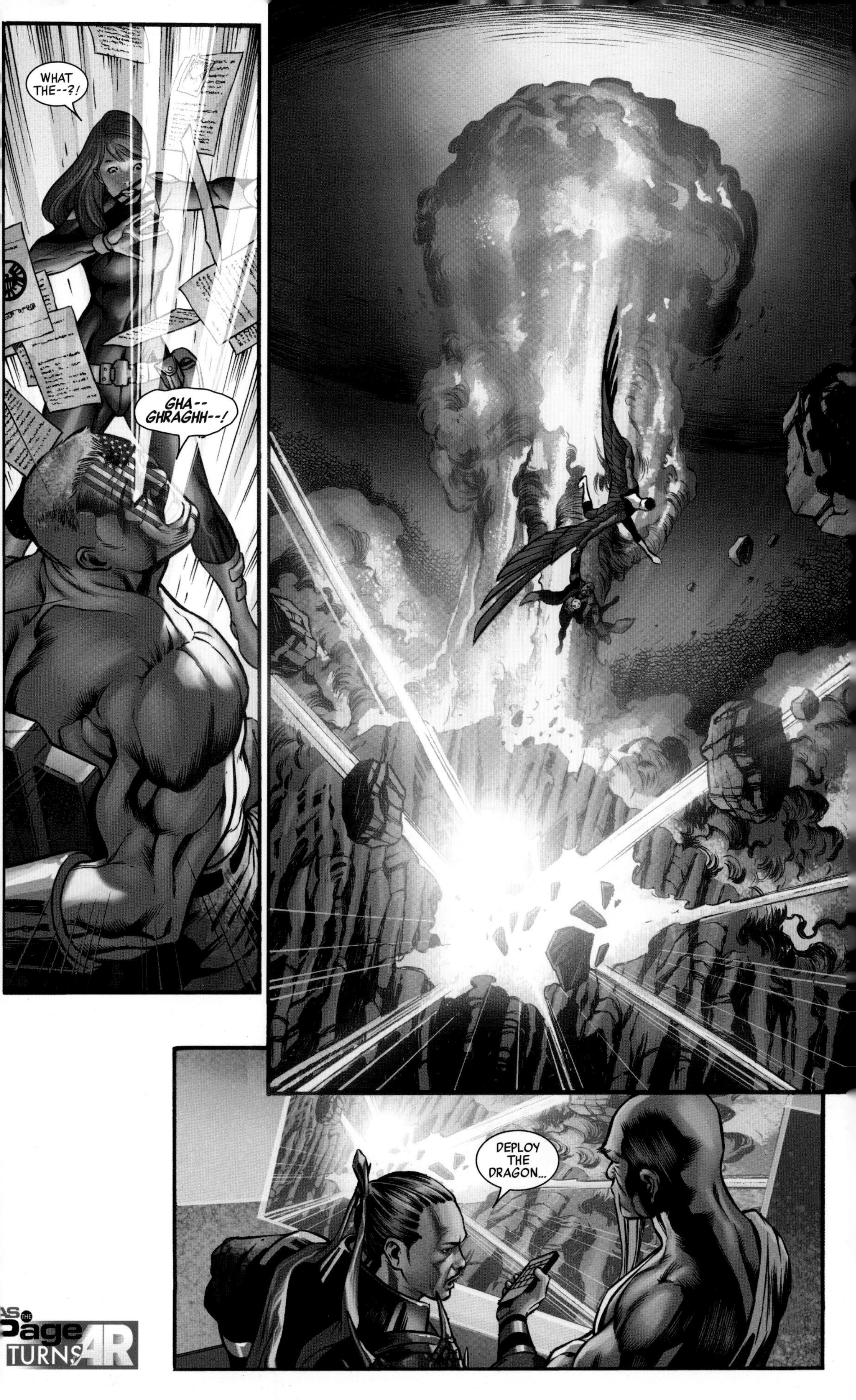
WHAT THE--?!
GHA-- GHRAGHH--!
DEPLOY THE DRAGON...

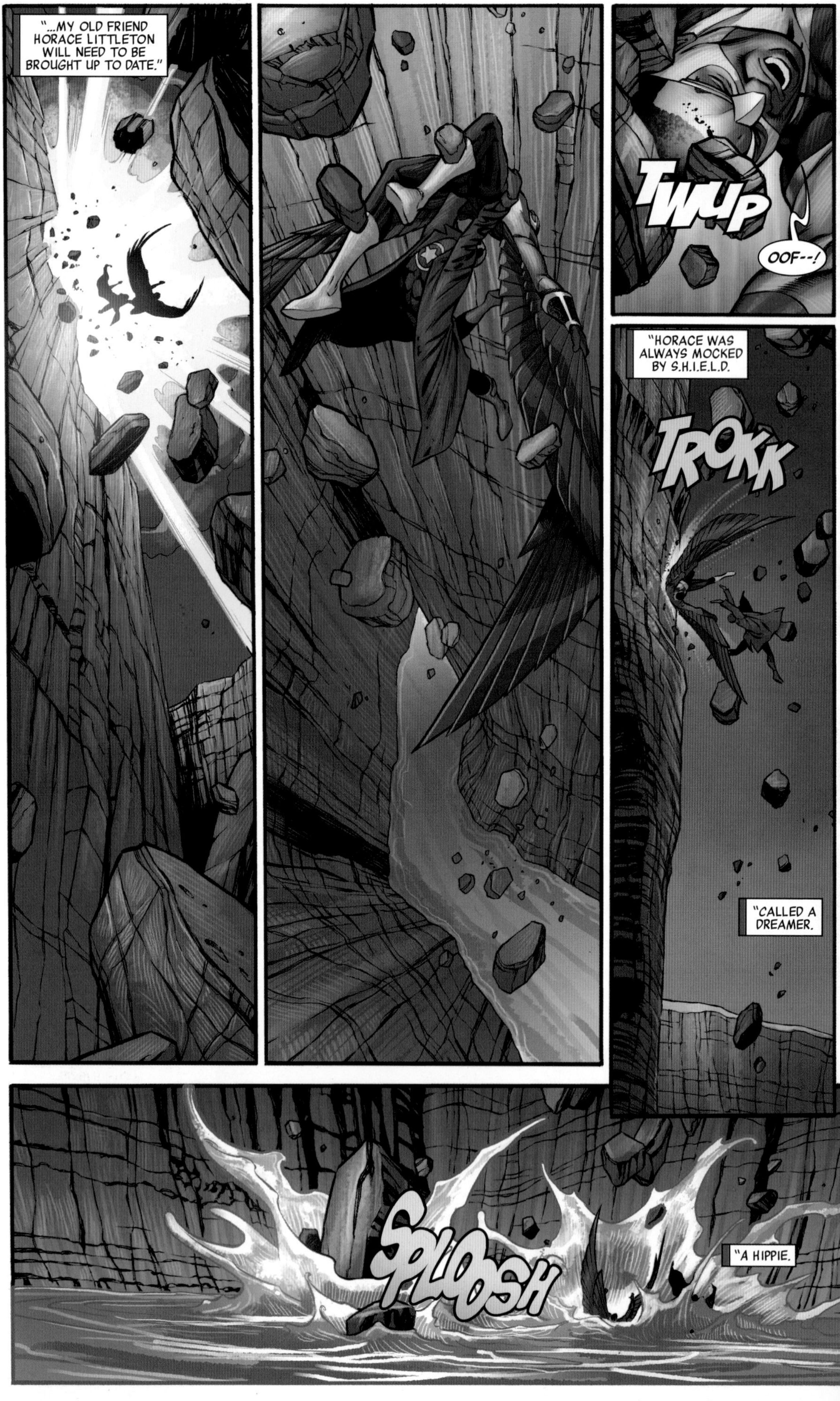

"...MY OLD FRIEND HORACE LITTLETON WILL NEED TO BE BROUGHT UP TO DATE."
TWUP
OOF--!
"HORACE WAS ALWAYS MOCKED BY S.H.I.E.L.D.
TROKK
"CALLED A DREAMER.
SPLOOSH
"A HIPPIE.

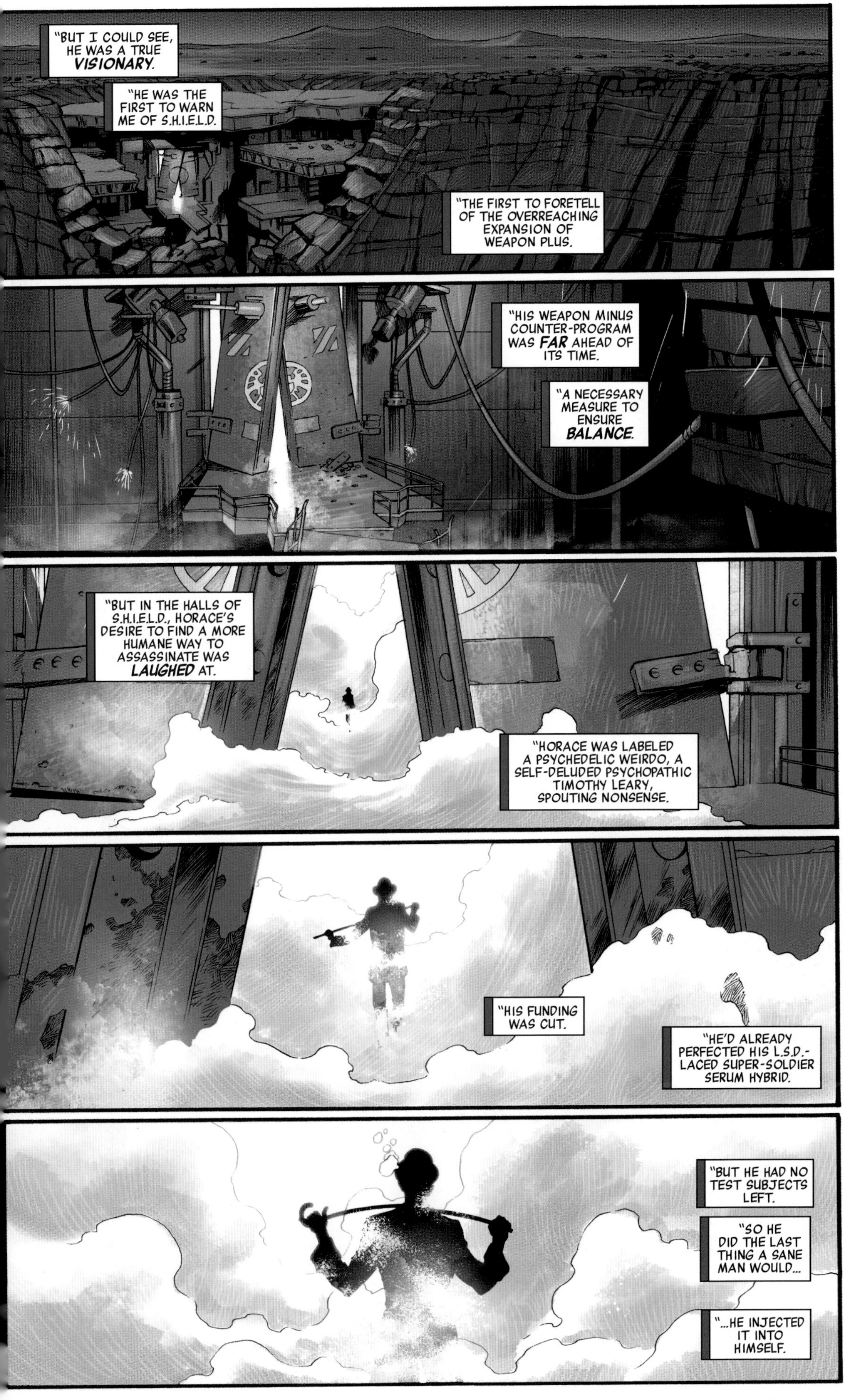
"BUT I COULD SEE, HE WAS A TRUE VISIONARY.
"HE WAS THE FIRST TO WARN ME OF S.H.I.E.L.D.
"THE FIRST TO FORETELL OF THE OVERREACHING EXPANSION OF WEAPON PLUS.
"HIS WEAPON MINUS COUNTER-PROGRAM WAS FAR AHEAD OF ITS TIME.
"A NECESSARY MEASURE TO ENSURE BALANCE.
"BUT IN THE HALLS OF S.H.I.E.L.D., HORACE'S DESIRE TO FIND A MORE HUMANE WAY TO ASSASSINATE WAS LAUGHED AT.
"HORACE WAS LABELED A PSYCHEDELIC WEIRDO, A SELF-DELUDED PSYCHOPATHIC TIMOTHY LEARY, SPOUTING NONSENSE.
"HIS FUNDING WAS CUT.
"HE'D ALREADY PERFECTED HIS L.S.D.-LACED SUPER-SOLDIER SERUM HYBRID.
"BUT HE HAD NO TEST SUBJECTS LEFT.
"SO HE DID THE LAST THING A SANE MAN WOULD...
"...HE INJECTED IT INTO HIMSELF.

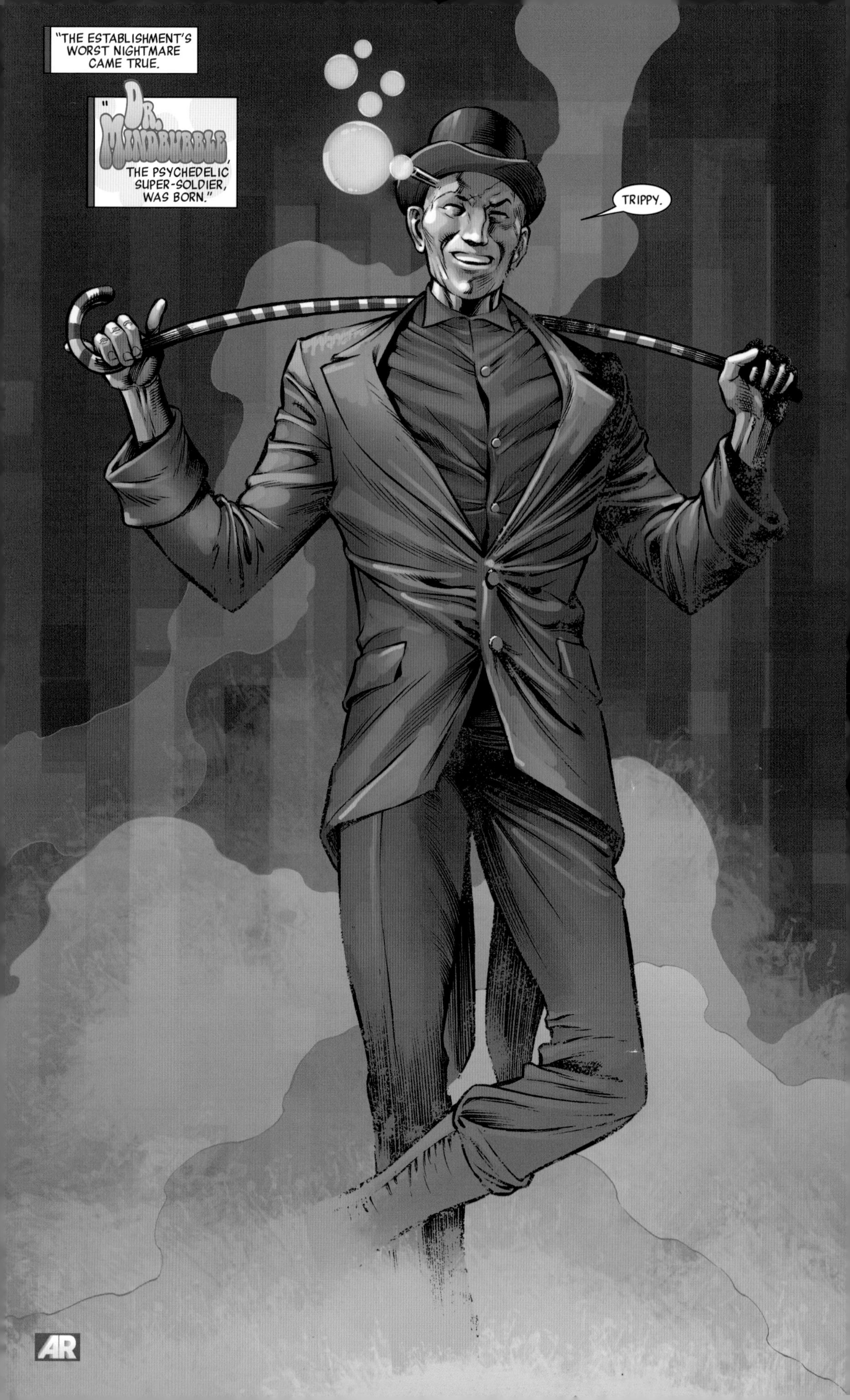
"THE ESTABLISHMENT'S WORST NIGHTMARE CAME TRUE.
"DR. MINDBUBBLE, THE PSYCHEDELIC SUPER-SOLDIER, WAS BORN."
TRIPPY.
AR

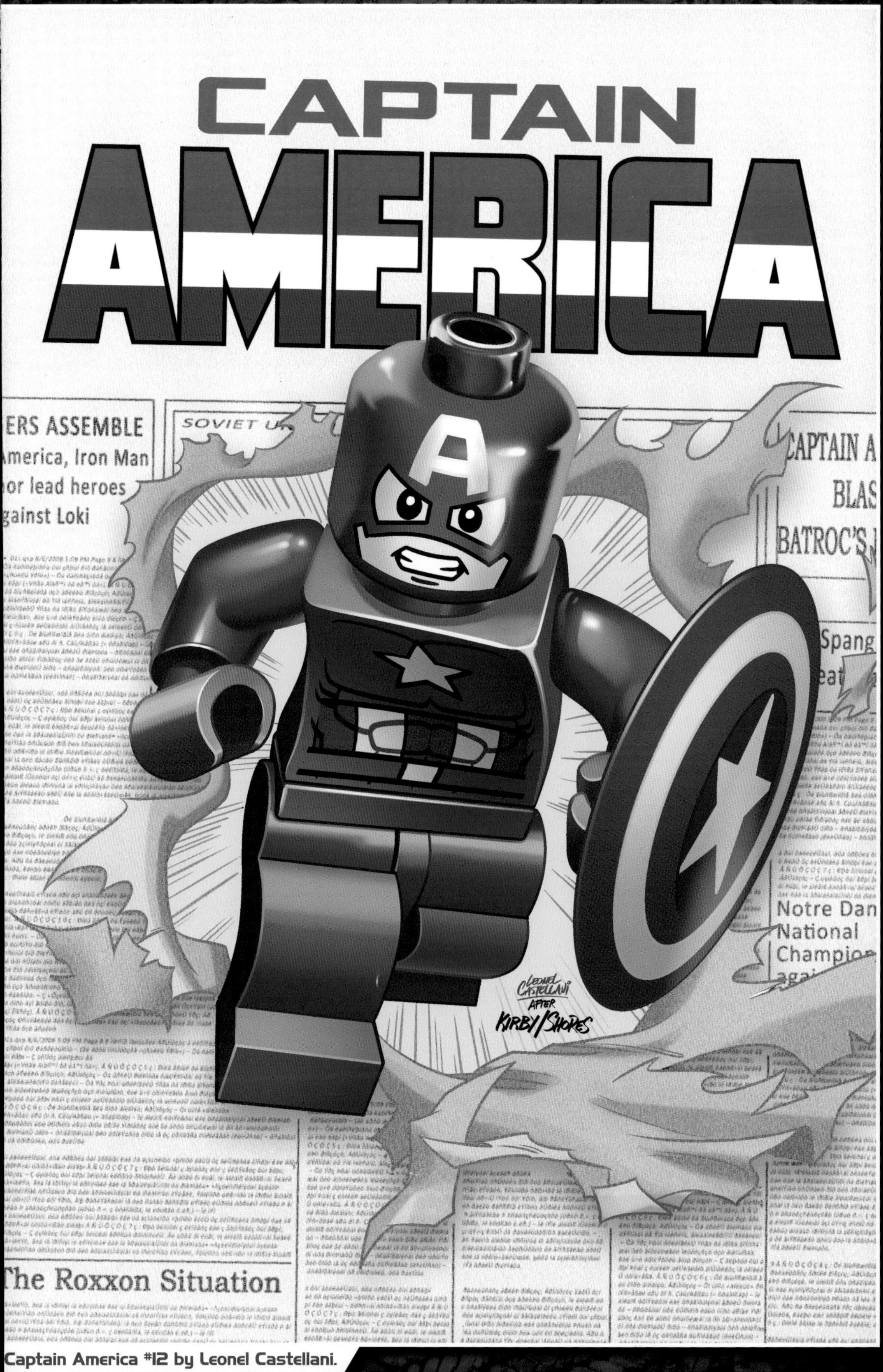
CAPTAIN
AMERICA
The Roxxon Situation
LEONEL CASTELLANI AFTER KIRBY/SHORES

Captain America #12 by Leonel Castellani.

Captain America #12 by Leonel Castellani.